PEGGY LEE

PEGGY LEE

A Century of Song

Tish Oney

ROWMAN & LITTLEFIELD
Lanham • Boulder • New York • London

Published by Rowman & Littlefield
An imprint of The Rowman & Littlefield Publishing Group, Inc.
4501 Forbes Boulevard, Suite 200, Lanham, Maryland 20706
www.rowman.com

6 Tinworth Street, London SE11 5AL, United Kingdom

British Library Cataloguing in Publication Information Available

Library of Congress Cataloging-in-Publication Data

Names: Oney, Tish, 1969–, author.
Title: Peggy Lee : a century of song / Tish Oney.
Description: Lanham, Maryland : Rowman & Littlefield, 2020. | Includes bibliographical references and index. | Summary: "One hundred years after the legendary singer's birth, this book brings to life the career of an iconic performer whose contributions to the Great American Songbook, jazz, popular music, and film music remain unparalleled. Tish Oney explores Lee's musical technique, and interviews with family, friends, and colleagues reveal new insights"—Provided by publisher.
Identifiers: LCCN 2020000898 (print) | LCCN 2020000899 (ebook) | ISBN 9781538128473 (cloth) | ISBN 9781538128480 (epub)
Subjects: LCSH: Lee, Peggy, 1920–2002. | Singers—United States—Biography.
Classification: LCC ML420.L294 O64 2020 (print) | LCC ML420.L294 (ebook) | DDC 782.42164092 [B]—dc23
LC record available at https://lccn.loc.gov/2020000898
LC ebook record available at https://lccn.loc.gov/2020000899

CONTENTS

ACKNOWLEDGMENTS

With my whole heart I thank God for fostering this vision and for giving me the strength, health, and necessary diligence to complete it. I offer sincerest thanks to John Chiodini for our years of collaborating onstage and off. He remains a joy to perform with and a dear friend, and I am tickled to consider this yet another collaboration we have created together. I sincerely wish to thank Holly Foster-Wells, Nicki Lee Foster, and Peggy Lee Associates, LLC, for their wealth of information, generosity, and encouragement to see this project through. I offer thanks to Mike and Peter Stoller for their time, insights, feedback, and contributions to this book. Iván Santiago-Mercado's online discography and videography provided a plethora of invaluable facts and details—thank you, Iván. Both Will Friedwald's and David Torresen's various writings, including liner notes within Lee's albums, supplied valuable insights and observations. I warmly thank my editors, Natalie Mandziuk, Michael Tan, and John Cerullo, for their guidance and help transforming this project from a long-incubating set of ideas into a published book. I lovingly thank my mother for introducing me to Peggy Lee's music when I was particularly impressionable. I extend sincerest thanks to my husband, George, for his support and sustaining encouragement. I thank the hundreds of professional musicians with whom I have worked over the years—thank you for the magic we have co-created and continue to create together! I thank all my teachers—

how blessed I have been to have been shaped intellectually and musically by some of the most outstanding minds and talents on the planet. Finally, I thank the thousands of audiences that have enjoyed and supported my music and the many fans who urged me to write this book. This is for you.

FOREWORD

John Chiodini

Tish called me one day and asked for an interview. I did not know her at the time. She was attending the University of Southern California and writing her doctoral dissertation on the "lyrical genius of Peggy Lee." She asked if we could talk about my experiences working with Ms. Lee in the studios on recording projects and live performances. Her focus was on Peggy Lee's creativity as a songwriter. We got together, and that led to the creation of not only the *Peggy Lee Project*, a touring show that highlights Peggy Lee as a songwriter, but also a wonderful friendship and professional partnership. In the ensuing years, Tish and I have recorded four CDs together and performed for live audiences nationally. The latest album, *Tish Oney with the John Chiodini Trio: The Best Part*, includes three songs that I co-wrote with Peggy Lee but that were never recorded by Peggy or anyone else.

I started working with Peggy Lee in 1979, recording a few tracks on her DRG *Close Enough for Love* album. I was subbing for another guitar player who couldn't make a certain date. I was recommended by Peggy's longtime friend, bassist Max Bennett. To promote the album on TV, it was sent to *The Tonight Show* and *The Mike Douglas Show*, among others, and the producers of those shows chose "It Was Just One of Those Things" as the song they wanted Peggy to perform. I had come up with a funky rhythm lick that Peggy liked, so I was invited to join her band to perform the song on the TV shows. After that, we played an engagement at the Westwood Playhouse. The band was great—Mike Renzi, Grady Tate, Jay Leonhart, and Mark Sherman. It was wonderful to play for Peggy Lee and be a part of that band. I stayed with Peggy for about ten years. There were many tours and three more albums, but the special part was co-writing songs and creating music with Peggy Lee.

Tish could have called this book *Anatomy of a Singer*. Anatomy, according to the *Longman Dictionary of Contemporary English*, is "a study or examination of a process in order to understand and explain how it works." This is what Tish has done in this book, what makes it unique: no gossip, no rumors—just enough personal information to propel the story of how Peggy Lee created her amazing music by connecting one period of her life to the next.

In the midst of studying the anatomy of Peggy Lee's music, how it was actually created, Tish reveals the recording industry at that particular time, especially how male dominance caused female artists to have a much smaller role. Peggy's approach would take decades to accomplish, although radio broadcasts helped her craft her skills as a pop diva, jazz singer, and concert and recording producer. Tish shows how Peggy always fought for musical artists and songwriters to receive the proper royalties for their work, from jukeboxes to film. Any one of us who collects royalties from the film industry has to acknowledge Peggy Lee's commitment and victory.

Tish details Peggy's sense of adventure. In film, as a singer, actor, composer, lyricist, and voiceover artist (as both a performer and a music creator), she always went her own way. She created her own music videos. She sang and collaborated with the other singers and songwriters of her time—just about everyone you could think of.

This book is like a series of short stories. Sometimes you hear about this or learn that. At other times something historic is happening. There are many surprises in these chapters. Tish's attention to detail is very compelling, and you want to keep reading.

A couple of my experiences working with Peggy Lee exactly mirror what Tish has written about in this book. For example, I witnessed what Tish describes about Peggy Lee's belief in visual appearance mattering as much as musical performance. When the lighting for a show was not what she wanted or expected, she would claim to enter a vortex, and nobody wanted to see that. The lighting had to be exact. No improvising.

Before I met Peggy, I didn't have a lot of experience working with vocalists. I played with the Boston Pops, the Buddy DeFranco Quintet, and the Maynard Ferguson Band. As an accompanist, I learned the music and played my part. Then I got the great opportunity of working with Peggy Lee. I experienced with her firsthand, as an accompanist and especially as a songwriter, that music and poetry are collaborative partners, that the lyrics are just as important as the composed music. As Tish explains in her book, this one idea was the overriding reason for the choices Peggy Lee made in creating and performing her music.

One last story. For tours, Peggy would spend a great deal of time deciding what kind of show she wanted to do and what songs she wanted to perform. Her music library at her home had every arrangement for her recordings. She would choose a song, tell me if there was something she didn't like about that particular arrangement, and we would try different ways to change it. Peggy was an excellent musician. She knew what she wanted to hear. After all, she spent her entire career working with the best writers and musicians. After choosing the songs, she would sequence the show. Then we would rehearse the show, usually at her home in Bel Air. Extreme detail and work went into planning and preparing her shows. That's what I love about Tish's book, the detail.

On a personal note, Tish and I have a special friendship. We have worked a lot of gigs as a duo. You really need to trust that other person in a duo. There's no one else. The way to earn that trust is by having your fundamentals together and then making good musical choices. The key word is *musical*. Tish and I always come ready to play. We know the music and have all the details down. But above that, we recognize in each other the same intent to make the music great, not only our own part. Because we have all this together, we can be spontaneous in our performance. Joyful.

Tish has written a great book. She has detailed the creative genius of one of our national treasures, Peggy Lee. Because of my close association with Peggy on many fronts (guitarist, band member, arranger for her quintet, co-writer of her songs, musical director on tours, co-producer, and friend), I can confirm that what Tish wrote about the creativity of Peggy Lee is what I knew about Peggy. I can say, without reservation, that if you want to know who Peggy Lee really was, you should read this book.

Tish has a vast knowledge and understanding of her subject and passes this on to the reader in an easy style that compels you to keep reading. The detail is amazing. You experience Peggy Lee's life through the lens of her creativity: every song, every show, every win, and every loss. This book is an excellent read for anyone and a special delight for Peggy Lee aficionados.

INTRODUCTION

The International Ballroom of the Beverly Hilton Hotel reverberated with tumultuous applause when Peggy Lee was introduced on May 9, 1994. That evening the Society of Singers awarded Lee an "Ella" Lifetime Achievement Award at their gala tribute event in Beverly Hills. When a microphone was brought to her table, Lee briefly addressed the audience from her wheelchair before launching into a tear-jerking rendition of her original song "Here's To You," a musical toast dedicated to those in attendance. The singer bid all within earshot her sincerest best wishes in several languages, ending with her favorite blessing, "angels on your pillows." The peerless timing, poignant phrasing, and gentle musical delivery that marked thousands of her performances quietly transformed into one of the last musical moments this remarkable artist would share with her adoring public.

During the course of her long and successful career, Lee grew into a globally beloved singer, composer, lyricist, voiceover artist, actress, and entertainer. The spectacularly diverse six-decade catalog of music she created represents one of the greatest artistic contributions by anyone to American music. Lee's remarkable work in big band swing, pop, jazz, blues, the "cool" school, radio, television, film, and theatrical music permanently changed the landscape of American popular music as well as the role and society's expectations of the female pop singer. Hailing from rural North Dakota, Norma Delores Egstrom would carve her own path as a force to be reckoned with in twentieth-century American popular music.

Lee's unmistakable contributions and genius among her peers in the recording and performing industries have heretofore been inadequately documented. Intending to correct this shortfall, I set out to write not a biography, but a book about Lee's music. While biographers relate surveys of an artist's life, times, and their best-known works of art, few dive deeply into the entire oeuvre of an artist as prolific as Peggy Lee. The lack of documentation of Lee's total creative work begs a volume dedicated to her music alone.

Lee's musical contributions included several hit songs, a wide, varied palette of albums, success in several genres, fourteen films, an autobiographical Broadway show, scores of radio and television performances including those she herself hosted, and thousands of outstanding live performances. She also contributed her own signature style of understated singing, impeccable phrasing, meticulous attention to pitch and rhythm, stagecraft, poise, and a level of preparation uneclipsed by her peers. Somehow, in previous books about Lee, these innovations and accomplishments received only cursory glances. While vastly different biographical accounts of Lee's life, marriages, successes, and personal failures have already been published, the facts pertaining to the artist's incredible musical productivity and accomplishments have remained largely understated. Interviews with collaborative musicians, composers, and colleagues of Lee have reflected on the artist's musical contributions, shedding new light on her motivation and unconquerable drive toward musical excellence.

Some questions arise when pulling the broad view of Lee's life into a purely musical focus. How did her voice and musicianship evolve over the course of her six-decade career? What did she leave in regard to musical posterity for fans and others who would follow in her footsteps? How did Lee interpret the Great American Songbook, jazz, blues, ever-changing popular music, easy listening, and theatrical music? What was Lee's significance as a lyricist of more than 270 songs? How did Lee continue to roll with the changing musical landscape as she aged? How did she somehow ensure ongoing posthumous success with a catalog of recordings still treasured by young audiences, television writers, and film music supervisors, now eighteen years since her death? Lee's centennial birthday is an appropriate occasion at which to address these questions and grant the artist due credit for her phenomenal contributions to American music. This book focuses exclusively on Lee's musical footprint and artistic legacy, beginning with an exploration of the true genius of the girl from rural North Dakota who would give us *A Century of Song*.

I

A VOICE FOR THE BIG CITY

In May 1920, just three short years after the first jazz record was made by the Original Dixieland Jass Band, a little girl who would forever change the development of jazz singing and American popular music was born in Jamestown, North Dakota, to Marvin and Selma Anderson Egstrom. Raised on a farm in the Midwest with no clear alternate pathway provided for her, Norma Delores Egstrom dreamed of becoming a professional singer like those she admired on the radio. Years later she shared in a personal interview that Maxine Sullivan, the African American singer who recorded the Scottish folksong "Loch Lomond" for Claude Thornhill's band, exerted a strong early influence upon Norma, albeit merely over radio waves: "She sang very lightly, like a painter using very light brush strokes. She communicated so well that you really got the point right away."[1]

Norma's mother sang beautifully, played the family piano, and encouraged her children to make music together at home. A classmate of the Egstroms commented that Norma's older sisters Della and Marianne had also possessed lovely singing voices but lacked the motivation to pursue music as a career.[2] Without any formal musical training, early in her teens Norma sought opportunities to sing in public. These community gatherings and talent shows eventually yielded her an opportunity to perform as a soloist on live radio close to her home in Jamestown. Introduced by a friend to Ken Kennedy, the music director at

WDAY in Fargo, Norma was scheduled to perform live on his show, but Kennedy insisted she change her name first. Moments before she began her song, he nicknamed her "Peggy Lee" and the name stuck.

Lee sang at school throughout her teen years and picked up a job working as a waitress at the Powers Hotel Coffee Shop in Fargo. She was soon performing two shows a day plus late shows on weekends at the establishment with organist Lloyd Collins, who regularly played requests for patrons. With this on-the-job training, she quickly built her repertoire to include a wide variety of music, from old folk songs to modern jazz and contemporary popular songs.

By the tender age of seventeen, Lee had grown restless in rural North Dakota. Her thirty-nine-year-old mother had died when she was four but remained a muse throughout the singer's musical life. Growing up in a troubled household with her alcoholic father and abusive stepmother, Min Schaumber, with whom she had a very strained relationship, Peggy yearned for independence. Loving the new popular music, which was strongly tied to jazz and swing, and possessing relentless ambition, she auditioned for a spot with Sev Olson's band in nearby Minneapolis, which led to a stint with a nationally touring dance band led by Will Osborne. She set off with a couple of bandmates for southern California as soon as an opportunity arose. In 1939 Lee managed to secure a performing date at The Doll House in Palm Springs and recalled that the noisy crowd would not quiet down enough for her to be heard over the din, so she instinctively sang more softly into the microphone: "I knew I couldn't sing over them, so I decided to sing under them. The more noise they made the more softly I sang. When they discovered they couldn't hear me, they began to look at me. Then they began to listen. As I sang, I kept thinking, 'softly with feeling.' The noise dropped to a hum; the hum gave way to silence. I had learned how to reach and hold my audience—softly, with feeling."[3] In a later interview, Lee described the concept of dynamic contrast as "one of the interesting things to me about music in general—how to change the colors and the moods and how to build up like an ocean wave and let it wash away and then be very quiet."[4] As patrons paused and became hushed in order to hear her, she discovered her knack for drawing listeners in by singing quietly instead of by increasing her volume. Fortunately for Lee, an influential hotelier, Frank Bering, witnessed this magical performance and offered Lee her next job at The Buttery Room, the nightclub inside his Ambassador Hotel in Chicago. It was in this room that Benny Goodman first heard Lee perform, shortly after his singer, Helen Forrest, had left the Goodman band. This stroke of good fortune placed Lee literally at the front of the most influential band of the swing era. Needless to say, her career was off and running.

Lee later described the sometimes difficult Goodman as a taskmaster whose musical demands were the highest of any bandleader in the industry. Goodman laid down strict rules each band member was expected to maintain including mandatory curfews, brutal tour schedules (one year the band performed fifty one-night-only concerts in succession, in different cities), and intolerance for imperfect musicianship. Goodman lived with music as his highest calling and took that calling very seriously. He expected his musicians to attain the highest possible level of musical execution for both live performances and recording sessions. While this may have created a difficult workplace situation for some, it lifted the musical quality of Goodman's band to admirable heights.

At first glance, Peggy Lee may have appeared to be just one of many attractive female singers fronting important big bands of the early 1940s. When she first joined the Goodman band as a replacement for soprano Helen Forrest, Lee dutifully sang in those same high keys. In that year's recordings, Lee's high-pitched, youthful tone matched the lightness and sunny approach of many other leading big band vocalists. Her early success with a lighter, higher tone proved Lee's versatility and raw talent, even without formal training or professional tutelage. When finally given opportunities to show off her lower, softer, bluesy approach though, her signature style began to bloom.

Lee first recorded with the Goodman band on the Okeh label owned by Columbia Recording Corporation. Her recordings from 1941 revealed the uncanny pitch precision, easygoing rhythmic sense, and relaxed delivery the artist would become known for throughout her life. Even with the higher relative range of this repertoire as compared with her later material, her exquisite tone quality was equal to or exceeded that of other popular singers of the period; plus she had an approach that was singular and original. She wasn't just talented, though. She was unique. While often compared with Billie Holiday, Peggy Lee possessed an unequivocally lighter and more vibrant voice in the early phase of her career. The pure, youthful, and healthy voice in Lee's 1941 recordings surprises those whose familiarity with Lee centers around her later radio hits from the 1950s and '60s. Over time, smoking took its toll on her pure vocal sound, and its nascent clarity gave way to the darker, slightly husky quality for which she became famous.

One early recording, "Elmer's Tune," made in August 1941, sported a bouncy swing feel with a lightness and jovial quality that Lee's teen-aged voice suited perfectly. The chromatic melody proved to be no challenge whatsoever for the pitch-perfect singer. Benny Goodman's lighthearted clarinet solo toward the end of the recording yielded a lovely response to Lee's cheery vocal chorus. Later that month the band entered the recording studio again to lay down "I See a Million People (But All I Can See is You)." This song possessed a melody featuring a couple of surprising pitches and matching harmonic turns in its returning theme.

The standard song delivery for the Goodman band (and many others in the swing era) involved playing a song (or a portion of it) instrumentally first, with the entire orchestra, then transitioning to a section for leading in the vocal soloist, often facilitating a key change. Such was the case with "That's the Way It Goes," recorded in September 1941. Following an instrumental reading through the first two iterations of the opening theme during which Goodman played the melody, an extended transitional section preceded Peggy's sung entrance. After Lee's gentle vocal chorus displayed an even, well-produced tone, Benny Goodman and the band repeated the tune more forcefully with a short call-and-response clarinet solo alternating with the band's answers. This coupling of roles functioned nicely as a coda to finish the song with a neatly arranged ending, furnished by the now legendary big band arranger Eddie Sauter.

As Lee gained more experience with the Goodman band and became more comfortable with her voice's expressive qualities, she began to embrace the emotion of each new song. In October 1941, Lee and the Goodman band recorded Duke Ellington's classic "I Got It Bad (and That Ain't Good)." Lee delivered a particularly feminine, pure rendition of this standard, in keeping with her youthfulness. Her musical precision and rich tone quality revealed her growing skill and ease with which she tackled the pressure of the recording studio. Although the simplistic approach to this bittersweet text sounded light and carefree in tone quality, the final eight bars suggested Lee's innate connection to the song's dark undertone. Demonstrating the journey from innocence in the sweet, mellifluous beginning section, Lee shifted to a voice of tragic experience in the final closing. Goodman's swinging improvised solo dripped with jazz style and overt blues wailing appropriate for the King of Swing. The band also swung masterfully, with no hint of rushing or overplaying. The incredible control required for an eighteen-piece band to execute meticulously timed swing in a manner that eased off each note without affecting the tempo filled this recording with the authenticity exclusive to the top band from the swing era.

This recording represented the first of many songs to reach the popular music charts during Peggy's involvement with the Goodman band. The single was released almost immediately after it was recorded and hit the music charts on the fifteenth of November 1941. Unlike today, songs or "sides" (three-minute single songs that occupied a whole side of a ten-inch-wide, 78-rpm record) were recorded and released relatively quickly, without the long processes of editing, mixing, and mastering that require many months of production in modern music recording. Recordings were presented to the public via 78-rpm singles, in jukeboxes, and on the radio as basically live versions of songs, even though a few takes might have been necessary to glean the best performance. Today even *live* albums are meticulously edited, mixed, and mastered before the public ever hears a note.

In the swing era, recorded music truly represented the newest offerings of modern songwriters, as songs may have been delivered by their composers or lyricists to bands on the same day they were to be recorded. Because bands were in the business of delivering the latest swing music to the public through both performances and records, frequent recording dates were the norm. Bands recorded a few times per month on average, and session musicians were paid modest fees for a day's work. These musicians were, of course, expert sight-readers, being required to perform music they had never seen before with accuracy, grace, and expertise. Many long careers were made for instrumentalists in New York and Los Angeles (where the major recording studios operated) who could read music well.

"My Old Flame" appeared on the Goodman band recording session list in October 1941. This blues-inflected ballad from Paramount's Mae West film *Belle of the Nineties* went on to become a jazz standard recorded by many singers after Lee. This song possessed a gently walking bass line, understated, with soft dynamics (until the more raucous trumpet solo halfway through), and a tenderly delivered melody and lyric by a golden-voiced singer. Here stood a preview of Lee's later penchant for singing at an extremely soft volume. The band joined her in creating a gentle, quiet form of swing that pleasurably moved as one unrushed, plaintive voice. Goodman's brief, high-pitched clarinet solo transformed toward the end of the recording into a fleeting double-time flurry, adding a passionate contrast to the previously easygoing, dreamy stroll of the song.

Irving Berlin's "How Deep Is the Ocean" enjoyed a medium swing interpretation by Goodman and Lee that stood firmly among the definitive versions of this famous tune. The introduction opened with an ascending minor riff played first by the low brass, then passed to the saxophones and finally to the trumpets at one-measure intervals over a steady bass walking quarter notes. Lee entered in a new key following this long instrumental storyline. Her lyrical contribution revealed beauty in the poetry Berlin infused within this timeless song. Lee's respectful delivery of the text kept with the tradition of the period. Lyrics were never interpreted by singers fronting a big band but were simply de-livered as purely and beautifully as their voices allowed. Interpretation and stylistic affectation were deemed inappropriate for singers of the big band genre. These permutations began to come into common use mostly by singers such as Billie Holiday, whose skills became best known within the context of the small jazz combo. As was typical of song recordings from the big band era, this song's wonderful lyrics were not repeated but only presented once, with instrumental openings and endings surrounding the prized lyrical content.

Using understatement, tenderness, and thoughtful phrasing to ex-press song lyrics, Lee found ways to cover her songs with a robe of alluring sensuality. Even as early as her first few sessions with the Ben-ny Goodman Orchestra, Peggy exhibited musical restraint, as heard in her first recorded hit, "Somebody Else Is Taking My Place" by Howard, Ellsworth, and Morgan. Her minuscule slides from note to note con-nected the lyrics and tones in an elegantly controlled, sophisticated manner. Lee's conversational quality revealed a thoughtful artist devel-oping a keen ability to communicate emotion and depth throughout the course of a song. She successfully matched the band's lighthearted, bouncy tone of this swing arrangement, even though the lyrics sug-gested that a more serious approach might have been appropriate. Lat-er in her career Lee would surely have modified her approach to this lyric in a way that preserved its heartbreaking sentiment, but she had not yet learned to assert herself in insisting that her arrangements con-sistently respect the intention of the text. As a result this recording exhibited a triteness and vocal indifference uncharacteristic of her later work, manifested in the vividly cheerful way she sang about being passed over for another lover. Nevertheless, the music prevailed, and the band's relentless swing led to a warm reception by the public and a hit song on the radio. Recorded November 13, 1941, "Somebody Else Is Taking My Place" debuted March 7, 1942, hovered in the pop music charts for fifteen weeks, and peaked at number one.[5] This marked the first of many number-one hits Peggy Lee would enjoy throughout her long career.

"Somebody Nobody Loves" followed suit as another sad story put to a carefree swing. We might wonder why the lyrics of such songs were not paired with more sensitive, somber musical accompaniment. These songs balanced out the happy, optimistic songs of the swing era without sacrificing the all-important dance beat. Lyricists knew that if they

Peggy Lee, 1943. *Photofest.*

could mold their texts to fit a danceable beat they had a better chance of hearing them performed by the most popular bands. In the early 1940s dance halls provided a primary form of entertainment, and American popular music was synonymous with swing. Most songs during this era required a danceable beat, regardless of the mood of the text. As a result, this period included a great many songs whose music would surely have been more somber if composed in a later period.

Most importantly, music from the early 1940s intentionally maintained a lighthearted and joyful mood to provide the American public with a needed distraction from reality. The shock and horror of World War II pervaded the everyday lives of American citizens as well as men and women serving in the armed forces. Performing artists, recording artists, and film actors often offered their services to the USO to support American soldiers, and upbeat songs played by leading swing bands served this cause very well. Inspiring and encouraging servicemen and their families back home became a ministry performed by American dance bands. Bing Crosby, a friend of and frequent collaborator with Peggy Lee, served the USO faithfully, and Lee did her part by providing upbeat music at wartime for radio and for American families awaiting the return of their beloved soldiers. As the war dragged on, optimistic dance music became a valuable, although perhaps ironic, offering to the American public provided by performing artists.

On the same day that Lee recorded the ironically upbeat "Somebody Else Is Taking My Place," she also recorded the Gershwin standard "How Long Has This Been Going On?" from the Broadway musical *Rosalie*, with the Benny Goodman Orchestra. This gently swinging ballad allowed Lee to showcase her innate expressive compass. She supported her voice with efficient energy, yielding superb resonance and tonal purity that suggested years of formal training. Lee's lovely rendition of this Gershwin gem allowed her to stand among the many other revered recordings of this song, including Lena Horne's 1945 recording replete with a light, fluttering vibrato that contrasted with Lee's slightly cooler, more emotionally charged version.

"That Did It, Marie," a heavily swinging tune recorded the same day, gave both Lee and Goodman an opportunity to allow their swing style to rise to a new level. Lee bent notes, employed ascending and descending smears and falls, and wrapped a thick sense of easygoing style around the humorous narrative personifying various band instruments. The lyrics described a saxophone's "jumpin' jacks" and urged "jump, jump, jump it through that trumpet." Goodman later poured on the blues during his improvised clarinet solo, wailing lines that drew the band into exuberant swing. Lee's vibrato (albeit light and gentle) came through as a hallmark of these early recordings. As her career developed, she would use less vibrato and focus more on smoothness of tone, phrasing, and rhythmic timing.

Later that same month, the Goodman band recorded "Winter Weather," which peaked at number twenty-four on the popular music charts. For this vocal duet, Lee sang the first chorus followed by an instrumental trip through the song. Benny Goodman then provided an improvised chorus, alternating with arranged passages for the full band. Following that, the male singer for the Goodman band, Art London (who later modified his name to "Lund"), sang the second verse before the band played a four-bar transition and Lee sang the reprise. This bouncy, optimistic song included interesting key changes, calling to mind the lyrical descriptions of unpredictable weather.

In December 1941 Lee and Goodman reentered the recording studio to record Johnny Mercer and Victor Schertzinger's "Not Mine," from the film *The Fleet's In*. This song, while still requiring a higher vocal range than Lee preferred in later years, gave Lee the opportunity to exercise a more womanly tone that sounded more at home in front of the microphone. Goodman recalled that when first hired, "[Lee] was so scared for about three or four months, I don't think she got half the songs out of her mouth."[6] Lee was not the only one growing more comfortable with their collaboration. During the improvisational solo for this song Goodman employed a double-time technique (briefly playing notes twice as fast), exhibiting exemplary control and obviously enjoying himself.

"Not a Care in the World," from Broadway's *Banjo Eyes* by John Latouche and Vernon Duke (arranged by Eddie Sauter), was recorded by the band in December 1941. This easygoing swing tune marched ever onward with Benny Goodman providing the opening melodic statement on his clarinet, unlike the contemporary tradition of a vocalist singing the first iteration of a song's melody. Keeping the focus on himself, Goodman often commanded the attention of audiences by being the first soloist featured, even if just to perform the melody ahead of the singer. This song was remarkable in its form, as it departed from the usual eight-bar sections. The opening theme (called A) was nine bars in length, so in this AABA format (in which B represented the contrasting theme or bridge), it yielded 9+9+8+9 measures in its total form, equaling thirty-five measures instead of the conventional thirty-two. While more typical for an art song five decades later, a song departing from an eight-bar main theme was highly unusual for 1940s popular music. The song also employed a melody that illuminated Peggy's ability to sing low passages with ease.

Also that month, Peggy and the Goodman band recorded the Johnny Mercer/Harold Arlen standard "Blues in the Night," from the Warner Brothers film by the same name. Lee's rather conservative rendition of this blues song represented an excellent example of the early Peggy Lee sound. In her later years, her approach to the blues became much earthier and more dramatic, and her voice more husky, breathy, and prone to quieter singing.

Accustomed to the rigors of having to share Capitol's studio time among many active artists, Lee recorded Rodgers and Hart's "Where or When" from the Broadway musical *Babes in Arms*, on Christmas Eve in 1941. Recording schedules also frequently stretched late into the night when deadlines loomed so that projects could be finished before opening the studio for a different artist or band the next morning. Peggy's "Where or When" peered into the future by revealing her use of an ultra-soft vocal technique that, years later, became Lee's go-to strategy for making audiences listen. Her enchanting and gentle approach on this early recording melded perfectly with the delicate celesta and piano accompaniment. The celesta was an instrument often used on radio shows and in certain types of ballads during this time period. Played at a keyboard, the celesta contained a series of metal bars struck by felt hammers operated by keys, yielding a heavenly tinkling sound. This tone quality commonly accompanied children's music, holiday music, and ballads with dreamlike texts to create an ethereal quality. Lee's understated approach and the slow, steady pace of this ballad suggested that the tenderness of a lullaby was the desired effect. Throughout the song, Lee provided a remarkably even softness and haunting beauty, spanning a wide range beyond an octave. She effortlessly traversed the difficult final phrases that slowly ascended stepwise all the way up the major scale. This recording's attention to vocal nuance and tonal consistency throughout a wide range represented Lee's finest example of vocalism to date.

That same day in the recording studio, Lee and Goodman laid down a track of the Jimmy McHugh and Dorothy Fields standard "On the Sunny Side of the Street," from Broadway's *International Revue*. Goodman bounced along through the opening melodic statement before Lee entered with an uplifting statement of her own. She managed to sing several low F's (far below the range of a soprano and lower than most altos were required to sing) without difficulty. Her stylistic choices to change a pitch here and to bend a note there yielded an enjoyable, rewarding romp through a very well-known song. Her sense of syncopation was also rich here, as she anticipated downbeats by selectively choosing to enter an eighth note early on some occasions, as was, and still is, respectful of the jazz or swing style.

"The Lamp of Memory" was a nostalgic tune that received its due attention by the Goodman band during their first known studio date of the new year in January 1942. Far from being a swing song, this romantic ballad rapt in melancholic wishful thinking had Peggy singing with a great deal of vibrato and old-fashioned sentimentalism. At that same session, Lee joined Art London again in a duet from the Paramount film *The Fleet's In*, singing "If You Build a Better Mousetrap." This clever tune by Johnny Mercer and Victor Schertzinger served as an adorable cat-and-mouse romp for any pair of songbirds. First Art lectured on all the techniques and tricks he knew to attract women. Peggy then described her recipe for dating success in a similar way, and both ended their litany of tips with the questions: "Why doesn't anything happen to me?" and "What's the matter with us?" During this storytelling foray, Lee showed her predilection for genuine swing feel, a keen sense of humor, and a vocal approach that was more spoken on pitch than sung. This last point described Lee's manner of singing throughout most of her life. Although that same day in the studio she sang with a more classical, traditional approach for "The Lamp of Memory," the duet revealed her preference for her unique style of storytelling.

Lee and Goodman recorded the ballad "When the Roses Bloom Again" at the same recording session in January. The inclusion of nostalgic pieces like this in a mainstream swing band's recording session (and live performances) illustrated the balance often sought by bands and recording companies to present to the public not only new, forward-looking material tailored toward youth, but also songs that appealed to those established, mature music consumers preferring music in the style of yesteryear. In this way the Goodman band appealed to more than one demographic. In catering to mature audiences, Peggy tended to modify her vocal approach toward the same classical technique she employed for tunes like "The Lamp of Memory."

Recorded in February of that year, the somber song in a minor key "My Little Cousin" began with an ethnic folk flourish by the trumpet reminiscent of traditional Jewish music. This ethnic folksong flair returned at the end of the song, during which Lee and Goodman performed together several times in well-rehearsed harmony a particular type of ornament (a *mordent*, or turn) specific to that cultural style. Considering Goodman's Jewish heritage and upbringing, the inclusion of this song may not have been surprising to some, although it certainly was not a frequent sound in commercial recording sessions of the early 1940s. Interestingly, the original Yiddish lyrics of "My Little Cousin," which expressed frustration and disillusionment on behalf of America's Jewish immigrants, were drastically toned down in translation. Instead of rocking the image of Jews in America, the text's focus changed to that of a romantic relationship. While Goodman clearly demonstrated a desire to reflect his ethnic heritage in his music, the reality of political stress likely influenced Capitol's repackaging of the song's message.[7]

This was not the first time Benny Goodman advocated for diversity and inclusion. Several years earlier, Goodman crossed racial barriers by organizing a mixed-race trio and quartet for recording and performing. Goodman had hired Teddy Wilson, an African-American pianist, and praised him as the finest jazz pianist in the business.[8] The trio and quartet also featured Caucasian drummer Gene Krupa (who had already performed in the Goodman band) and African American vibraphonist Lionel Hampton. Goodman was known throughout the music business as leading one of the first racially integrated music ensembles in American history, so his decision to record a song with strong Jewish inflections shortly before the U.S. entry into World War II was neither surprising nor insignificant.

"The Way You Look Tonight," a classic standard by Jerome Kern and Dorothy Fields, fell onto the list of songs to be recorded by Goodman and Lee in March 1942. This delightful love song from the RKO film *Swing Time* fit Lee's knack for imbuing a ballad with beauty, tenderness, and sincerity. In this recording she gave attention to each tone, enlivening each note with grace and innocence. She slightly delayed several phrase entrances as though in the midst of an extemporaneous conversation. This manner of *backphrasing*, either intentionally delaying the start of a lyric phrase until after the musical phrase has already begun or anticipating the musical phrase by singing the lyric early, was an expressive technique first used by Billie Holiday, who learned it from saxophonist and mentor Lester Young. Lee followed suit quickly, staying at the forefront of stylistic trends. Certainly aware of Billie's style, Lee possessed her own expressive compass as well. Creating a trancelike atmosphere within the song, she wove her musical lines in a spellbinding fashion mirroring the text. The impression she gave through her relaxed gliding from note to note suggested hypnosis experienced while gazing at her lover, yielding a dreamlike desire to remember that moment forever. The celesta accompaniment added a sparkling twinkle of magic to the total sound on the recording, and this meshed well with Lee's delicate voice. The song peaked at number twenty-one on the pop charts in June of that year.

Irving Berlin's "I Threw a Kiss in the Ocean" yielded a charming swing tune for Lee to explore with Benny Goodman and his big band at one of their March 1942 recording sessions. It opened with a full band fanfare followed by a brief, energetic clarinet solo punctuated by trumpet hits, the low brass provided the finish to the introduction with a vocal lead-in transition driven by the saxophones. The trumpets continued to punctuate the melody sung by Lee in alternation with low brass responses, as though she were having a conversation with separate sections of the band. This turn-taking texture created a sense of equality between the band and the singer that contrasted with the more common texture of lead vocal backed by accompaniment that prevailed during this period. This recording illustrated Goodman's and Lee's willingness to explore different musical textures in their recording output. A piano solo provided additional textural contrast, followed by a trombone solo and then a clarinet improvisation offered by Goodman. The band rejoined for a big finish, with a tasteful extension played by the piano and walking bass.

Recorded in March 1942, "We'll Meet Again" by Ross Parker and Hughie Charles hit the pop music charts in May, peaking at number sixteen. This nostalgic but lightly swinging song gave Lee a chance to share her optimistic spirit and encouraging personality. The lyrics promised a future meeting after time spent apart from one's dearest friends. For many years this song has continued to grace retirement parties, family reunions, and class reunions as an anthem of hope for enduring friendship. Having resonated strongly with older music fans drawn to the music of yesteryear, the song enjoyed significant popularity in the early 1940s and beyond. Lee approached this lyric in a straightforward and sincere manner, showering her sunny disposition upon the music to match the hopefulness contained in this sentimental text.

"Full Moon" (also known as "Noche de Luna") was recorded on the same date in March. It arrived on the music charts in June and peaked at number twenty-two. A moderately fast song, it opened with a heavily swinging big band sound followed by a gently moving clarinet solo, and after another interjection by the full band, it tapered into a more delicate vocal tune perfectly suited for the vulnerable feminine voice of the young Peggy Lee. Beginning the vocal chorus in an up-tempo Latin style and falling into swing feel eighteen bars later, the tune provided both exotic and laid-back flavors for fans of different styles. The Latin flair returned at the very end to provide unity and cohesion to the piece—an ode to the power of the moon to influence romance. Lee and Goodman found a good match for their talents in this sentimental swing song blending both older and newer styles.

"There Won't Be a Shortage of Love," an unissued single finally released on the Columbia Legacy series in 1999, came into being in March 1942 courtesy of Lee and the Goodman band. This cute ditty followed the format of several other swing songs recorded by this band, as it was arranged by pianist Mel Powell, who held the responsibility of arranging several of their recorded songs. Goodman offered a taste of the melody in a brief solo following a fairly quiet opening with Mel Powell playing flowery piano lines amid short brass hits and a swath of soft padding by saxophones. Powell's tasteful arranging ability showed a great depth of variety, giving young Lee a sense of what might be possible for her own songs and arrangements later in her career. The timely lyrics described various food shortages, rising taxes, and other sacrifices suffered by Americans during the lean years of World War II. As always, this swing band managed to keep even wartime messages light and danceable, pointing to the abundance of love to be enjoyed in the midst of such relative lack. Even with this extremely positive spin on the plight of working American civilians, the song was never released to provide the encouraging message it sought to deliver.

In May 1942 the Goodman band entered the studio again with Lee to record Irving Berlin's classic song "You're Easy to Dance With," from Paramount's *Holiday Inn*. With the success of Fred Astaire's timeless version taken directly from the movie musical, it is no mystery why this somewhat less polished rendition was never released. Although an adorable song, the arrangement did not lend itself to improving the original enough to endure as an alternate version.[9] Although Lee sang her vocal line acceptably, her opening phrases sounded less stable and confident than usual, and she seemed to be less vocally prepared for this selection. This song may have been cut from an album (or a series of singles) before a final edited version was made. Masters never meant to be heard by the public tended to be less polished than fully rehearsed, edited recordings. Even before the days of painstaking, months-long editing processes that current songs undergo, major studios like Columbia and Capitol went over final cuts with a fine-tooth comb to ensure a high standard of quality.

The slow, charming ballad "All I Need Is You" that Lee and the Goodman band recorded in May 1942 sounded as if it belonged to years gone by rather than to the leading styles of the day. Deftly sung by Lee (even in the passages befitting a soprano), the song included wide melodic leaps landing the singer in a higher vocal range than was usually performed in jazz and swing. A jazz or swing song's performance keys were, and still are, generally selected with the singer's spoken voice range in mind. This ensured that the lyrics came through clearly and differed from the emphasis of classic genres like opera, where the power of the voice was more important than the clarity of lyrics. Since jazz, swing, and popular singers' voices were amplified in performance and recording, they could place a greater emphasis on lyrics. As this need to amplify one's own voice quickly waned at the dawn of the technological age, voices with excess vibrato and projection fell out of vogue. By contrast, soft, sultry voices like Lee's became popular, and gentler vocal stylization began to evolve among the popular, swing, and jazz set.

Along with many other bands, the Goodman band participated in war bond rallies in New York to assist with the war effort. Returning to New York to perform at the Paramount Theater in May 1942, Lee and Goodman wowed audiences with their renditions of "Where or When" and "Sing, Sing, Sing," Goodman's swing era anthem. Back in 1937 the

Goodman band had recorded this Louis Prima standard, clocking the recording at over eight minutes—way past the usual three-minute limit for radio play. The song was instrumental in continuing the swing frenzy begun on August 21, 1935, at the Palomar Ballroom in Los Angeles. Goodman ushered in the swing era that evening with the national radio broadcast of his live concert at this colossal dance hall attended by twenty thousand dancers. With the help of AM radio's long wavelengths traveling hundreds of miles farther than modern FM radio, and a string of DJs devoting their airtime to broadcasting the concert, the event blanketed the nation in swing. One of the most influential concert performances in music history, Goodman's Palomar debut ushered in a whole new genre of popular music and made Benny Goodman one of the first American pop culture stars. Even though other bands (notably Duke Ellington's) had been playing swing for years already, the public awareness and appreciation among white audiences was sealed that evening. Goodman later commented about the song: "'Sing, Sing, Sing' (which we started doing back at the Palomar on our second trip there in 1936) was a big thing, and no one-nighter was complete without it."[10] Thereafter, Goodman's audiences expected to hear the song whenever he appeared. New York's Paramount Theater crowd responded with the usual appreciation accorded to this era-defining hit.

During an interview with George Christy in 1984, Peggy Lee related that she was a fan of Lil Green, "a great old blues singer."[11] Being in the habit of playing Green's recording of "Why Don't You Do Right?" repeatedly in her dressing room at the Paramount, Lee heartily accepted Goodman's offer to create an arrangement of it especially for her. In July 1942 Peggy and the Goodman band entered the recording studio to record the song that would change the trajectory of Lee's career. Charting in January 1943, Lee's rendition of the song stayed on the popular music charts for nineteen weeks, peaking at number four. The success of the recording led to a spot in a film for Lee and the band. Their scene from *Stage Door Canteen*, in which they played the song in its entirety, became a famous moment in music history, announcing the arrival of Lee as a new solo recording artist. The vital importance of this recording to Lee's ensuing career cannot be overstated. Her perfor-mance of "Do Right," as it was often called, unveiled Lee's unique soulful blues and swing sound in a key aligned with her speaking voice. Lee infused her rendition with a respectful nod to the style of African American singers of the time while delivering her own original stylistic interpretation. Any skeptics as to whether Lee had merely copied Billie Holiday's sound were silenced after hearing Lee's signature style devel-op over decades.

"Let's Say a Prayer" was the final recording made while Lee was with the Goodman band. Recorded in July 1942 but not released until 1999, this patriotic wartime anthem was Lee's swan song with the top swing band in America. Opening with a long instrumental section, Lee's vocal chorus rendered heartfelt sentiments asking God to bless young men fighting for American freedom. She coupled this blessing with an exhortation to listeners to actively pray not only for "somebody's boy" but also for the nation. Lee poured sincerity and precision into this song as she delivered its patriotic and spiritual message.

Unfortunately for this and many other outstanding swing bands, the American Federation of Musicians declared a recording ban to com-mence immediately after July 31, 1942. The ban continued for Colum-bia Records until 1944, eliminating further opportunities for more re-cordings to be made by union musicians. The union hoped that the strike would yield artist royalties from jukeboxes and radio stations play-ing music without paying for it. The strike backfired when no fair reso-lution was found to compensate musicians. Sadly, this unfortunate situ-ation has continued to the present day. Modern songwriters continue to lobby Congress to rectify this long-unjust situation.

Interestingly, the ban did not extend over the contracts of singers, which was a major reason young Frank Sinatra's career launched during this period. Singers were not required to join the union, so they could continue to record, albeit with non-union musicians. The monopoly that ensued for Sinatra upon his release of a slew of new recordings during the ban ensured that those recordings received radio play, since radio stations had nothing else new to play. Established union bands could not compete and many established singers, faithful to and standing by their union bands, waited for the ban to be lifted before returning to the recording studios. This reality gave Sinatra, an emerging non-union singer untethered by band loyalties, a greater advantage and career boost than that of any other singer in American pop music history. Although the Goodman band did not record during this time period, it continued to perform with Lee until she left the band in March 1943.

In addition to jump-starting Lee's career and releasing several hit songs, the Lee-Goodman collaboration yielded another huge benefit for Peggy. In the summer of 1942, guitarist Dave Barbour joined the Goodman band and quickly became a new love interest for the chanteuse. In March 1943, having defied Goodman's rule against band members becoming romantically involved with one another, Barbour and Lee left the band and soon married. Barbour became the first collaborative composer with whom Peggy wrote a long string of songs. For the moment, though, Peggy was content to simply enjoy being Mrs. Dave Barbour.

2

A CAPITOL IDEA

Peggy Lee's career as a major-label recording artist began and ended at Capitol Records, spanning twenty-nine years. She spent five of those years sharpening her jazz chops in the studios of a major competitor that became well known for its outstanding jazz talent. Overall, though, Lee's home was with the Capitol family throughout the 1940s, '50s, '60s, and into the '70s. She began winning the hearts of her fans even from her earliest days.

Toward the end of her tenure with the Benny Goodman Orchestra, on December 30, 1942, Peggy returned the Paramount Theater in New York for a special performance. This engagement happened to include the solo debut of a young singer who had recently left the Tommy Dorsey Band to actively pursue a solo career. Bob Weitman, the manager at the Paramount, booked this performer as an additional act on the bill. When Goodman dryly announced the entrance of this young singer, Frank Sinatra, the theater erupted in girlish hysteria akin to that accompanying Beatles concerts a couple of decades later. Both Lee and Sinatra would soon enjoy worldwide renown and stardom as fellow artists on the roster of a new label called Capitol Records. While the Paramount introduction may have left an indelible first impression upon both artists, their common link to Capitol would not commence for several more months.

In February 1943 the Goodman band spent six weeks performing in Hollywood. While there, Lee gave Goodman her notice of intention to leave the band, as she and Dave Barbour (who had already been fired for fraternizing with the singer) planned to marry. Another take on the story was that Dave had simply quit and asked Lee to marry him at the moment he informed her of his leaving.[1] Either way, the Barbours tied the knot in March of that year, and their daughter Nicki would arrive in November. In the meantime, Peggy found contentment in her domestic roles of wife and soon-to-be mother.

Producers at Capitol Records became interested in signing young Peggy Lee following the success of her hits with the Goodman band, especially "Why Don't You Do Right?" which led to a video spot for Lee and Goodman in the film *Stage Door Canteen*. The film spot consisted of a scene containing a full performance of the song with the camera on the band and singer. The film's popularity created some of the first inroads for Lee's talent to be seen and appreciated on a national level. Just prior to the film's release, the song itself rose slowly and spent almost five months on *Billboard*'s Top 30 chart in 1943, creating an unusually long period for the hit and its singer to bask in the public's consciousness.

Lee's subsequent successful recording dates as a guest vocalist with ad hoc bands also created allure strong enough to attract Capitol's producers. Concert dates and radio performance opportunities continued to roll in. Lee, however, was committed to her new job as wife and mother and harbored no plans to return to her former mode of employment. She engaged her musical interests by writing songs with her husband. Dave eventually convinced Peggy to return to her career, feeling strongly that with such talent she would one day regret leaving the stage for a purely domestic life. Her husband was sensitive to the fact that Lee's recent difficult childbirth and an ensuing hysterectomy would prevent her from ever having more children. Dave's unflagging encouragement toward his wife to pursue a music career under such sober realities at home showed a support of his spouse's best interests that was well before its time. As a result of Dave's support, as well as the reality that the Barbours needed the money, Lee began accepting some performance and recording offers while turning others down as she sought balance between her home life and occasional work. This part-time music lifestyle proved to be short lived. As her daughter grew stronger, Peggy began to accept more and more offers to perform and record, effectively taking her career to the next level. Before Nicki reached her second birthday, Lee had fully returned to a life of music.

Peggy signed with Capitol Records toward the end of 1944 to begin an immensely successful solo career. Holding an active recording contract with Capitol for an impressive twenty-three years, Peggy Lee remained the longest-signed female artist that ever worked with this label. At the time her contractual arrangements began, she also signed with General Artists, a professional booking agency. Capitol Records indulged the Barbours to some extent, allowing many of their co-written songs to be recorded along with the other songs Peggy was given by the session producer. Some of the better-known Barbour-Lee collaborations included "I Don't Know Enough about You," "It's a Good Day," and "What More Can a Woman Do?" Each of these songs would eventually be recorded by Peggy with Dave Barbour and His Orchestra.

In November 1943 and January 1944 Capitol put together an ensemble called The Capitol Jazzmen to celebrate the end of the musicians' union recording ban. Peggy Lee was called to participate in the second session. She initially declined but then accepted after receiving a second invitation. One song selected for this session was "That Old Feeling," an Academy Award–nominated Sammy Fain and Lew Brown song from the film *Vogues of 1938*. In Lee's version the song was accompanied by celesta, saxophone, bass, and drum set. This enchanting song suitably reintroduced Peggy to her talent for recording. Two months after enduring a cesarean section to deliver her only child, Lee infused a delicate passion and expressive technique into her tone as she wove the aural tapestry of this classic song. Lee's tenderness matched that of saxophonist Eddie Miller as they gently related the story of a long-ago love reawakening. Lee's heartfelt rendition of this jazz standard took its rightful place as an important early recording of it, long before Chet Baker contributed an up-tempo swing version to delight the ears and hearts of jazz aficionados a decade later, followed by Frank Sinatra, for whom it scored a hit in 1960.

In "Sugar," another standard Lee recorded at that first Capitol recording session, Lee's darker, huskier vocal quality came through in her heavily swinging interpretation. Her slightly naughty sound (produced simply by singing in a spoken pitch range, or alto range, with a wide expressive and stylistic compass) replete with slides, smears, and note bending yielded many sexist comments about her singing from the men who recorded with her. This disrespectful reception by men of Lee's singular, bold style that sounded incredibly sexy while being marked with appropriate jazz sensibility constituted a challenge with which she would have to cope throughout her life. The male-dominated music industry unjustly judged female singers as sounding like tramps and whores if they sang low with a husky, emotionally charged tone. Likewise, the industry judged female singers to be pure, angelic canaries if they sang in a soprano register with a slightly more classical approach. This prejudice was expressed in comments made by the producer, Dave Dexter Jr., at the recording session during which these two recordings were created: "Peggy Lee could sing like a little girl in a church choir or a husky-voiced, tired old whore." By contrast, Dexter considered Lee's sweet and innocent rendition of "That Old Feeling," which required her to sing in a higher register, "pure angel food."[2] Music columnist and DJ Eddie Gallaher published: "Peggy is not the girl you'd run into at a high school prom. Her voice is more that of the girl in the smoke-filled room at a truckline café or at a juke joint along a Texas highway."[3] On another occasion a band member stated, "This chick sounds like a drunken old whore with the hots."[4] As tempting as it might be for some to consider such descriptions of Lee's wide range of expression to be complimentary, one must remember that male singers (basses or tenors) would never have been given equally disrespectful judgments based on their expressive additions of smears, slides, changes in tone quality or range, or jazz ornaments. Being among the first Caucasian women to sing in the soulful, down-to-earth manner of her black blues and jazz contemporaries, Lee was exposed to criticism, sexism, attempted physical assault on her person, and other injustices purely on the basis of her talents and how she chose to use them. Enduring gender prejudice and assumed to be an easy sexual target based on her huskier singing style and alluring stage presence, Lee was chased backstage at the Paramount Theater by a group of male audience members. In response to Sinatra's debut at the same performance, female patrons screamed and swooned. He was viewed as an untouchable idol, she as an objectified target to be played with and possessed. Lee quickly learned by this dichotomous injustice that she needed to protect herself from her audience and began to withdraw to a safer internal space. The safety Lee enjoyed in the recording studio became a creative haven she would return to for the rest of her life.

New American Jazz was the title of the four-disc album that was released from the first two recording sessions (November 1943 and January 1944) by The Capitol Jazzmen. The producer's note in the album stated that no arrangements were used for the sessions. Instrumentalists and vocalists simply came and played or sang as they wished in an extemporaneous fashion. As jazz required improvisation, this absence of written charts ensured that the final product was, indeed, new American jazz. The album was only the third album ever released by Capitol, preceded only by *Songs by Johnny Mercer* and *Christmas Carols* (featuring St. Luke's Choristers). In addition to Peggy Lee, vocalist and trombonist Jack Teagarden contributed vocals to songs on the *New American Jazz* album, although the two were not in the studio simultaneously for this session.

"Ain't Goin' No Place," a heavy twelve-bar blues song also sung by Lee at her first Capitol session, was essentially spoken on pitch in the traditional manner of blues singing. Shining through in a few places, her upward-inflected speech style clearly betrayed a nod to the inflection style of Billie Holiday. One also heard the influence of the Empress of the Blues, Bessie Smith, in the strong, assured, full-voiced approach Lee used to sing this female-empowered text. Blues songs often possessed a repeated first line with a contrasting text in the third line that drove home the point raised in the first phrase. This twelve-measure form sometimes included, as in this example, a stop chorus after the first or second chorus, during which the accompaniment suddenly stopped. Musical rests (when the instrumentalists did not play) were then used to call attention to important words in the text. Immediately following the "stop" section an instrumental interlude led up to the final stanzas or verses. Lee finished this tune with a spoken question often attributed to her style. Collaborative composer John Chiodini asserted that Peggy was, in some ways, "the first rap artist," frequently choosing to speak during a song for a particular desired effect.[5] In this case she likely improvised her final spoken thought: "Why don't you come on home, baby?"

"Someday Sweetheart" was also recorded at Lee's inaugural Capitol session with The Capitol Jazzmen, featuring a clarinet solo by Barney Bigard. This song matched the swing style she had first explored with her previous band, the Benny Goodman Orchestra. This piece required a lighter, sweeter-sounding approach than the blues song previously described.

The musical and stylistic distinctions Peggy routinely made in the recording studio deserve mention. The three styles exhibited at this single recording session over four songs—blues, swing, and romantic ballad—each received a singularly authentic rendition and approach. While most singers would have sung all four selections with the same vocal color, breath support, technique, diction, and overall sensibility, Peggy Lee by this time in her career began to consider a song's background, theme, rhythmic feel, and appropriate storytelling angle. Her thorough efforts to make distinctions among her recordings resulted in a wildly varied catalog of repertoire. She infused her singing with enormous attention to subtlety, nuance, and understated expression. This ability to distinguish appropriate differences among songs grew as her musicianship and interpretive prowess matured. Sarah Vaughan, who recorded Lee's "What More Can a Woman Do?" admired Lee's vocalism: "I like those nice breathy tones Peggy gets on her low notes." Count Basie's singer Joe Williams was likewise "captivated" by Lee's rendition of "You Was Right, Baby," which he first heard in a Chicago race record store that grouped Lee's single among those of black artists.[6]

Lee's ownership of her studio performance style grew enormously over the course of her career. Once, while working with Goodman, she expressed a desire to slow down and soften a new arrangement of Gershwin's "But Not for Me," but rather than concede to her suggestions, Goodman discarded the song entirely. Similar scenarios followed for Lee as her career climbed into new territory. Record producers at Capitol would eventually allow her to bring original songs and other material preferences to the sessions but generally reserved for themselves the final decisions about song lists and which masters would make it to an album. Likewise, as a young Capitol artist she would determine what approach to use for each song, but the bulk of the repertoire decisions would be producer-driven. Lee worked tirelessly to gradually grow her autonomy as an artist, but in the male-dominated music industry, her goal would take decades to accomplish.

From the Capitol Jazzmen session, one song in particular received extensive radio airplay. "That Old Feeling" mesmerized Lee's fans because of the way she filled it with expression and meaning. She became so sought after from the success of this record that she hired her first manager, Carlos Gastel, to help shape her solo career. Shortly thereafter, Lee recorded a few sides with Bob Crosby and Orchestra, possibly in conjunction with a guest appearance on Crosby's radio show. These included Harry Warren and Johnny Mercer's song "On the Atchison, Topeka and the Santa Fe" and Jimmy Van Heusen and Johnny Burke's adorable song "It's Anybody's Spring." The first began with the unmistakable sound of an orchestral depiction of a locomotive engine and train whistle (provided by a chorus of woodwinds) throughout the long introduction. When Lee entered, her youthful exuberance contrasted brightly against the more mature baritone voice of Bob Crosby. Lee's lighthearted tones brought the song to life while Crosby's counterpoint balanced her energy with intentional coolness. In "It's Anybody's Spring," Lee sounded remarkably different, using more vibrato than usual, as if copying Bing Crosby's style (for whom the song was written by Jimmy Van Heusen for the film *Road to Utopia*). This marked an interesting choice for Lee in interpreting this swing song—instead of her usual swing groove and spoken-on-pitch style, she mysteriously deferred to a previous style used when she had to sing in higher keys. Given her greater success with a more spoken style when singing swing, this rendition seemed out of place, amateurish, and inconsistent next to her more successful work, but it may have represented an experimental, transitional period when she was discovering her own voice. When readying herself for this session, she possibly had been modeling Bing Crosby's film rendition because she sang it (note-for-note) exactly as the composer wrote instead of interpreting it with her signature stylistic touches.

In December 1944 Dave Barbour and His Orchestra entered the recording studio with Lee and recorded a charming ballad, "Baby (Is What He Calls Me)." Already, fans heard the mature Peggy Lee sound replete with thoughtful interpretation and expression packaged in a lower, slightly husky tone quality. Lee's signature breathy vocal production would become her calling card, by which she would become known and loved worldwide. The first Barbour-Lee collaboration to be recorded, "What More Can a Woman Do?" was also undertaken at this 1944 session, and it fully utilized the breathy voice Lee had grown accustomed to using in favor of the earlier pure, high, and youthful tone resplendent with innocence and clarity. In coming into her own sound, Lee sacrificed some of the pristine finish heard in her most youthful records but gained a unique, earthy sound she felt was more her own. Lee's penchant for smoking cigarettes intensified the huskiness of her tone. Over time this approach to singing was firmly cemented into Lee's style, and there was no turning back. Fortunately for Lee, this novel sound exactly fit the persona she exhibited onstage, so she made the most of her unique musical niche.

"What More Can a Woman Do?" exemplified a slow and lovely original ballad and painted a picture of devotion typical of Lee's lyric-writing style. So often, Lee approached songwriting from the standpoint of total commitment. While other writers may have stopped short of saying the obvious message (leaving a bit to the imagination), Peggy unapologetically wore her proverbial heart on her sleeve, holding nothing back. This self-revelatory lifestyle allowed her warmth and expressive depth to stay honest and vulnerable throughout her career.

In December 1944 Dave Barbour and His Orchestra recorded "A Cottage for Sale" by Willard Robison and Larry Conley, with Lee singing vocals. The master was never released as a single until it appeared in 2008 on *Peggy Lee: The Lost '40s & '50s Capitol Masters* album. This session marked Lee's first enterprise as a solo Capitol artist. Lee's initial entrance displayed temerity, and her voice bobbled slightly in a couple of places, which may have accounted for the fact that this track was cut from Capitol's list of songs fit for release. Her usually secure centering of the pitch lapsed in a few places at the mercy of a fluttering vibrato. Still, much of the song was beautifully rendered, and Lee's confidence seemed to sharpen as she progressed through it.

Shortly thereafter, Lee and a jazz quartet led by Dave Barbour recorded an original blues song called "You Was Right, Baby" that showcased Lee's outstanding bluesy style and flirtatious expression. In this song (with Barbour's quartet backing Lee's vocals), both Lee and Barbour showed the peak of their performing abilities. Barbour's guitar solo flaunted his ability to maintain an understated groove while exploring the tension between the flat and natural thirds that define the blues. He then tapered his guitar seamlessly back into the texture, making room for Lee to finish the piece. Lee balanced her true confidence in this style with artistic note choices, using a half-spoken, half-sung manner of communicating her text.

Peggy credited Great American Songbook composer, singer, and early Capitol executive Johnny Mercer for encouraging her to write her own songs and for suggesting that Barbour and Lee record their original songs at Capitol sessions. Agent Carlos Gastel had encouraged the Barbours to play their originals for Mercer, and Lee heartily welcomed the songwriting veteran's suggestions and advice. As Iván Santiago-Mercado explained in his exhaustive Peggy Lee discography, Peggy remarked: "When they talked us into recording, we didn't have any material, so Johnny said, 'Do those things I heard—those are great.' So we did them, and they were hits . . . 'What More Can a Woman Do?' and 'You Was Right, Baby.'"[7] These two songs ended up on opposite sides of a Capitol 78-rpm single that spent ten weeks on the *Disc Hits— Box Score* best-seller music charts affiliated with *Cash Box* magazine. "You Was Right, Baby" peaked at number eleven.

In 1945 Peggy Lee joined Dave Barbour and His Orchestra to record another 78-rpm record, titled "Waitin' for the Train to Come In," by Martin Block and Sunny Skylar. This was issued for the Armed Forces Radio and Television Service along with selections featuring Dick Haymes and Frank Sinatra, in addition to other artists. This dragging ballad aptly described the painfully slow passage of time as one waited hour after hour and day after day for a loved one to return. The song stayed on *Billboard*'s charts for fourteen weeks beginning in November 1945, peaking at number four. Lee's relaxed and easygoing manner, as mirrored in the companion ballad on the reverse side, "I'm Glad I Waited for You," beautifully expressed the sentiment of a faithful woman awaiting the return of her beloved from the war. This latter song on the second side also attained chart positions, in March 1946, reaching number twenty-four on the *Billboard* list.

Billboard represented the gold standard of popular music's record sales and radio spins—a song's weekly ranking could be viewed in both parameters, and its overall success depended on the combination of both. *Billboard* measured, and still measures, popularity of a song relative to the other songs in the current week's market. *Billboard* magazine featured its first "hit parade" in 1936, and a plethora of song charts followed in ensuing years. The charts soon reached around the world, and awareness of the fast-paced change occurring in American popular music spread internationally in part thanks to the weekly change-up of *Billboard*'s top songs, eventually known by 1958 as the Hot 100. Since then other charting services evolved in an effort to grow readership for other publications competing in the pop music industry.

In December 1945 Lee recorded "I Can See It Your Way, Baby" with the Dave Barbour All-Stars. This easy swinging ballad allowed Lee to purr her lyrics gently into the microphone. The song showcased Lee's ability to persuade using her feminine charms and musical nuances, emphasizing the consequent phrase balancing the title, "but please see it my way tonight." The song attained a level of sexy playfulness that Lee would build into her style.

At, presumably, the same session, Lee and Barbour recorded one of their best-known original hits, "I Don't Know Enough about You." This slow swing tune employed elements of the blues amid clever lyrics that explored an angle of male-female relationships that had not been described in other songs. Elucidating details about human interaction in new ways that resonated with millions of people seemed to be a challenge to which Lee often rose in her songwriting: "I read the latest news, no buttons on my shoes, but baby I'm confused about you . . . I know a little bit about biology and a little more about psychology . . . but I don't know enough about you." Through this song, Lee and Barbour succeeded in marrying music to lyrics in a way that pleased listeners and earned them millions of fans. Debuting on the *Billboard* charts in May 1946, the song peaked at number seven.

Lee and Barbour explored the process of writing songs together in various ways. Sometimes she would write lyrics and he would set the completed lyrics to music, as in "What More Can a Woman Do?" At other times she would compose words to complement Barbour's simple musical ideas, and occasionally they would sit down together to work on composing words and music at the same time, contributing their thoughts and creating a song simultaneously, building upon one another's ideas. John Chiodini expressed that his collaborations with Lee followed this same three-way songwriting paradigm, and Lee "said she loved this because this was the way she used to work with her first husband, Dave Barbour."[8] Generally, Barbour would then arrange and orchestrate the music for performance or recording purposes. Later in her career, other members of the band (usually the pianist or big band conductor) would assume that responsibility.

In late 1945 Peggy Lee was called to a recording session in Hollywood in order to sing the vocal tracks for two Disney songs that were yet to be released in the film *Make Mine Music,* originally planned to be a sequel to the legendary 1940 Disney film *Fantasia.* While classical music claimed the equivalence of a leading role in *Fantasia,* popular music occupied an equally important role in the 1946 counterpart. Although Lee played no part in making this film, nor its soundtrack (Dinah Shore and The Andrews Sisters performed these songs on the soundtrack), this session independently created two promotional recordings for radio release ahead of the film. The songs "Johnny Fedora and Alice Blue Bonnet" and "Two Silhouettes" were accompanied by the Charles Wolcott Orchestra. The film represented a wartime compilation of short animated skits (much like *Fantasia*) put together to create a feature film, while Disney's primary film staff finished serving in the army draft. Released in theaters in 1946, *Make Mine Music* was never reissued; instead it was sliced into ten shorts used in Disney's televised shows.

In April 1946 Peggy's solo career as a Capitol Records artist rose to new heights with "Linger in My Arms a Little Longer," which became her fourth hit for the label. Dave Barbour and His Orchestra provided an easy swinging accompaniment to her gently crooning voice. According to *Your Hit Parade Singles Chart*, the song hit the charts in September and spent three weeks there, peaking at number eight. "Baby, You Can Count on Me," the song on the other side of the 78-rpm record, was also recorded at the same session. This swing tune included a line in Spanish (a translation of the song title), which represented Lee's first foray into music with strong Hispanic or Latin qualities. She would later explore this Spanish theme many times in original songs like "Mañana" and "Caramba! It's the Samba." Her keen ear for languages and interest in singing with heavy linguistic accents led Lee to record music highlighting various cultures more frequently than most other pop singers of her generation.

In July 1946 the Barbours recorded two of their original collaborations: "Don't Be so Mean to Baby" and "It's a Good Day." The first was a slowly swinging song in which a woman begged her man to treat her with more kindness. It possessed a sense of earnest yet dignified pleading, as if Lee were asking for mercy on behalf of all ill-treated women. This version was held in the Capitol vaults for decades, finally seeing the light in 2008 when several unreleased masters were unveiled on the long-awaited album *Peggy Lee: The Lost '40s and '50s Capitol Masters*.

"It's a Good Day" became an anthem for optimism long associated with Lee and would be used as a theme song for her radio show in forthcoming years. This wonderful up-tempo swing tune championed all that was fun and joyous about an ordinary day. In it, Lee encouraged the listener to embrace both the day and a positive outlook, to get going, and to be thankful for all the beauty and opportunities that this new day brought. The recording included a trumpet solo, a guitar solo by Dave Barbour, and a clarinet solo during the interlude before Lee returned for the final vocal reprise. "It's a Good Day" first appeared on the *Billboard* charts in January 1947 and peaked at number sixteen. Capitol released this recording as a single in 1947, 1948, and 1951. Other labels, RCA Victor and Columbia, released their own competing versions of this Barbour-Lee composition. The song resonated so much with so many listeners that it remained relevant and cherished for multiple decades following its initial release. Other singers recorded it, including Dean Martin, Vic Damone, Perry Como, Bing Crosby, and the author of this book. Lee herself performed it on television four times as a duet with Bing Crosby, and Judy Garland performed it on her televised variety show in 1963. "It's a Good Day" has appeared in several film soundtracks, including *Scent of a Woman* (1992), *U Turn* (1997), *Blast from the Past* (1999), *World's Greatest Dad* (2009), and *Pete's Dragon* (2016), and on television in episodes of *Malcolm in the Middle*, *The Marvelous Mrs. Maisel*, and *Wilfred*. Its universal appeal, catchy tune, and direct, positive message cemented its ongoing relevance for subsequent generations.

One song recorded at the same session, "I've Had My Moments," ended up being rejected for commercial release but was eventually included as part of the 2008 posthumous album mentioned above. Lee's

overall performance was clean, expressive, and beautifully complemented by celesta, piano, and bass, but she anticipated her final note, singing
it slightly early. This altered the timing of the pianist's penultimate
chord, which created an awkward musical moment and possibly accounted for the rejection of the track. Lee recorded "I've Had My
Moments" five times in the 1940s, more than any other song. She recorded the song twice for radio broadcasts and two other times at Capitol for commercial release (July 1946 and November 1947), although
only one of the three recordings made at Capitol was released prior to
2008.

On July 15, 1946, Peggy's voice appeared on a recording of "A
Nightingale Can Sing the Blues," for which the Frank DeVol Orchestra
was credited. Some uncertainty remains as to whether Lee actually
attended the DeVol session or whether her vocal master from a June
session, featuring Dave Barbour and His Orchestra, was inserted instead. Either way, the final product yielded a delightful symphonic
rendering of a romantic, bluesy ballad with a flute soloist providing
birdlike fluttering and calls in response to Lee singing the title lyric.
Lee's natural, gentle stroll through this storytelling song coaxed the
listener into a virtual forest glade to observe the birds and trees so
clearly painted in this orchestral landscape.

In July 1946 Lee recorded her fifth hit song, "It's All Over Now."
Backed by Dave Barbour and His Orchestra, Lee imbued this medium-
slow swing tune with a heartfelt story about falling prey to a lying beau.
She navigated swinging semitones and employed fall-offs at the ends of
notes to ornament her melody with jazz inflections teeming with authentic swing style. Halfway through, the band moved into a double-
time feel, causing a ramp-up of energy and a sense that the music
moved twice as fast, during which Lee naturally transitioned into a
matching rhythmic sensibility. (This double-time feel was and still is a
technique used by bands to add energy to the middle of ballads—the
music's harmony and melody move at the same rate as before but feel
more energetic, with a busier undercurrent of rhythm and musical activity.) The music then tapered into the original slow swing feel for the

end of this well-executed song. It entered the *Billboard* charts in November and attained number ten status.

Lee's version of the scandalous song "Aren't You Kind of Glad We Did?" by George and Ira Gershwin never made it to the *Billboard* charts, being banned from radio airplay by networks due to its lyrics being strongly suggestive of a sexual encounter. Moreover, two other duet versions of the same song were allowed radio play. Judy Garland and Dick Haymes performed it for the Decca label, and Vaughn Monroe and Betty Hutton recorded it for Victor. The duets allowed the male characters to assume much of the responsibility for the described indiscretions, leaving Lee's solo version to show her simmering alone in the song's shocking implications. Lee certainly did simmer in this recording, bringing a sensuous, unapologetic, and surprisingly open conversation about sex to the masses in a musical package. Lee forged new ground here in respect to recording subject matter universally deemed unsuitable for public discourse, and it would not be the last time. Whereas many other singers shied away from controversial subjects, Lee welcomed opportunities to explore new frontiers, even if they raised more than a few eyebrows.

In September 1946 Lee returned to the Hollywood studio at Sunset and Vine, again with Dave Barbour and His Orchestra, to record "He's Just My Kind" by Floyd Huddleston and Mark McIntyre. This slow-moving ballad provided plenty of interpretive ground for Lee's masterful ballad singing. Her uncanny knack for expression and nuance proved reliable here, yielding a rich example of sensitivity, musicality, and feminine charm with a distinctively jazzy tone. The song was released as a 78-rpm single with "It's a Good Day" on the other side.

Also that month, Lee participated in a massive recording undertaking for a Capitol album called *Jerome Kern's Music*, featuring a host of other artists. Lee recorded "She Didn't Say Yes" for this project, which was originally released in 78-rpm format on four discs. It was later released as a 10-inch LP disc and as an EP (three 45-rpm discs). Johnny Mercer, Martha Tilton, The Nat Cole Trio, Margaret Whiting, The Pied Pipers, and Paul Weston were among the stars called in for this album, which may have been an effort by Capitol to proactively produce music by their top artists in anticipation of another recording ban.

Indeed, in October the American Federation of Musicians once again engaged in disputes with record companies over wages and contractual agreements, threatening a second debilitating strike. This caused the studios to schedule far more recording dates than usual for artists on their rosters. Fortunately, by October twentieth the parties had reached a settlement, and the recording schedule relaxed again. Four songs were recorded during this period by Peggy Lee and Dave Barbour: "When Irish Eyes Are Smiling," "Birmingham Jail," "Don't Be So Mean to Baby" (again), and "Swing Low, Sweet Chariot." Recording masters of the first and last in this list were cast aside and never released until many decades later. Without the urgent need for new material, Capitol may have simply dismissed these recordings and moved on toward new, contemporary material. This session's version of "Don't Be So Mean to Baby" was released in 1948 (the previously recorded version was not released until sixty years later), and "Birmingham Jail" went public in 1951.

"Birmingham Jail" boasted an easy swinging rendition of this traditional American folk song. A refreshing new take on this well-known song lent the arrangement some historical value. The bouncing swing beat and Lee's down-to-earth style lent new contemporary American relevance to the folk song genre as interpreted by the best swing musicians of the time period. "Don't Be So Mean to Baby" was recorded again, replacing the horn section featured in the July recording with a guitar solo in October. The couple had booked a recording session in New York during a string of concerts at the Paramount Hotel and hired an unknown combo of performers. Both versions of this original song were vocally similar, although Lee presented the melody in a naturally expressive speech-like manner appropriate for the song's moderately slow swing style, so each version inhabited its own unique character. Lee's extemporaneous approach to recording jazz and blues possessed much freedom and originality by this point in her career, making the recording of identical iterations of the same song highly unlikely. Thus, the song versions possess differences, both in arrangement and in vocal delivery.

The couple recorded eight masters (all jazz or blues) during the New York recording session in October 1946. Four were ballads and four exhibited a medium swing feel. Music historian Iván Santiago-Mercado has asserted that these eight songs may have been intended for a Lee-Barbour album, as eight tracks often comprised a full album in the 1940s. However, no such album ever transpired for these masters, so some were stored in the Capitol vaults until their eventual release in 2008. These songs included: "When Irish Eyes Are Smiling," "Swing Low, Sweet Chariot," "It's the Bluest Kind of Blues (Nuages)," "You Can Depend on Me," "Trouble Is a Man," "Music, Maestro, Please," "Birmingham Jail," and "Don't Be So Mean to Baby."[9]

Upon returning to Los Angeles, the Barbours lost no time in commencing with the recording routine. Recorded in November 1946, "Everything Is Movin' Too Fast" hit the *Billboard* charts in February, peaking at number twenty-one, and gave the Barbour-Lee songwriting team their third hit. This medium-fast swing tune relied heavily on the blues and displayed clever lyrics about the ever-increasing pace of modern society. With its catchy melody and relevant words, the song found its niche in the canon of late 1940s swing music. It also may have served as a harbinger of trends to come—rock and roll was around the corner, and swing's days were numbered. "Everything Is Movin' Too Fast" sent the clear message that Lee wished the world would slow down to a more easygoing, comfortable pace.

In January 1947 Lee recorded "Speaking of Angels," a romantic ballad played by Dave Barbour and His Orchestra, featuring the gentle accompaniment of flutes, clarinets, other subtle woodwinds, and muted horns. At the same session, they recorded the Gershwin/Buddy DeSylva classic "Somebody Loves Me" for a Capitol compilation album titled *The Beloved Songs of Buddy DeSylva*. Several other recording stars appeared on this album, including Johnny Mercer, Martha Tilton, The King Cole Trio, The Pied Pipers, and Margaret Whiting. This 78-rpm album contained four discs of music by some of the finest Capitol recording artists of all time, yet, unfortunately, it has never been re-leased on compact disc for twenty-first-century aficionados to enjoy.

In March of that year, Peggy reunited with Benny Goodman to create a recording of "Eight, Nine, and Ten," a simple swing tune with a melody consisting of a repeated tonic note. This time Goodman and Lee recorded with a smaller combo rather than with their previous eighteen-piece jazz orchestra. The Benny Goodman Sextet, featuring Dave Barbour on the guitar, proved to be in line with the trend of downsizing bands. This trend continued through the late 1940s and beyond, both for financial reasons and due to the fact that big bands generally were becoming less popular in favor of small jazz combos and rock bands. A simple rhythm section—guitar, bass, drum set, and a horn or singer—soon replaced the larger ensembles. Goodman later recorded another version of this song with his own voice providing the vocal part.

In April, Lee recorded "Chi-Baba, Chi-Baba" (also known as "My Bambino, Go to Sleep"), which climbed to number ten on the popular music charts. Perry Como's version of this song reached number one. Lee's version began with a gentle swing reminiscent of a rocking cradle; it then transitioned to a fast and furious double-time section, returning again to a lullaby-like finish with male backup singers providing sup-port, singing the song title while Lee spoke a mixture of Italian and English to the infant receiving this serenade. At the same recording session Lee performed "Ain'tcha Ever Comin' Back?" which was also recorded by Frank Sinatra. Both Sinatra's and Lee's versions spent one week on the *Disc-Hits Box Score* music chart.

On July 3, 1947, Lee and Barbour recorded another original collabo-ration, "Just an Old Love of Mine," a slow ballad with a melancholic nostalgia for days and relationships gone by. Lee's tender, unhurried, soft vocal approach to this musically rewarding piece left the listener in a reverie of blissful relaxation, as if she lulled her audience to sleep—something she was truly capable of doing, whether in a live perfor-mance room filled with people or in a recording studio. Other versions of this popular Lee-Barbour song were recorded for Columbia Records by Doris Day, for RCA Victor by Tommy Dorsey, for MGM by Billy Eckstine, and for Majestic by Dick Farney. Lee's take on this ballad reached number thirty-four in the popular music charts and stayed for two weeks during the month of October. "Just an Old Love of Mine" and its popularity among studios and recording artists furthered the Barbour-Lee songwriting team's credibility and clout in the pop song-writing business.

Although Peggy was in wonderful voice during this recording date, her lovely performance of another song, "Why Should I Cry Over You," remained locked in Capitol's vaults until the album *Rare Gems and Hidden Treasures* was finally released in 2000. Joined as usual by Dave Barbour (this time with a group of unknown musicians billed as the Dave Barbour All-Stars), Lee displayed exuberant swing in full-voiced style.

Peggy Lee and Dave Barbour in rehearsal. *Photofest.*

Why so many seemingly high-quality masters remained unreleased for over five decades seemed peculiar, indeed. Lee, however, had little decision-making power in regard to what masters landed on albums or singles that Capitol released for sale or radio broadcast. At this point in her career, Lee, along with countless other artists, had to defer to Capitol's producers and company executives who decided which masters to use and which to toss. Being female made her influence even smaller with regard to the record executives' decisions. Several of Lee's original songs were recorded at Capitol sessions but never made the final cut for albums or singles, although she was fortunate to have been allowed to release *some* of her own compositions early in her career. Her songwriting prowess was already proven by the number of other mainstream artists (both at Capitol and at competing labels) who recorded her songs, namely Sinatra, Martin, Day, Vaughan, Cole, and others. That her originals had produced genuine hits may have further persuaded the record producers to include her songs in their album releases.

"'Is That All There Is?' is not just the title of a hit song recorded by Peggy Lee . . . It's also a question long-time Lee collectors have posed throughout the CD era."[10] Peggy Lee fans all over the world rejoiced when the albums *Rare Gems and Hidden Treasures* and *The Lost '40s and '50s Capitol Masters* were finally made available to the public. EMI took on the latter project with cooperation from Capitol Records archivists and Lee's granddaughter Holly Foster-Wells leading the charge. These archived recordings bore merit of their own and constituted an important additional catalog of Lee's output. Scores of previously unheard tracks that Lee had recorded many decades earlier finally took their rightful places in her canon of recorded music. Aficionados and scholars of music from decades past obtained a much greater sense of Lee's total musical and artistic output when the plethora of unreleased songs gained their due hearing alongside well-worn recordings her fans remembered as big hits. Music critic Jack Garner wrote of this posthumous project: "Through the 39 tracks, Lee stokes the fires that ultimately lead to 'Fever,' her late-'50s megahit. If you only know Peggy Lee from her later hits, check out this early material. This lady was a winner from the get-go."[11] Nashville music writer Ron Wynn asserted that the same collection revealed "Lee's deep blues roots [. . .] her ease working with small combos or larger orchestras and her ability to elevate novelty fare and disposable period piece bits into memorable, explosive productions. Lee . . . displayed outstanding phrasing and enunciation and covered songs from Irving Berlin, the Gershwins and Cole Porter. It's rare so much quality music remains obscure, but there's absolutely nothing disposable or generic about anything included."[12] *New York Sun*'s Will Friedwald gushed: "It is unimaginable why Capitol Records would have kept these gems in the can for almost 65 years; they are considerably better than a lot of the contempo songs the label did release during these years."[13]

The first Capitol Records era in Peggy Lee's career spanned the years 1946 to 1952. This was followed by a five-year stint with Decca beginning in 1952 and ending in 1957, after which she moved back to Capitol for an impressively long stretch from 1957 to 1972. No other female artist held a Capitol recording contract for as long as Peggy Lee held her consecutive contracts. This reality proved the immense value Peggy brought to the Capitol brand and to the catalog of American popular music that was enjoyed each day through radio broadcasts, jukeboxes, and records played in the homes of her adoring fans. As early as 1947, Peggy Lee was well on her way to becoming the jazz and pop diva she came to embody.

3

CAPITOL HITS AND *THE PEGGY LEE SHOW*

Lee's career as a Capitol Records artist continued to flourish and grow immensely. By 1947 she was enjoying regular session calls for Capitol, putting forth increasing numbers of hit records, and gaining national fame as a leading singer of popular music. One song hailing these transformations, "There'll Be Some Changes Made," Lee recorded with Frank DeVol's jazz orchestra in August of that year. Lee's bluesy approach revealed her ability to embody traits of various blues singers who preceded her (from Bessie Smith's vocal power to Billie Holiday's inflections) as well as her talent for packaging those traits into her own unique style and sound. This unique, expressive style enhanced Peggy's live performance polish and elicited invitations to appear as a guest on radio shows that later gave rise to television variety shows.

Radio shows were all the rage in the mid-1940s through the 1950s and were hosted by famous entertainers including Bing Crosby, Jimmy Durante, Woody Herman, and eventually, Peggy Lee. Highlights from Lee's show often included her performances of songs associated with other artists, like Nat King Cole's hit "Somewhere along the Way," and Louis Armstrong's "A Kiss to Build a Dream On." Performances from hosted radio programs represented a crucial connection between leading pop musicians and their American fans. These shows finally gave way to widely popular television variety shows filmed before a live studio audience and hosted by stars such as Bing Crosby, Judy Garland, Ed

Sullivan, Dean Martin, and many others. Among a slew of interesting skits and other acts, these radio and TV variety shows broadcast hundreds of impromptu performances showcasing the top entertainers of the day.

On September 12, 1947, Lee joined fellow Capitol artists Johnny Mercer, Benny Goodman, Margaret Whiting, The Pied Pipers, and Paul Weston and His Orchestra at Radio Recorders in Los Angeles to record a new patriotic Irving Berlin song, "The Freedom Train." This post-war song featuring an all-star cast of singers celebrated American freedom. The song experienced an unusually rapid turnaround between composition and commercial release, not only by Capitol Records, but also by its chief competitor, Decca. The latter studio enlisted Bing Crosby and the Andrews Sisters to provide an immediate recording for the airwaves. During a conversation with disc jockey Fred Hall, Lee shared a humorous story of this Capitol session during which uncontrollable giggling temporarily stopped the process:

> And one time we had an all-star group of all the singers on the whole label on that record. And something happened. We got the giggles in the middle of trying to record this thing, and one would laugh, and then two more, and finally about ten of us were laughing, and it got to be where you can't stop laughing. And we finally had to absolutely stop the session and take a half-an-hour break to get ourselves straightened out.[1]

This recording provided short solos by each of the stars as well as a beautifully harmonized pop choral arrangement for them to sing together. Although the record may have had commercial potential, in her autobiography Margaret Whiting referred to it as a "bomb."[2] Even so, this recording survived as an example of the unified front American recording artists put forth to the public at large in the postwar years.

Throughout the summer of 1947, amid intermittent recording sessions, Lee hosted the second season of a radio show sponsored by Old Gold cigarettes titled *Rhapsody in Rhythm*. Broadcast on Wednesdays at 9:00 p.m. between June 11 and September 17, this show boasted Lee as hostess and female singer, sharing hosting credits with male singers Johnny Johnston (also signed to Capitol Records) and Buddy Clark. Jan Savitt and His Orchestra provided accompaniment for the singers as well as instrumental numbers in both classical style (with spiced up arrangements) and swing. The second season's premiere received positive reviews from *Variety* magazine:

> The 1947 edition of Old Gold's summer show is fresh, easy to take and welcome. A good compilation of popular music items, it has variety in entertainers as in music styles, and is expertly put together, despite the disarming, engaging informal attitude of handling. (This) premiere started off smoothly, apparently effortlessly, in an easygoing introduction of participants . . . to set the summer's mood and tempo. Johnny Johnston doubled as emcee and singer and did both well. His romantic style blended well with Peggy Lee's sultry type of song.[3]

The second season of *Rhapsody in Rhythm* comprised fifteen episodes, each a half hour in length. Unfortunately for modern fans, the episodes have not been made readily available, if they exist at all.

That year Peggy co-hosted the third season of *The Summer Electric Hour* with clarinetist/singer Woody Herman. Prior to this season the show's music centered around opera and was therefore hosted by performers with operatic voices, but when the third season arrived, producers abandoned the operatic context and instead chose a contemporary pop slant. They hired Dave Barbour and His Orchestra to provide arrangements for Lee and Herman. Recordings still extant from those half-hour episodes include "The Lady from 29 Palms," a comic duet for Lee and Herman featuring a swinging performance by Barbour's group in front of a live audience. Lee performed the jazz standard "I Can't Give You Anything but Love," "Ask Anyone Who Knows," and "Cecilia," another duet with Woody Herman. During this collaborative episode Lee exhibited a perfect rhythmic groove while Herman's harmony amply complemented Lee's secure melodic lines.

Radio icon Bing Crosby extended no fewer than forty-nine invitations to Lee over eight years to join him as a guest on his popular radio show. The two shared several duets and scripted skits, giving Lee plenty of experience managing the challenges of performing for radio broadcasts. In the 1947–1948 season, comedian Jimmy Durante featured Lee as his radio show's primary singer. Hired frequently to perform at both NBC and CBS studios, Lee held a corner on the radio market and became familiar with the ins and outs of that industry while she honed her studio session prowess at Capitol and built up her live performance skills in concert appearances.

Back in the recording studios at Capitol, Lee continued to churn out singles like "Sugar," referencing the sugar rations of wartime, and "Golden Earrings," which took a path through a minor key and expressed an exotic, melancholic journey of a gypsy. Here Lee demonstrated her ability to cast a spell throughout a song, reveling in a dark, foreign aural landscape. This recording experienced so much success that it became prized as one of the top three songs of 1947. It peaked at number two on the *Billboard* chart and ran for eighteen weeks.

"Them There Eyes" fit the bill for yet another jazz standard Lee recorded, albeit with descending smears distinctly reminiscent of Billie Holiday. This energetic arrangement lent itself nicely to Lee's effortless and ebullient swing. Lee's text-based improvisation on her second chorus exhibited her complete transformation of the song's melody and rhythm in a climactic romp of expressive freedom. In text-based improvisation, the text is sung but the singer changes notes and rhythms, departing in varying degrees from the melodic and rhythmic organization dictated by the composer. Lee's recording of "Them There Eyes," particularly her second chorus, has remained a worthy study for aspiring jazz singers seeking to improvise without using scat syllables. Over the years, Lee became more and more adept at this style of jazz improvisation.

Lee performed a long string of songs on the radio through the summer of 1947, including several well-known staples of American popular song: Gershwin's "Somebody Loves Me"; the romantic Van Heusen/

Burke song "As Long as I'm Dreaming"; the classic "On the Sunny Side of the Street," as a duet with Woody Herman; and the Barbour-Lee standby "It's a Good Day." In return, CBS showered upon Lee, Herman, and Barbour the hype often apportioned to radio stars via publicity photos and articles, promoting their *Summer Electric Hour*.

A couple of months following the close of the summer radio show, Lee joined ten Capitol Records instrumentalists in an unusual project titled "Ten Cats and a Mouse," for which each performer played an instrument he/she was not known to play. Dave Barbour played trumpet and Lee played drums while the rest of the crew traded instruments among themselves. They cut two sides, "Ja-Da" and "Three O'Clock Jump," which received favorable reviews even with the obvious handicap ascribed to each musician. The entire undertaking was formed as a response to the second Petrillo Ban on commercial recordings by union musicians. James Petrillo, the leader of the American Federation of Musicians, had instigated the 1942–1944 ban and enacted another in 1948 to try to obtain better royalties for musicians through pressuring record companies to improve compensation. Since musicians expected to be bound by these union rules after December 31, 1947, shenanigans surrounding the controversy caused various musical curiosities like this recording to be released in the autumn months in anticipation of the ban. Knowing the story behind the recordings made listening to them all the more pleasurable and humorous. The group's passable performance on secondary instruments rendered the recording of "Three O'Clock Jump" an important moment in music history, which modern audiences and industry professionals would be wise to comprehend. The point was clear—that in order to attract the finest musicians, to maintain the highest musical standards, and to obtain the best recordings possible, musicians needed to be fairly compensated for their work, or else mediocre, substandard music should be expected.

Lee recorded the comic song "Caramba! It's the Samba," in November 1947. It described a dancer's wish to hear the band play any dance except for a samba (which the band of course played). Its exotic Spanish flavor yielded an energetic, fun tune with an ethnic twist that Lee loved to explore. The biggest-selling record of 1948 was another Spanish-inflected song recorded on the same day, an original Barbour-Lee collaboration called "Mañana." This song, in which Lee imitated a person with a heavy Mexican accent, yielded a huge hit for the Barbours, but it also brought a slew of criticism and even a lawsuit. Many Hispanic listeners expressed offense at how Lee's performance depicted Latinos. Her pronunciation contained exaggerated ethnic inflections and lyrics based on what some felt perpetuated a culturally insensitive stereotype (that Hispanics were typically lazy). Prior to nationwide awareness about cultural sensitivity, Lee was clearly naïve about how her flagrant depiction would be received by the Hispanic population. However, the cool reception by the demographic portrayed taught a lesson to all musicians and artists about the need for empathy and discretion whenever performing music that reflected, or especially, caricatured, other cultures.

The lawsuit occurred not due to racial or cultural quibbling but as a matter of copyright infringement. The Barbours were accused by multiple parties of plagiarizing sections of "Mañana" and spent years defending their case through the American court system. The first accusers, Harry Kirby McClintock (a singer of folk music) and publisher Sterling Sherwin, claimed that the Barbours copied music from their 1932 song "It Was Midnight on the Ocean." The lawsuit was eventually abandoned following a court investigation that deemed the disputed melody to be in the public domain. The second accuser, Luis Fronde Ferrazzano, claimed, in February 1949, that "Mañana" sounded too much like his 1929 song "La Rifa." Due to lack of evidence, however, a case against the Barbours never materialized. Five months later, Walter C. McKay (also known as former vaudeville performer Hats McKay) sued the Barbours for plagiarism of his "Laughing Song," which he had never recorded nor officially published.[4] The lawsuit finally ended in court on November 22, 1950, when Lee and Barbour prevailed. Without solid proof of prior publishing, the plaintiff could not show that the defendants had actually stolen his song, and moreover, the court determined that it was unlikely that Lee or Barbour had ever seen or heard McKay perform "Laughing Song." Peggy and Dave were finally able to put the matter to rest and keep the royalties from their all-time best-selling song to themselves.

"Mañana," Lee's eleventh solo hit recording, graced the popular music charts in January 1948, remained on the charts for twenty-one weeks, and spent nine of those weeks in the number one position. This song was a million-selling record for Capitol and earned the *Top Disc Jockey Record of the Year* accolade from *Billboard*. A second Spanish-inflected master, "Laroo, Lilli Bolero," appeared on the charts in April of that year, peaked at number fourteen, and constituted Lee's four-teenth solo hit. This easygoing Latin number possessed a simmering energy that splashed with exotic flavor in its unique percussion sounds and Spanish guitar licks. Once again, Lee proved her versatility in nail-ing the gentle, straightforward, understated approach needed to pull off a recording with a Brazilian sensibility. "Caramba! It's the Samba" also debuted on the charts in June, reaching as high as number thirteen. These three Latin-inflected songs demonstrated both Lee's interest in and prowess for delivering songs as diverse in color and cultural flavor as one could find on the American airwaves.

In November 1947 Lee recorded "All Dressed Up with a Broken Heart," which landed on the charts in January 1948 and reached num-ber twenty-one—her twelfth solo hit. The song boasted Dave Barbour's robust jazz orchestra providing a lighthearted, joyful accompaniment in spite of the bittersweet lyric. Lee hinted at the blues with a few discreet smears and whines mixed into her straight-ahead bouncy swing. She entertained a satisfying call-and-response game with the band in which they responded to each of her three declarations of love with a sassy figure in the brass. This recording may be one of the finest and most worthwhile, yet one of the least well-known big band hits of the late 1940s. Having been released on the flip side of the "Mañana" 78-rpm single, the song received some airplay of its own but was greatly over-shadowed by the enormity of the hit on its back.

That November Lee also recorded "While We're Young" with Hal Schaefer on piano. The two recorded the ballad out of time (*rubato—*

without a steady beat) in a darkened studio. Dave Barbour provided a few harp-like guitar chords at the beginning and end but allowed the pianist and singer to play the rest of the song by themselves. Schaefer related that Peggy had trouble finding the mood for the piece and asked for the studio lights to be turned off. "I don't own it, yet," she asserted.[5] In that pitch-dark setting, the duo found an expressive palette on which they both painted a beautiful aural spectrum of colors and delights. Both utilized a malleable sense of time to illustrate how poignant time-less love can be in certain significant moments, and they musically moved together in a dance teeming with romance and passion. This recording aptly displayed Lee's genius for molding musical time and space and delving deeply into a beautiful song. Penned by Alec Wilder, William Engvick, and Morty Palitz, "While We're Young" was finally released by Capitol in 1949 on the B side of "Similau." Several other studios concurrently released their own versions of the song (usually on B sides), not the least of which featured the up-and-coming male singer Tony Bennett.

In December 1947 Lee entered the recording studio again with The Benny Goodman Orchestra to record "For Every Man There's a Wom-an," by Harold Arlen and Leo Robin. The opening section, a rich ballad set in a minor key, presented a somber story narrated through an understated vocal simmer provided by Lee. When Goodman entered after the vocal chorus, the meter adjusted to a double-time feel, sug-gesting that the music began to move at a faster pace, but only tempo-rarily. Lee returned to the texture posing a poignant final question, "Where is the one for me?" This recording scored the eleventh hit for Lee and Goodman as a combined team, but it was their first on the Capitol label, which Goodman had joined that year. *The Disc Jockey's Pick* on *Billboard* placed this collaboration as number six on the popular music chart in February 1948. In June, Columbia reissued the pair's "Somebody Else Is Taking My Place," a number one hit from 1941, yielding a number thirty placement the second time around.

In September 1948 Peggy Lee began her next radio show stint with *The Chesterfield Supper Club*, which aired on weekday evenings. This fifteen-minute presentation boasted hosts Perry Como and Jo Stafford before Peggy joined the ranks. Como hosted Mondays, Wednesdays, and Fridays, while Stafford hosted Tuesdays and Thursdays. When newcomer Lee joined the team, Thursdays were given to her and Stafford kept the Tuesday hosting slot. Three different orchestras were featured to accompany these three stars—Dave Barbour conducted the orchestra backing Lee. Paul Weston (conducting for Stafford) and Mitchell Ayres (conducting for Como) rounded out the outstanding entertainment lineup. Lee's weekly commitment with *The Chesterfield Supper Club*, filmed in Hollywood, enabled her to frequent another radio show (for NBC) hosted by her iconic friend Bing Crosby. Crosby's show, *Philco Radio Time*, extended guest spots to Lee on a semi-regular basis. When Peggy hosted the *Chesterfield* show, she was fortunate to have top talent joining her, including Nat "King" Cole, The Mills Brothers, and Frankie Laine. The show was broadcast in Hollywood at 5:00 p.m. and aired on the east coast at 9:00 p.m. One clear advantage for Lee in hosting this nationally broadcast show was the opportunity to showcase her original songs. Lee appeared forty-seven times on the *Chesterfield* show, thirty-seven as hostess. Historian Iván Santiago-Mercado chronicled 151 musical performances by Peggy Lee during her tenure with *Chesterfield*, her third major radio show assignment.[6]

Repertoire that Lee performed on her first show in March 1946 included "You Was Right, Baby" and "I Don't Know Enough about You," two Barbour-Lee compositions, plus her previously released "Waitin' for the Train to Come In." Having a weekly opportunity to nationally broadcast performances of studio hits on the radio served as a distinct advantage to Perry Como, Jo Stafford, and Peggy Lee, as their radio performances produced even more fans and cemented their rapidly increasing fame. The network studios and commercial sponsors (in this case, Chesterfield cigarettes) milked the star power of their show hosts for all that they could, and for good reason. Having recording industry stars speak personally to their national audiences during radio broadcasts of their performances drew listeners to those networks by

Peggy Lee and Perry Como recording a *Chesterfield Supper Club* broadcast, circa 1948. *Photofest.*

the tens of thousands in those days, before television abducted the attention of America's media consumers.

Both Lee and Stafford exited *The Chesterfield Supper Club* at the close of the same 1948–1949 season, in the same week of June. Many radio stations were facing decline at the end of this decade. The oncoming television variety show boom loomed in the near future, casting doubtful shadows over the fate of radio programming. In the absence of steady radio work between 1949 and 1950, Lee and Barbour underwent a busy performance tour through major cities across the nation. As they traveled, the couple enjoyed guest spots on various radio shows in Chicago, New York, and Los Angeles amid concerts of their career hits and recent releases.

During the spring of 1951, after years of struggle with Barbour's alcoholism and months of stressful touring, the couple dissolved their marriage. This new arrangement resulted in Lee promptly moving to New York to pursue new opportunities in radio. By June of that year, CBS had extended Lee an invitation to host a summer radio show. What came to be called *The Peggy Lee Show* consisted of two distinct series from 1951 to 1952. The first, a summer series titled *The Peggy Lee Rexall Show*, became alternately known as *A Date with Peggy Lee*. This two-month venture attracted such guest performers as young Capitol artist Mel Tormé and prominent songwriter Walter Kent. In Capitol's studios, Lee and Tormé had recorded four duets between 1949 and 1951, combining their songwriting talents for two of those songs. The duo began performing together during this time period and continued to be matched as co-performers for large live concert events until nearly the end of Lee's career several decades later. Lee and Tormé appeared together several times in 1951: in the first episode of her new *Peggy Lee Rexall Show*, on television co-hosting *TV's Top Tunes*, and guest singing in the television program *Songs for Sale*.

Variety magazine reported that Lee intended to introduce a new song in each episode of her *Peggy Lee Rexall Show* in a segment titled "Peggy's Preview."[7] For her inaugural episode, Lee welcomed Walter Kent, composer of a soon-to-debut Broadway musical titled *Seventeen*. Kent performed as a duet with his hostess the best-known song from that forthcoming musical, "After All, It's Spring." Singing this song on Lee's debut show provided a plug both for the new musical (due to open in just four days) and for its composer. Interested in promoting this fellow songwriter, Lee performed the song again later that same month. While the song may not have earned standard status, *Seventeen* enjoyed 182 Broadway performances and scored an original cast recording on the RCA Victor label. Lee displayed this form of camaraderie toward fellow songwriters consistently throughout her career, championing their songs and benefiting from other singers who recorded and performed her own. Lee understood the importance of supporting her colleagues at this fairly early stage of her career and continued to show her commitment to lifting up the creative work of others.

The 1951 model of *The Peggy Lee Show* ran for thirty minutes on CBS Radio. An edited version of the show, lasting fifteen minutes, was later prepared for Armed Forces Radio in 1953. Lee's original set list included "After All, It's Spring," "Mañana," and "It Never Happen'd to Me" as pieces contained within the first episode, along with "All of Me," "Too Late Now," and a duet with Mel Tormé, "We Kiss in a Shadow." Tormé also contributed "Mister and Mississippi" as a solo piece. "Mañana" and "It Never Happen'd to Me" were omitted from the AFR's abbreviated program presumably in order to meet the necessary time constraints. Subsequent episode guests included Art London, Don Cornell, Louis Prima, and Benny Goodman. Song repertoire varied from little-known new pieces to well-established standards. A wonderfully comic swinging arrangement of "Shanghai" was a crowd-pleasing number that Lee reprised more than once on her show. Well-known songs she performed included "Try a Little Tenderness," "That Old Black Magic," and "Too Young."

On July 15, 1951 Lee performed "Make the Man Love Me" on the air. Just months after her recent divorce, Peggy delivered a heartbreaking rendition of this song about trying to force the affections of a lover by promising to make a man happy and declaring her desire to keep him just as he is. This would not be the last time Lee wore her heart on her sleeve with regard to her music. Many of her songs, both originals and covers, were extremely relevant to her current life circumstances. She opened the live broadcast of this song, in which her singing voice trembled with urgent intention, by introducing it with the following words: "Right now I've got myself a tune—a song that needs no talking about, just singing."[8] The jazz orchestral accompaniment included a plaintive harp strumming its delicate, ethereal music, not to be outdone by Lee's moving performance.

That day's broadcast also called for Lee's performance of "Too Young," a song that became a standard after countless singers released their own interpretations. Nat Cole achieved a hit with this tune that, for many, remained the definitive version. Lee's live radio show version featured the harp as prominent in the overall orchestral texture whereas in Cole's version the strings and piano predominated. The radio show recordings included a live studio audience wildly applauding after each song, and the recording quality betrayed the limited ability the studio possessed at the time to balance the sections and to adjust recording levels adequately. Lee's impressive performing talent rose above those challenges and displayed her lovely vocal instrument, musicianship, and expression in spite of the limitations exacted upon her and the instrumentalists. The limited technology available allowed little to no attention to balance, timbral adjustments, equalization, compression, and editing of the recorded tracks. Add to that the ambient noise resulting from the audience, musicians, tech crew, and moving parts in the room, and it is a wonder that any decent recordings exist at all. Indeed, *Peggy Lee: At Last—The Lost Radio Recordings* was a triumph not only for recovering Peggy Lee's live radio work but as an important archive documenting the radio shows of the mid-twentieth century.

"It Never Happen'd to Me" was a Spanish-inflected song included on this radio broadcast date. Living in southern California, Lee knew many Spanish-speaking people, and her fascination with the dialect of English they spoke as well as their traditional music propagated song after song in her repertoire in which she imitated their speech. This charming and humorous piece set in a medium tempo created a striking ethnic contrast to the other popular songs featured in this episode of *The Peggy Lee Show*.

By this stage in her career Lee had grown aware of the importance of carefully sequencing her songs for live performance. She thoughtfully placed songs in an order that balanced one another—ballads; Latin pieces; swing tunes; fast, energetic pieces; and blues—and organized them in new, refreshing ways to maximize variety and enjoyment for her listeners. Even today the ripple effect that Peggy Lee began in her manner of selecting songs for jazz festival appearances, public concerts, and nightclubs (in her later years) can be traced back to her earliest appearances on her radio show. She routinely included one new song along with several that were currently popular, and she always combined them in ways that engaged the audience throughout the entire presentation. She avoided tiring the audience's ears by playing back-to-back songs having the same tempo, style, or key. Contemporary singers (the author included) continue even today to follow this model created by Peggy Lee and other great singers. Their recipes for the successful design of song lists facilitated maximum listener enjoyment and attention.

July 1951 likely produced the *Peggy Lee Rexall Show* episode guest starring Johnny Mercer. Archives indicating the exact recording date no longer exist due to the subsequent modification and reordering done by the Armed Forces Radio Service. During this time period little thought was given to the preservation or precise archiving of created works including films, albums, recordings, or radio broadcasts. For this reason, exact details surrounding the origin dates of many works created during this era and previous eras may be dubious. At some point during the course of Lee's first self-titled show, she recorded "Come On-A My House," "These Foolish Things," "Ac-cent-tchu-ate the Positive," and "Go, Go, Go," quite possibly while Mercer served as Lee's guest.[9]

Years later arranger Billy May shared a story about Mercer coming to his house to hear Peggy Lee's version of "I Remember You," which May had arranged: "I was really kind of proud of the arrangement, and Peggy Lee sang good, and it was a wonderful rendition of the song . . . he liked it so much he started to cry."[10] Biographer Philip Furia revealed that Mercer often "burst into tears, particularly when he heard a song he loved."[11] Having begun working together in the earliest days of

Capitol Records, Mercer and Lee enjoyed a high level of mutual respect and admiration throughout both of their professional lives.

"Come On-A My House" contained a fast tempo and a text requiring a heavy Hispanic accent. The energetic swinging accompaniment beautifully complemented Lee's rhythmic precision and carefree manner of tossing off difficult pitch intervals with briskness and ease. In authentic Lee style, she included a humorous spoken question at the end: "Hey, where you goin'? To Rosemary Clooney's house?" Clooney had recently attained a major hit with this song, so Lee was quick to inject a joke about it as a comical closing.

In her radio recording of "These Foolish Things" Lee infused the tenderness she usually reserved for timeless ballads. This gentle-as-a-whisper approach that first belonged to Lee has since been imitated by countless singers since Lee made it part of her standard practice. "Go, Go, Go" represented an energetic romp between Lee and the band, during which they engaged in a literal call-and-response dialogue using the song title (Lee sang it, and the band shouted it back) over a smooth and simmering samba groove. This danceable tune was less a quality composition and more a rowdy dance number that provided good contrast with the standards also performed on the show.

The Peggy Lee Rexall Show aired seven episodes on CBS between June and July 1951 as a substitute program during the vacation period for the *Amos and Andy Show*. Immediately following the close of the Rexall-branded series, Lee was given a yearlong program of her own called *Club 88 Starring Peggy Lee*, which debuted on Christmas Day. The new show as well as the previous Rexall stint featured musical direction by Russ Case, the bandleader and arranger affiliated with Perry Como. The first forty-two episodes of Lee's self-titled radio show (December 1951–May 1952) were broadcast from CBS New York studios, giving Lee the opportunity to also appear as a guest on Ed Sullivan's original *Toast of the Town*, *TV's Top Tunes*, and *Songs for Sale*.

As before, Lee began her new show in the spirit of showcasing new talent as well as her own. On the Christmas broadcast, she welcomed a new harmony act called The Four Lads. Over the next few years this group ended up recording a few big hits and then continued to perform nostalgic music for several decades. On this episode Lee chose to sing the poignant, enduring ballad "Try a Little Tenderness." This radio version (with tinny piano and harp accompaniment) came off remarkably delicately and with sincere honesty, as if she sought to gently melt icy attitudes and soothe strained relations between the sexes. While thousands of artists have recorded this priceless standard, Lee's delivery of the song as a straightforward, heartfelt, exquisitely gentle plea for a peaceable truce stands as a prime example of her ability to combine musical excellence with emotional sincerity and elegance. That she accomplished this definitive version with unsurpassed vocal control on an essentially live radio broadcast rather than in a recording studio further proved what an accomplished and virtuosic performer she had become.

A subsequent episode guest-starred twenty-one-year-old hit maker Richard Hayes, who sang his latest hit song "Out in the Cold Again," which he had recorded for Mercury Records and which had peaked at number nine in October. Hayes also sang "I've Got My Love to Keep Me Warm" as a duet with Lee. On the next installment of *Club 88*, pop singer Johnny Ray joined Lee, and the two performed an Irving Berlin duet, "Slumming on Park Avenue," while Ray also promoted his latest hit single.

Lee also performed "Undecided" on this broadcast, a song usually associated with fellow jazz diva Ella Fitzgerald. While Lee's version was a bit slower than that of Fitzgerald, it possessed plenty of sass and jazz style. Lee infused this wonderful tune with her own attitude, replete with slides, whining lyrics, and moments of listening to the band's responses instead of filling in all the words. All in all, this performance represented a highly unique and impressively swinging take on this well-known song. Had it been a studio version (with technicians available to balance, tune, and equalize the instruments before, during, and after recording, as necessary for studio tracks) this performance may have offered some competition for Ella's famous rendition. The vocal performance as it was certainly measured up nicely.

Guests featured on *The Peggy Lee Show* in early 1952 continued to be primarily of the young male persuasion and included The Golden Gate Quartet, Robert Q. Lewis, Tommy Edwards, and a newcomer to RCA Records, Harry Belafonte. Singer Merv Griffin (who later became a well-known TV personality, producer, and real estate mogul), vibraphonist Red Norvo, and jazz pianist Barbara Carroll also visited Lee's show early that year, contributing strong musical numbers to her broadcasts.

Composer and jazz pianist Mary Lou Williams brought her trio to Lee's show to accompany the singer on a Williams original, "Pretty Eyed Baby." This pleasantly swinging performance allowed both Lee and Williams to show off their sizeable talents. Williams performed a tastefully crafted piano solo midway through the piece. Lee's enjoyment of this song was evidenced in her expressive vocal inflections as the two bounced their way through this happy tune. Williams returned to Lee's show in April, performing "Fine and Dandy" with her trio and "I Got Rhythm" with Lee at the mic.

Broadway singer Larry Douglas joined Lee for an episode in March 1952 for a charming duet performance of the Gershwin standard "Let's Call the Whole Thing Off." The energetic entertainer Louis Prima returned to *The Peggy Lee Show* as a special guest that month, too, singing the jazz favorite "Basin St. Blues" as a duet with Lee, and again in April to join her in performing "My Baby Just Cares for Me." Pop singer Jackie Paris also graced Lee's stage that spring, as did Johnnie Ray, who sang "Walkin' My Baby Back Home" with Lee in classic duet style. Several other one-time guests and multi-episode returning artists enjoyed Lee's company for the New York series of broadcasts of *The Peggy Lee Show*. As the series tapered toward its final east coast episode, Italian American crooners Alan Dale and Johnny Desmond shared the honors as Lee's final guests. The first half of Lee's radio series signed off with a Desmond-Lee duet, "Let's Get Away from It All," in anticipation of the migration of her show to the west coast.

Shortly after the final episode wrapped in the New York studio, Lee moved back to southern California to begin working on her first leading role in a film—she was cast as Rose in *The Jazz Singer*. Francis "Sonny" Burke handled the music direction of the Los Angeles version of the radio show, which represented a serendipitous meeting of the minds, since Burke later became a close colleague and collaborative composer with Lee for Disney's huge animated feature film *Lady and the Tramp*. Lee rose to the challenge of hosting her successful radio show alongside a burgeoning career in film music, which included acting, voiceover work, and film scoring.

The second half of *The Peggy Lee Show* broadcast forty-seven episodes from Los Angeles. Burke and Lee welcomed Hollywood heart-throb Dick Haymes, on May 6, 1952, as their inaugural episode's guest artist. Haymes sang "Nice Work if You Can Get It" as a solo and "Walkin' My Baby Back Home" as a duet with Lee. *Club 88* (the alternate name for Lee's show) next featured a young Liberace as its esteemed guest, just a couple of months prior to the opening of the pianist's own television show. Bandleader Bob Crosby was soon to follow. Crosby hosted a radio show called *Club 15* that alternated broadcast time slots with Lee's *Club 88*.

May 20, 1952, boasted the arrival of Hoagy Carmichael to *Club 88*. This visit represented the first of four *Club 88* broadcasts dedicated to specific American songwriters. This first composer tribute show set the precedent, followed by all the others in which Lee and her guest performed a medley of the composer's original hit songs. Carmichael's visit included a medley melding the timeless "Georgia on My Mind" with "I Get along without You Very Well." Additional selections included "Ole Buttermilk Sky," a delightfully lighthearted, fully orchestrated joyride for the orchestra and soloist, as well as a straightforward rendition of Carmichael's major hit "Skylark."

Carmichael had won an Oscar for his "In the Cool, Cool, Cool of the Evening," sung by Bing Crosby in the 1951 film *Here Comes the Groom*. Early in his career, his 1927 composition "Stardust" gained him an immortal standard in the Great American Songbook. Regarding this beloved song, the composer offered: "And then it happened—that queer sensation that this melody was bigger than me. Maybe I hadn't written it at all. The recollection of how, when and where it all happened became vague as the lingering strains hung in the rafters of the studio. I wanted to shout back at it, 'maybe I didn't write you, but I found you.'"[12] In 1930 he recorded "Georgia on My Mind," "Lazy River," and "Rockin' Chair," and he moved to Hollywood in 1936 to try his hand as a film musician. In the midst of a successful career as a film scorer and actor, Carmichael had hosted his own self-titled radio show that first aired in 1946 on CBS, so Lee's radio tribute provided familiar territory for this widely acclaimed recording veteran.

Former Capitol Records pal Johnny Mercer was the next composer featured. He returned to collaborate with Lee on May 27, bringing a medley of well-known songs like "Blues in the Night," "One for My Baby," and "Ac-cent-tchu-ate the Positive," as well as two stand-alone songs, "That Old Black Magic" and "Come Rain or Come Shine." The medley featured Lee and Mercer taking turns singing a string of songs Mercer contributed to the Great American Songbook. Mercer's legacy as a Capitol Records founder, lyricist, and singer lent him much clout in the radio industry. His songs had been consistently recorded by scores of singers, so Lee naturally gravitated toward Mercer as a logical choice for her show's featured composer series.

Musical greats based in Los Angeles appeared week after week with Peggy, growing her personal network and her show's star power. Red Norvo returned for a virtuosic vibraphone performance, followed by trombonist, bandleader, and composer Tommy Dorsey. Lee performed her latter guest's biggest all-time single, "I'll Never Smile Again," from his amazingly prolific 286-hit career. Desi Arnaz visited *Club 88* in June 1952, singing Lee's 1948 hit "Mañana" with her as a duet, providing a bit of linguistic authenticity for this Spanish-infused song. Lee's impressive cadre of illustrious guests for her radio show seemed to know no bounds.

After a string of featured musical performers, Lee's next composer showcase (August 12) fell to Matt Dennis, who contributed his standard "Everything Happens to Me," along with a medley that showcased his "Angel Eyes" (with lyrics by Earl Brent), and "Let's Get Away from It

All," among others. A capable pianist, Dennis accompanied himself and Lee on this broadcast. Dennis had also written "The Night We Called It a Day," which Frank Sinatra had recorded (along with the other pieces already mentioned) when he worked with the Tommy Dorsey Orchestra early in his career. Dennis's songs (most often sporting lyrics by Tom Adair) provided Sinatra with excellent material that both suited his voice and represented a fine, original voice in songwriting for the early 1940s. The quality and poignancy expressed in Dennis's songs provided Sinatra with a fitting paradigm through which the young singer's fans would fall in love with the artist who became known alternately as "The Voice," "Ol' Blue Eyes," and "Chairman of the Board."

Fellow Capitol artist Nat "King" Cole followed Dennis as the featured guest on Lee's next show, performing "Johnny One-Note" with Lee and "Somewhere along the Way" by himself. Back in 1947 Lee had been invited as a guest on Cole's radio show, *King Cole Trio Time*. By the time of this 1952 broadcast, Lee had returned the favor six times. Clearly one of the greatest accomplishments of the 1940s and '50s radio era was bringing the best music performers together in one place to create outstanding collaborative performances on a variety of star-hosted weekly shows.

The August 21 installment of *Club 88* rounded out Peggy Lee's four composer tribute shows, highlighting Frank Loesser. Together, Lee and Loesser performed a medley of duets including some of his best-known Broadway staples: "If I Were a Bell," "On a Slow Boat to China," "A Bushel and a Peck," and "Baby, It's Cold Outside." Lee also performed the composer's "My Darling, My Darling" on this episode as a brief once-through reading of a slow, nostalgic ballad strongly suggestive of romance and sweetness. Loesser had firmly established himself as a leading Broadway composer, penning enduring songs from *Guys and Dolls*; *How to Succeed in Business without Really Trying*; *The Most Happy Fella*; and *Where's Charley?*, among several others. Churning out reams of songs and musicals, Frank Loesser was a highly sought-after composer in the early 1950s. Lee loved to perform new songs from Broadway as often as she could. Honoring Loesser on her show for his compositional achievements helped elevate his stardom while giving Lee an opportunity to showcase many of his songs herself.

Lee's consistently heartfelt interpretation of ballads such as "My Darling, My Darling" could hardly be eclipsed by other singers of the time. She had mastered the art of purring and nearly whispering her tones into the microphone, even in live performances with large bands. She managed to keep the band volume low enough to enable her incredibly soft and tender vocal stylings to stand out over the instrumental music, even in a radio setting. These abilities to lead a band and to know how to adjust volume, timbre, and nuance to perfectly suit the song, venue, and audience at hand were rarely as polished in the hands or voices of other singers.

Club 88 Starring Peggy Lee welcomed many fabulous performers during its brief two-year tenure on the air. Jud Conlon's Rhythmaires made their fifth appearance in September 1952, followed by several other guests, including the longtime radio host Bob Crosby and Lee's current co-star in the feature film *The Jazz Singer*, Danny Thomas. Woody Herman returned to share another fine performance with Lee. Popular Hollywood actor Gordon MacRae and his archrival, actor-singer-dancer Gene Nelson, each appeared on back-to-back episodes. Nelson's talents led him to star on Broadway and to direct several hit television shows in the 1960s and '70s. The attention he received on the radio with Peggy Lee helped to further his budding career.

During Lee's stint with *Club 88*, she developed the routine of reciting poetry to lead off many of her song performances. Her fascination with well-put-together words was not surprising considering her enormous strength in interpreting song lyrics. Not all singers possessed a particularly poetic sense, but Peggy certainly did. Not only did she adore reciting poetry on her radio broadcasts, she endeavored to write poetry herself. She eventually wrote a book of privately published poems titled *Softly, with Feeling* (1953) from which a new Peggy Lee song composed and recorded by the author, "Burn It Slow," resulted in 2007. For Lee, music and poetry were collaborative partners, and the lyrics of a song held as much importance as the composed music—

sometimes more. Toward the end of her run with *Club 88*, she recited poetry by Rudyard Kipling, T. S. Eliot, Samuel Taylor Coleridge, and Robert Browning, among others, elevating the importance of poetry on her show to nearly equal status with music.

Club 88 aired twice weekly, on Tuesdays and Thursdays, over a forty-five-week period beginning on Christmas Day 1951 and ending October 28, 1952. It featured fifty-five guests and over four hundred memorable performances by its hostess. Episodes from *The Peggy Lee Rexall Show* and *Club 88 Starring Peggy Lee* were rebroadcast in 1953 by the Armed Forces Radio Service, albeit not in their entirety. Those segments that were rebroadcast by AFRS were preserved, but unfortunately, the original broadcasts from which those came were neither kept nor archived. The AFRS called the rebroadcasts, simply, *The Peggy Lee Show*. Thanks to those rebroadcasts, some of the recorded material from Lee's radio shows was preserved. It is from these that modern listeners may hear a portion of her outstanding radio performances, poetry readings, and displays of her many roles: emcee, interviewer, bandleader, featured vocalist, and hostess to a huge variety of guest performers. From these radio broadcasts Lee further crafted her skill set as a pop diva, jazz singer, concert and recording producer, and well-rounded performing artist.

Lee's continued success as a Capitol Records artist flourished alongside her early 1950s stint as a radio host. Few other singers showed a penchant for honoring living songwriters to the extent that Peggy Lee did, as displayed by her consistent presentations of their works in both her live performances and her media productions. Using the platforms available to her, most especially radio, Lee helped create national awareness about the contributions of living composers of Broadway, popular music, and jazz, as well as poets, television personalities, actors, and other entertainers. Her efforts in this regard may well point to her being among the first important advocates of performing artists and their vital work in American arts and culture.

4

EARLY ALBUMS AND THE DECCA YEARS

Having gained six years of recording experience and scoring several hit singles for Capitol, Peggy Lee was given her first opportunity to record a full solo album in November 1947. This was the first of several, which eventually led to Lee recording one of the top ten jazz vocal albums of all time, albeit for a different label. Her inaugural solo album, *Rendezvous with Peggy Lee*, represented an early milestone in her distinguished career. *Rendezvous* sported Lee's take on six standards from the swing era, including "Why Don't You Do Right," "I Can't Give You Anything but Love," "Them There Eyes," "Stormy Weather," "'Deed I Do," and "Don't Smoke in Bed." The album found success, rising to number two on the *Billboard* charts, and showcased Lee's keen talent for swing and improvisation. Featuring Dave Barbour and His Orchestra, *Rendezvous* became expanded more than once to accommodate the changing technology that produced longer albums. This title compiled first six, then eight, then twelve songs in its successively growing number of tracks.

In the original six songs, Lee explored the range of possibilities of text-based improvisation. Staying true to the original text, Lee played with new melodies and rhythmic combinations of notes, restructuring the timing of how the lyrics interacted with the music. The first *Rendezvous* began and ended with two of the songs most closely associated with the style of Billie Holiday, to whom first credit for this type of vocal improvisation had been traditionally ascribed. While Holiday certainly exploited this technique liberally in her recordings, she was by no means the only working singer employing its charms.

"Don't Smoke in Bed" was penned by Willard Robison, Barbour, and Lee. When Robison became seriously ill before credits for the song were finalized, Barbour and Lee decided to decline writing credits as a gift to Robison.[1] In this recording Lee unequivocally demonstrated a dark, tragic quality and a vowel color and inflection similar to those used by Billie Holiday. These similarities drew disapproval from some critics, including Holiday herself. Holiday's bassist, John Levy, expressed "When Peggy Lee came around, Billie would say, 'why don't you find some other way to sing?'" Replying, "It's because I love you. I love everything you do," Lee confessed to mimicking her idol.[2] She eventually had to learn to avoid overt copying of Holiday in order to forge a path more distinctly her own.

Founded in 1942, Capitol Records maintained a secure and steadily growing presence in the American popular song recording industry as a private company managed by three individuals: artist/songwriter Johnny Mercer, songwriter/film producer Buddy DeSylva, and businessman Glenn Wallichs. By 1948 Capitol had gone public, became a corporation with countless shareholders, and sold millions of records. Author Philip Furia quoted arranger Billy May in his book *Skylark: The Life and Times of Johnny Mercer* as saying, "John got upset when the company got so successful. He liked it when it was just a little company, and he could write a song in the morning and record it in the afternoon and have it a hit a week later. . . . He got mad when they started competing with the majors and everything like that. . . . And Glenn (Wallichs) was, of course, the other way. Glenn was a business man: 'Let's get ahead here and make it.'"[3]

Peggy Lee served Capitol as a primary force in the development of the young recording powerhouse. Her rendition of the Victor Young gem "Golden Earrings" brought Capitol a top-three single of 1947. "Mañana," released the same week that "Golden Earrings" peaked, became her first million-selling hit. Mercer's dream of staying in control of the company's growth was not to be. With the phenomenal success of its young artists at the outset of their long careers (not the least of which included Frank Sinatra, Nat King Cole, and Peggy Lee), and the correspondingly influential technological advances moving the needle from 78-rpm records (allowing only one song per side) to long-playing albums, the startup company had nowhere to go but up. Up, up, up it went.

Another Lee hit that set Capitol Records apart from the rest of the competition entered the popular music charts in April 1949 and peaked at number seventeen. "Similau," Lee's twenty-first solo hit, boasted unusual subject matter and a highly exotic sound set squarely within the controversial topic of an overt sexual encounter. Sounding like a pagan incantation, this song opened as a percussion feature with precise stickwork and drums. Lee played with minor and major tonality while delivering poetic lyrics alluding to physical intimacy. Backup male chanters and the growing loudness of a drumbeat created the impression of a tribal ceremony reaching its apex upon which Lee elicited a resonant yell toward the end of the recording. Here she ascended a full octave and completed an expressive melodic turn using the harmonic minor scale. The strange, hypnotic song began and ended with the striking of a gong in the manner of the commencement and closing of a pagan ceremonial rite. Lee's attraction to recording such sexually provocative songs ultimately contributed toward her conflict at Capitol, resulting in her decision to pursue a recording contract elsewhere.

In March 1949 Lee recorded "Bali Ha'i" from Rodgers and Hammerstein's Broadway hit *South Pacific*. This song explored a melodic raising of the fourth scale degree (known by jazz musicians as a "sharp eleventh"), which modified the major scale in a manner that painted an exotic, hypnotic veil over this famous show tune. Incessant beating of drums in the background provided a traditional folk flavor suggesting an island-tribal origin. Lee's gentle, expertly controlled singing suggested the right amount of volume and neutral tone color to induce a trance-like state in her listeners. Her version of this Broadway song debuted in May and peaked at number thirteen on the popular music charts. Once again, Lee had fully explored an opportunity to capture listeners using a spellbinding quality in her song interpretation. This quality (and her uncanny talent for it) became more and more interesting to her as the years rolled on, both on a personal and a musical level.

"Bali Ha'i" was one of two songs Lee recorded for the Capitol compilation album *Songs from Rodgers and Hammerstein's South Pacific* in 1949. The other, "I'm Gonna Wash That Man Right Outa My Hair," involved Lee using a smooth quasi-spoken singing style over a trumpet-heavy big band arrangement. A great deal more conversational in style than the original Broadway version, this rendition presented a matter-of-fact attitude and a brusqueness from the band reflecting a sharp-edged resolve of a woman intent on forgetting a man.

At the same recording date, Lee also logged in a version of "(Ghost) Riders in the Sky," which she took all the way to number two on the popular charts. The song had previously been recorded only by men (originally Gene Autry, for the film *Riders in the Sky*), so her success with it may have surprised some, but her interpretive angle shifted to a darker, more haunting concept than the simpler, straightforward delivery of her male contemporaries. Her version utilized a percussive driving rhythm suggesting the galloping of horses, coupled with wailing background singers imitating the sounds of whistling wind.

In November 1949 Lee entered Capitol's recording studios to collaborate with another Capitol artist on a couple of duets. Mel Tormé was called upon to provide the male voice for Lee's recording of "Bless You (For the Good That Is in You)" as well as "The Old Master Painter." The latter song revealed the pitch precision of each artist in quick-moving lines that locked together in perfect harmony, rivaling any of the harmony-singing family trios of the 1930s and '40s (particularly the Andrews Sisters or the Boswell Sisters). The duet entered radio play in January 1950, reaching number nine on *Billboard's* charts, amounting to hit number twenty-four for Lee and number eight for Tormé. It was no wonder that Tormé and Lee continued to perform together throughout the decades following these early Capitol sessions. Their voices blended brilliantly, and their recordings highlighted the breadth of each singer's talent. Lee and Tormé's collaborations produced one exquisite joint effort after another.

February 1950 turned out to be a very good month for Lee. "The Old Master Painter" achieved top-ten status during the same week that she had three other hits simultaneously occupying top-ten chart placements in various regions. These included the swing standard "Sugar" and a Barbour-Lee original called "My Small Señor," which sported strong Mexican inflections and included Barbour's Spanish-style guitar performance beneath Lee's accented vocal performance. "When You Speak with Your Eyes," yet another original with a Latin beat and laid-back attitude, completed the quartet of February hits. Dave Barbour and the Guadalajara Boys accompanied the latter two songs. Based on these successes, 1950 looked to be a very fruitful year for the Barbours.

That year and the following year proved to be fruitful recording years, indeed. Lee maintained a heavy recording schedule at Capitol and churned out several more radio and jukebox hits. In July 1951 Lee and Tormé were booked together to record more duets for Capitol. "Don't Fan the Flame" permitted the duo to show off their talents for both swing and 1950's blues-inflected pop music. Each singer was featured as a soloist in the verses and then joined forces to form a harmony-singing duo in the refrain. "Telling Me Yes, Telling Me No" provided a nostalgic waltz that allowed each artist to exhibit their romantic crooning in a ballroom-dance style.

The Lee-Tormé duet period in the late 1940s and early '50s reflected a trend prevalent throughout the recording industry favoring the pairing of male and female solo artists. During this period duets were in vogue, whereas solo female voices of the soft, gentle variety were trumped by the Broadway-belt or novelty styles trending in midcentury America. Since Lee had never been a belter, Capitol wisely broadened her repertoire and recording versatility by featuring her with the velvety-voiced Tormé (commonly known among jazz aficionados as the "Velvet Fog"). Their combined talents produced some of the most artistic and delightful pop duets ever recorded and enabled both to continue churning out popular hits.

In 1952 Peggy decided to make a move from Capitol Records to one of its primary competitors, Decca. Several factors likely influenced this decision. Her recent split with her husband may have created a desire for a change of scenery. Also, Capitol executive Alan Livingston believed that Lee was underappreciated by the label for her consistent artistry and potential for continuing to produce hits.[4] Her most productive years up to this point had been 1947–1948, but she was by no means finished at this point in her career. Rather than staying and fighting for the attention she deserved, she made the decision to go where she would feel more appreciated and where her talents could blossom further. Another reason for the switch may have been purely geographical. Her increasing opportunities on television had led her to New York, where Decca had a strong presence. The bulk of Capitol's activity remained in Los Angeles, so when Lee made the decision to move to the east coast, her concomitant move to a stronger leader in the recording industry in that new home city made good sense.

Another primary reason Lee departed from Capitol concerned her desire to record Rodgers and Hart's "Lover." Arranger Gordon Jenkins had prepared a novel representation of this song using Lee's input based on a 1935 French film called *La Bandera*, during which the protagonist sang a song in Spanish accompanied by horses galloping and flags waving.[5] Lee earnestly wanted to perform the Broadway song using an aural atmosphere inspired by the movie. Jenkins and Lee got to work, and the resulting arrangement proved to be well received by live audiences at New York's hottest nightclub, the Copacabana, where Lee had a steady engagement. In her autobiography Lee related that Decca executives attended one of those performances and loved her rendition: "I was at the Copa at that time, and one night Sonny Burke came in with Milt Gabler of Decca Records, and when they heard me sing 'Lover,' they got excited. 'We must have this.' 'Would you record it?' I asked. 'Of course,' they said. So I left Capitol for five years and went with Decca."[6] Having already been refused by executives at Capitol when she proposed a recording of this fabulous arrangement, Lee was poised to accept the competing label's offer. As her Capitol contract was ending, her five-year contract with Decca (1952–1957) began a new chapter in her career.

The move to Decca was fortuitous for Lee in several ways. Not only did the new studio offer her a fresh environment with new colleagues and new challenges, but the artistic license and respect she longed for at Capitol were granted to her in more generous amounts at Decca. Furthermore, Decca was no stranger to the jazz recording scene. While Lee had left the company of Sinatra, Stafford, Whiting, Mercer, Tormé, Cole, and other superstar pop performing and recording artists, she was now moving into a milieu of more straight-ahead jazz than was available at Capitol. Decca had already scored bragging rights for chart busters and jazz legends Ella Fitzgerald, Bing Crosby, Louis Armstrong, Dick Haymes, Louis Jordan, Al Jolson, Guy Lombardo, and Jimmy Dorsey. Peggy Lee was well primed to cut the finest jazz recording of her career in this supportive and musically satisfying environment.

Lee's envisioned arrangement of "Lover" required several percussionists plus an orchestra. It rendered a frenzy of energy from instrumentalists playing at breakneck speed in multiple metrical patterns. The song was organized as a samba, a Latin form in cut time that facilitated a busy layering of rapid percussion patterns that formed the bedrock of the piece. Lee performed the song in a high belt style. This was a unique departure for her, yet it displayed her dexterity and versatility of range and vocal approach. The pattern of horse-galloping sounds was readily apparent in the orchestration, and the chromatic descent of the vocal line in the melody lent itself to the frenzied, almost disorganized effect of this super high-energy song so unlike the tamer recordings other artists were releasing. "Lover" required a very high level of musicianship to perform well, in addition to an unusual level of vocal intensity from the singer. Lee poured her heart, soul, and emotions into the expression of this passionate text. As she promised Capitol, this song turned into a million-selling hit (not immediately, but over time) and sold 250,000 copies over the first two weeks of its release. It occupied the *Billboard* charts for thirteen weeks, claiming the number three spot. Though the composer, Richard Rodgers, initially resented

Lee's unorthodox rendering of his song, he eventually came around to appreciate her innovative interpretation of his works. Lee quoted Rodgers in her autobiography as having told her at long last: "You interpret my songs any way you like. I trust your taste."[7]

On the flip side of "Lover" Decca's producers placed Lee's rendition of "You Go to My Head," a relaxed rendering of this jazz standard that was so out of time (not aligned with the orchestral beat) that listeners got an authentic sense of the character's inebriated state described so succinctly in the lyrics. Lee succeeded in performing the text like a drunkard, slowly shuffling her way to the door of a tavern following an evening of overindulgence. The performance was in no way sloppy, though. Rather, it delicately presented the music and lyrics in a way that suited them perfectly, creating just the right touch of realism.

"Lover" became first a huge hit for Lee in 1952 and then the title of her 1964 Decca album, which compiled several of her first recorded singles for the label. In fact, the 1964 album represented Lee's complete collection of solo masters recorded in 1952 for Decca. "Be Anything (but Be Mine)" was recorded in the spring of 1952 and was the first single Lee scored on the music charts with her new label. It peaked at number twenty-one on the *Billboard* charts and represented a very sensitive rendition of this song, which was recorded simultaneously by several artists at competing studios. Gordon Jenkins provided the orchestra, choir, and musical direction for Lee's Decca session. This recording captured Lee's mastery of subtle nuance, tasteful lyricism, and vocal control.

In April 1952, at the same session during which Lee recorded "Be Anything," she recorded the enchanting single "I'm Glad There Is You," which exhibited no less sensitivity or delicateness. This song's extraordinarily slow tempo predated the bebop era when extremes in tempo (either intensely fast or extremely slow) prevailed, proving both Lee's ability to hold her own among the jazz crowd as well as her relevance as a cutting-edge jazz artist in the early 1950s. Her simmering energy never waned, and she proved once again her prowess for holding listeners transfixed all the way through a ballad with the skill possessed only by the greatest singers in the business.

Also recorded in April, Cole Porter's brisk classic "Just One of Those Things" offered Lee a burning tempo and a first-rate jazz orchestra with rhythm section to accompany her. Her outstanding sense of rhythm allowed her to take liberties in departing from the band's steady tempo to experiment with timing her lyrical phrases outside the parameters of the musical phrases (a term called *backphrasing*). This technique required a singer to mentally keep track of her place in the form, as well as the band's. Backphrasing was employed in "Lover" as well as in this up-tempo arrangement. Less skilled vocalists got lost in the song's form when they attempted to stray from the fixed eight-bar musical phrases, but true professionals were (and are still today) more than capable of keeping two sets of phrases in mind at all times—the unchanging musical phrases and the malleable lyrical phrases that can be timed before, during, or after the phrases that the band played. Mastery of this technique continues to separate the pros from the posers in modern jazz singing.

In addition to the masters that later were collected into the *Lover* album, in 1952 Lee recorded a couple of duets with her Decca colleague Bing Crosby. These included her third hit for the label, "Watermelon Weather." A cute, slowly swinging tune, the song allowed an easygoing pairing of two of the finest voices in America. Matching adorable, almost-rhyming lyrics ("meander," "veranda," and "hand her") in an every-other-line passing back-and-forth manner marked this nostalgic duet that resonated with the postwar fascination for music that soothed and comforted the heart. This heartwarming duet peaked at number twenty-eight on the popular music charts during the summer of 1952. In order to promote this single, Lee sang it on the radio as a guest in Crosby's *Chesterfield Presents the Bing Crosby Show*, which aired on June 18.

For the next week's episode, the pair tantalized listeners with the other duet recorded at the same Decca session, "The Moon Came Up with a Great Idea Last Night," which featured one singer at a time

Peggy Lee and Bing Crosby in *Mr. Music* (1950). *Paramount Pictures/Photofest.*

singing lead, while the other sang a response in a backup manner throughout the first verse. In the second chorus, the two sang together in charming harmony. Whenever these two stars were paired, a worthwhile listening treat resulted from their collaboration. Both of these songs, although obscure today, reward repeated listening.

One more duet recorded by this duo bears mentioning: "Little Jack Frost, Get Lost" was recorded by Crosby and Lee from a live radio show performance. This holiday novelty song featured the Rhythmaires singing background for the pair of lead singers. A clever swing tune, it contained some holiday appeal in the wintry theme as well as in the instrumental interlude bearing the spritely sounds of high woodwinds (piccolos and flutes) and plucked stringed instruments sounding fresh from the spirit of "Sleigh Ride." This recording preserved a slice of music history not to be missed, and a song quite worthy of reviving.

Peggy Lee's inaugural album with Decca came as a result of a concomitant film project, *The Jazz Singer*. Since co-star Danny Thomas worked as an RCA recording artist, both competing labels sought to jump onto the film hype by releasing albums compiling songs their artists sang in the film. RCA released *Songs from The Jazz Singer*, a recording of Thomas singing most of the songs from the movie, including those performed by Lee. The Decca recording, *Selections Featured in the Warner Bros. Motion Picture The Jazz Singer*, included just the four songs Lee sang as a solo artist in the film and was considered an EP (extended play) rather than an LP (long play) record because of the limited number of songs it offered. Lee wrote two of the songs used in the film: "This Is a Very Special Day" and "I Hear the Music Now," which was based on a theme from the 1851 opera *Raymond, ou le secret de la reine* by Ambroise Thomas. "Lover" and "Just One of Those Things" rounded out the quartet of songs on the Decca recording. "I Hear the Music Now" was recorded in December 1952 and included a fully symphonic orchestration with heavy strings and a somber romantic poem set in a minor key. Lee rose to the challenge of matching this heavy accompaniment with a fuller tone and her characteristically mesmerizing denouement reserved for such poetic songs. The song itself exhibited Lee's versatility as a songwriter, revealing her capability of penning meaningful lyrics of a serious nature atop an operatic theme. Impressively fitting, her lyrics complemented the hundred-year-old music appropriately and tastefully. Modern fans may appreciate that both the RCA and Decca EP recordings were combined into a 2005 reissue by Sepia Records titled *Danny Thomas and Peggy Lee Sing Songs from . . . The Jazz Singer*.

The Victor Young-Peggy Lee songwriting collaboration "Where Can I Go without You?" was recorded in February 1953 to become Lee's eighth Decca hit. First appearing on *Billboard*'s charts in March 1954 (having been ignored by the studio for a year), it peaked at number twenty-eight. A gem in Lee's songwriting canon, this piece has remained one of the most beloved of Lee's originals. A poignant ballad that told a definite story, the lyrics related a tale of a world traveler whose exotic experiences were constantly dampened by the sad realization that the ghost of a past love haunted her. The sophisticated string orchestra accompaniment lent a touch of romantic elegance to the composition that enhanced the heartfelt, poetic lyrics. Lee successfully expressed a feminine vulnerability that set this text apart from so many others. Not merely nostalgic, this song sounded as though it came from a deep experience of lovesick grief coupled with a worldly occupation that involved frequent travel. It hailed from Lee's own life story, and her manner of singing it revealed an emotional transparency few other singers possessed. Interestingly, Lee's granddaughter, Holly Foster-Wells, related that Lee preferred Nat King Cole's rich, symphonic recording of this song even more than her own.[8]

At this point in history, *Billboard*, being more interested in the popular hits of the emerging rock and roll era, failed to see the relevance of reporting radio play of adult contemporary radio stations. For this reason, many of the important songs released after 1950 by the great crooners and singers of the previous decade were largely ignored in the music charts, hurting record sales and the staying power of many fine artists as well as their well-written songs. This trend, unfortunately, continued for many years, limiting the renown such compositions could attract. Hence, few of Lee's subsequent original songs gained chart reporting at all, even though they were amply broadcast on adult standard radio and enjoyed in jukeboxes and private homes during those years.

Lee's sixth Decca hit was a self-written novelty song, "Who's Gonna Pay the Check?" for which Lee wrote both words and music. Also recorded in February 1953, the song hit *Billboard* charts in May, rising to number twenty-two. Caricaturing an Italian-American accent, Lee essentially spoke this simple melody's lyrics on pitch. The Dave Barbour Orchestra was credited with accompanying Lee on this Decca single. This song further expanded Lee's reputation for imitating the linguistic idiosyncrasies of various ethnic groups.

Concomitant with her prolific recording career, Lee continued to perform for appreciative live audiences. On tour Lee played her latest recorded material as well as hits audiences recognized as her own, and she traveled with a lighting designer to consistently set the proper mood at each venue. Lee's harpist, Stella Castellucci, commented: "The nightclubs we played in Los Angeles and on tour were elegant and refined. . . . My first time as a musician with Peg was an engagement for two weeks at Ciro's [1953] . . . one of the most fashionable night-clubs. . . . She performed with minimal lighting. We all got used to playing our instruments in near darkness."[9] The year 1953 brought Lee and her traveling band performances in Lake Tahoe, Las Vegas, and the Hollywood Bowl. Castellucci continued: "Peg was soloist and the first nightclub singer to appear at the Bowl. *Hollywood Bowl Magazine* de-scribed Peg as thus: 'Miss Lee . . . offers one of the warmest show personalities in the entertainment field, plus a voice that is exquisite in tone and quality.'"[10]

In April of that year Lee embarked upon a recording project that would produce a top-ten jazz vocal album of all time—her peerless and legendary collection *Black Coffee*. This album represented the crown-ing achievement of her Decca years, the most acclaimed album of her entire career, and one of the very first concept albums ever produced. This compilation initially appeared in a ten-inch, long play record for-mat with only eight songs. The enormous success of this modest record-ing compelled Decca executives to propose an expansion and rerelease of the album a few years later to include a total of twelve songs. The augmented album was crafted in the new twelve-inch disc medium that remained prevalent in fans' living rooms for nearly three more decades. Songs subsequently added to this project in 1956 included "It Ain't Necessarily So," "You're My Thrill," "There's a Small Hotel," and "Gee, Baby, Ain't I Good to You?"

Black Coffee began with the title track, an artistically unparalleled version of a classic standard whose origins hailed from a traditional blues phrase spun into a song by W. C. Handy, then passed along to Mary Lou Williams in her song "What's Your Story, Morning Glory?" before being presented as a Sonny Burke composition on this album. The song's repetitive melody and harmonic motion reflected the mundane, cyclical daily routine expressed by the lyrics. Lee's casual delivery of these rightly supplied the appropriate mood and angle through which listeners peered to find a story that resonated with daily living. Lee put on no pretentions. Her raw, unapologetic, matter-of-fact attitude displayed in this housewife's lament placed her in the living rooms of her listeners, speaking directly into their hearts with realism and sober sincerity. The song aptly introduced the rest of the album's tracks by giving listeners an indication that this album represented something completely different than any they had previously heard. This concept album was bittersweet—it personified a woman's experience of loving a man whose reliability and trust remained in question. It was to jazz what *verismo* was to opera—dream-burning realism. The progression of songs relayed the heartbreak, bliss, and pain of authentic, vulnerable love as well as the awareness and acceptance that this love was no paradise.

Track two on Lee's supreme album fell to a Cole Porter standard, "I've Got You Under My Skin," a brisk and energetic swing rendition that Lee shaped in new and interesting ways. Her timing and phrasing played with the rhythms. She explored the expressive compass of text setting to achieve original ways of emphasizing important words. Lee balanced her natural, conversational approach of pronouncing sentences with an aurally artistic paintbrush that presented the lyric as a beautiful work of art.

"Easy Living" involved a delightful give-and-take between crooning Lee and the swooping muted trumpet lines of Pete Candoli, who responded to Lee's every phrase during the first half of the song and then again to her last few phrases. Their *rubato* (out of time) approach at the bridge created a lush effect of hypnotism, during which the audience hung on Lee's every word. In this way, this recording beautifully captured one of the signature qualities that characterized so many of Lee's live performances.

Track four on *Black Coffee* revealed a super-fast arrangement of another Cole Porter standard, "My Heart Belongs to Daddy." The piece opened in a samba feel and moved into a fast swing style after the first chorus—a combination of styles unlike those appearing on prior recordings of this traditionally easygoing swing tune. Lee's timing of her lyrical phrases was amazingly conversational and not lined up exactly with the musical phrases the band was playing. The freedom she displayed in her timing choices revealed her total command of the energy and mood that enveloped the whole band's performance. The outstanding solo commentary performed by trumpeter Pete Candoli around Lee's lyrics greatly intensified the sizzling effect. The piece showcased two performers in constant musical dialogue with one another. During the swing break, throughout which the band performed the refrain again in a fast swing style, both Candoli and Lee performed simultaneously in a corporate improvisational style reminiscent of Dixieland. The soloists matched the band's gradually building exuberance and intensification of energy. This rendition of "My Heart Belongs to Daddy" was what modern jazz performers would call a "barn burner," to indicate the intensely fast tempo and intricate, masterful musical precision required to execute the music cleanly. By this point in Lee's career, her fans knew they could expect at least one of these burning songs on her albums. Her immense success with "Lover" (which also could be called "burning") set the stage for her victories over other unusually fast, intense arrangements. "My Heart Belongs to Daddy," though only two minutes long, created a peak of intensity halfway through the record that left her audience begging for more. Lee's versatility, shown so vividly on this album, became increasingly impressive as fans completed their listening of the fourth track. Her astounding versatility helped this recording become one of Decca's finest all-time jazz records.

In stark contrast, "It Ain't Necessarily So," from George Gershwin's masterpiece opera *Porgy and Bess*, served as a stylistically sophisticated fifth track. Beginning as a slow ballad with a heavy sense of swing, the song periodically broke into an abrupt fast swing and just as suddenly returned to the original slow tempo. Lee was even successful in pronouncing the Gullah dialect–inflected "Ain't Nessa . . . Ain't Nessa" series of four repeated lyric motives at the end of the piece as authentically as anyone who had ever sung them. Her unusual use of bluesy pentatonic descending runs (common for blues and pop singers of that period and still used today) were indicative of the wide range of stylistic tools at her disposal. As this brand of ornamentation was never previously part of Lee's style, this recording destroyed all preconceived limitations regarding the singer's capabilities. This type of unexpected and completely uncharacteristic adornment of her musical lines may have prompted bandleader Raymond Scott, when hearing a blindfold test featuring this album in a *Down Beat* interview, to comment: "It must be Billie Holiday, but it is so accurate, precise, and artistic, that I can't believe it."[11]

"Gee, Baby, Ain't I Good to You," in the author's estimation, represents the first track on this album that actually does resemble the voice of Billie Holiday. However, rather than portraying Peggy Lee as a copycat, this track may have simply displayed yet another extreme in her many talents so evident on this album. The fast, almost out-of-control vibrato at the ends of words and phrases, the occasional upward-scooping note that has no place in the melody but rather functions as an exclamation, and the heavy blues with a lyric soaked in sorrow and self-pity all strongly suggested the vocal, musical, and lyric-interpreting approach of Lee's contemporary, Billie Holiday. Framed as a tribute rather than an imitation, this song's inclusion on *Black Coffee* may have been Lee's way to honor a fellow singer known throughout the world for her own unique contributions to the singing of jazz and popular music, and certainly an important direct influence upon Lee herself.

Composer Willard Robison wrote the next song on *Black Coffee* specifically for Lee to sing. His "A Woman Alone with the Blues" appropriately fit among the other songs on this concept album and provided another node of rest from the frenzy of some of the faster jazz selections. This easygoing ballad was not truly a blues song but was composed in the form and style of a contemporary jazz or pop ballad from the 1940s or early '50s. The powerful lyrics beautifully suited both Lee's mood for the album and her life story. This piece served the album as the song that tied all the others together in its unifying theme of a woman's lot in a flawed love relationship. Sounding more like herself here than in the previous track, Lee approached the lyrics with honesty and tenderness as well as with an earnest passion that spoke more of sincerity than of impressive technical skill. Ever the consummate translator of music into pure emotion, Lee successfully brought her authentic sentiments to the forefront in this humble outpouring of the feminine heart.

For the next song, "I Didn't Know What Time It Was," Lee wisely chose to include the seldom-performed introductory verse. The verse gently and innocently provided a backdrop for the storyline concept of the album. She conceded in this verse that when she was young, she exhibited naïve idealism in regard to love. The song began as an out-of-time (rubato) ballad, facilitating for Lee the opportunity to ebb and flow her lyrics word-by-word at a pace she extemporaneously decided. It then moved into a medium-fast swing style during which Lee demonstrated confidence in delivering this decisive, self-assured lyric. The beauty of this text lay in its ambiguity—nothing was actually stated, only insinuated. In the context of the other songs on the album, however, the song presented a point of view of one who had learned from her mistakes and would no longer be hesitant in making decisions to look after her best interests. That being one listener's interpretation, the charm of music includes the ability to cull from a song many different meanings. This riddle was not lost on Lee. Placed immediately after "A Woman Alone with the Blues," "I Didn't Know What Time It Was" effectively illustrated a woman's coming of age and entering a state of revelation toward self-empowerment.

Lee's devastatingly compelling introduction to "(Ah, the Apple Trees) When the World Was Young" (no less than two full minutes in length) created an entrancing backdrop for the comparatively brief core of the song, which lasted only a minute. In this noteworthy case, Lee heightened the importance of a song's introduction to represent its own set piece and relegated the rest of the song to function as a denouement, a tapering-down ending. Having no repeated sections, this exquisite offering within the LP offered recitative-like ruminations having to do with the loss of innocence and the transcendence of an inexperienced child into a wiser state of being. Pete Candoli's clever muted trumpet quips, especially when depicting Lee's text about a hive of bees, provided slices of comic relief within this otherwise serious soliloquy.

"Love Me or Leave Me" as track ten on this album provided a necessary release of tension created by the previous songs' expostulations about dashed hopes and maturity gained through heartbreak. This lightly swinging tune was deftly swung by Lee and the band. Candoli again contributed adorable backtalk to Lee's lyrics, taking turns with pianist Jimmy Rowles on the second time through the form, while Lee presented the lyrics in a freer, extemporaneous manner that rivaled the improvisational skills of the finest jazz vocalists of the time. This brief track offered the album an upbeat moment of carefree grace that arrived just in time to rescue the album's light/dark scale balance from excessive melancholy.

Lee then draped her mysterious spell over "You're My Thrill." Using an extreme sense of rubato, the song was so out of time during the introductory verse that listeners were forced to hang on every syllable. Taking full advantage of words like "strange," Lee capitalized on her ability to weave the full meaning of a word into a picturesque aural spectrum, assisted by the otherworldly timbres of harp and vibraphone. The essence of the song was enveloped in a reverie created by Lee and her musical compatriots in a way that resembled hypnotism.

Presenting "There's a Small Hotel" as a lighthearted waltz with harp, xylophone, piano, and bass accompaniment, then moving into a straight-ahead swing before returning to the original instrumentation of the opening waltz, Lee and her entourage brought refreshing touches to this beloved Rodgers and Hart standard. The back-and-forth playfulness of the waltz appearing in alternation with swing style and the continuing ping-pong match between the styles through the end of the piece created an incredibly delightful and unpredictable finish to this stunning album.

The charm of this legendary album stemmed from many factors, not the least of which was the sheer breadth of Lee's interpretive and vocal powers displayed among the selections. She whispered and soared, moaned and swung, purred, pleaded, and phrased poetry with equal skill. Just when it seemed that flawless swing must be her strongest skill, that theory was dashed in the shattering poignancy of her ballads, the lighthearted joy of a waltz, and the sizzling drive of an intense samba. Lee's unsurpassed powers to shape a phrase, to create and inhabit a song's essence, and to meaningfully time silences between words, filling them to overflowing with poignancy, were never exhibited to a more impressive degree than they were in *Black Coffee*.

Beyond this pivotal recording, Lee went on to record several more successful albums and a number of singles under the Decca label, including her next project, *Songs in an Intimate Style*. Recorded in September 1953, this compilation included Lee's recent chart single, "Baubles, Bangles, and Beads" from Broadway's *Kismet*. The album also featured several ballads, notably two Victor Young and Peggy Lee collaborations, "How Strange" and "Where Can I Go Without You?" A comic novelty tune bearing a striking resemblance to the *Kismet* title, "Apples, Peaches, and Cherries," rounded out the octet of intimate songs with a flash of humor.

In late 1953 Lee suffered an unfortunate collapse due to exhaustion and was placed on a four-month mandatory medical hiatus from all work activity. While recuperating in Palm Springs, Lee made plans to create a more peaceful lifestyle for herself. Her return involved planning a unique album featuring harp and harpsichord accompaniment, which was finally recorded in 1955. Musical musings on Chinese poetry (translated from seventh-to-ninth-century sources), folk songs, Irish songs, sea chants, and children's songs inhabited this unconventional album, called *Sea Shells*. The project was not released until 1958, after her contract with Decca had expired. Regarding reasons for the delay, harpist and arranger Stella Castellucci stated that Lee intended to add more tracks, so she did not push for its release. Also, given the dim commercial response to the album, Decca may have hesitated to put it forward when it was deemed likely to yield little financial gain. Today the album is considered a cult favorite of Lee's most devoted fans.[12]

Lee's next albums, *Miss Wonderful* (from 1956, conducted by Sy Oliver) and *Dream Street*, furthered her recording legacy with Decca, although the latter album was recorded quickly over two days (June 5 and 7), possibly to fulfill the singer's contractual obligations to the label prior to her departure from it. *Dream Street* featured Peggy singing fully orchestrated arrangements like "Too Late Now," a dreamy ballad that erupted unexpectedly into a flurry of Latin rhythmic activity. A new venture through "My Old Flame" also appeared on this album in addition to the namesake for the album, "Street of Dreams." The latter recording master was noteworthy in the extreme ultra-soft singing Lee employed, getting so close to her microphone that her mouth noises were amplified along with her quiet singing voice. "Dancing on the Ceiling" represented a similar example of the barely audible caressing of notes that Lee employed on this album. The virtuosic flourishes displayed by piano soloist Lou Levy provided an energetic contrast to Lee's lush, long lines, so subtly sustained.

"I've Grown Accustomed to His Face" (from Broadway's *My Fair Lady*) provided evidence that Lee employed more vibrato than usual on this classical-slanting album replete with rich orchestrations. Her vibrato matched the richness of the orchestra without causing her to lose her characteristic tone quality. Her impeccable taste and authenticity of style required that she adjust to the style of music she was singing as well as to the size and timbral spectrum of the ensemble. The result was a glowing demonstration on this album of yet another dimension to Lee's versatile technique, showing her mastery of singing with an orchestra.

During her Decca years, Lee recorded a number of additional albums, some of which the label released to take advantage of the singer's concurrent appearances in films, including compilation recordings of songs from *The Jazz Singer*, *Lady and the Tramp*, and *Pete Kelly's Blues*. Overall, Lee produced ten singles for Decca that rose to top-thirty status as well as one million-selling hit ("Lover"). She also recorded her most renowned album *Black Coffee* under this label. Peggy Lee's success at Decca represented a pinnacle of her career leading into even more hitmaking at her former stomping ground, Capitol Records. The singer decided to return to Capitol in 1957 and continued to record under contract there until 1972, making her the longest-contracted female artist in Capitol's history. It seemed the move to Decca only cemented Capitol's resolve to bring one of its brightest recording stars back home.

5

A FLAIR FOR FILM

Throughout the 1940s, '50s, '60s, and beyond, popular music artists who graced the radio waves frequently added their star power and performance excellence to Hollywood films via acting roles or cameo appearances, and less frequently through writing music for film soundtracks or scores. Peggy Lee was no exception in this regard. Lee's varied experiences in the film industry included recording songs for use in films, performing songs in film scenes, scoring, composing theme songs, contributing lyrics to preexistent instrumental movie themes (both before and after film releases), and performing cameos, voiceovers, and full acting roles. Unlike her contemporaries Frank Sinatra and Bing Crosby (and most other popular musical artists who were regularly engaged to sing and act in films), Lee was called upon to perform a wider variety of services to filmmakers. Being a universal artist in the sense of doing many things well, Lee successfully managed her diverse roles as singer, actor, composer, lyricist, and/or voiceover artist for several films. This important distinction of working as both a performer *and* music creator set Peggy Lee apart from nearly all her competition in that era.

Early in her career Lee was offered small acting roles and singing spots in a number of film shorts and feature films. The first, released in 1943, involved Lee performing with the Benny Goodman band in *The Powers Girl*. For this brief spot in a dance hall scene, Lee sang "The Lady Who Didn't Believe in Love" by Jule Styne and Kim Gannon.

Later that year, *Stage Door Canteen* was released, featuring a timeless performance by Lee with the Goodman band in "Why Don't You Do Right?" This entrancing film clip revealed the unique style, swing sense, stage allure, relaxed confidence, and complete performance package that young Peggy embodied. It foreshadowed her brilliant career and enduring presence as a jazz diva in the changing music industry. Her performance evoked a smoky, breathy vocal quality meshed with a sweet, youthful sound beautifully housed in rhythmic precision and deliberate yet easygoing swing. Her coy smile exuded her sheer enjoyment of making music. Lee's manner of "tossing away" certain word endings provoked comparisons with the interpretive singing style of Billie Holiday, who certainly exerted significant influence upon Lee. However, the final product, Lee's legendary video/sound recording of "Why Don't You Do Right," became a synthesis of Lee's own tools: cool singing style and subtle influences rather than slavish copying.

In the Paramount short film *Midnight Serenade* (1947), Lee undertook her first acting role. Albeit brief (the film itself lasted only eighteen minutes), she performed four songs: "I'm in the Mood for Love," "Sugar," and Barbour and Lee's "You Was Right, Baby" and "It's a Good Day." Dave Barbour not only played guitar on the bandstand during this film but also contributed a line. Family movies of the Barbours with young daughter Nicki complemented the film footage of the band's performance. This short marked the film debut of "It's a Good Day" and first introduced to the public the Lee and Barbour songwriting team.

Other film appearances included Universal's *Banquet of Melody*, a musical film short from 1946 in which Lee delivered the only line of spoken text throughout the film in addition to performing her two musical numbers "I Don't Know Enough about You" (another Barbour/Lee original song) and "Don't Blame Me." The Matty Malneck Orchestra provided music, and a quintet drawn from the orchestra provided the backdrop for Lee's performances.

In 1950 Lee made a cameo appearance in the Paramount film *Mr. Music*, starring Bing Crosby. Lee and Crosby sang the charming duet

"Life Is so Peculiar" in a party scene during which their voices inter-
mingled in a comedic and seemingly effortless conversation. Their
evenly matched singing talents combined to create an unforgettable
performance that entertained through the overlapping and turn-taking
of a friendly discussion set to music and choreography. The pitch-perfect delivery of a jumping, lightly swinging melody and the improvisational, casual playfulness of this delightful duo shone brightly in this
pivotal moment in film history when two of the finest singers in the
world met for a swinging, joyful romp.

During the 1950s, while frequenting the top nightclubs and performance stages around the world, Lee was presented with numerous
opportunities to contribute music, generally in the form of lyrics, to
several film scores. Lee's various film credits included a wide variety of
film genres, spanning the spectrum from westerns to mysteries and
musical dramas to animated children's films. Throughout her career
Lee composed song lyrics for at least fourteen films, yet her recorded
performances of others' compositions have been added to so many films
that enumerating them all is difficult. *The Bullfighter and the Lady*
(1952) boasted the song "How Strange," Lee's very first song composed
for a film, co-written by Victor Young. Regarding Lee's work with this
composer, Lee's daughter stated: "She loved working with Victor
Young. They have quite a few songs together that are really gorgeous."[1]
In this case Lee's lyrics were added to the preexisting theme after the
film was released, and the song later appeared on the silver screen in a
Republic film titled *The Woman They Almost Lynched* (1953). This
song displayed Lee's breathy, melancholic delivery of eerie, ephemeral
lyrics above a foundation of strings, distant choral background voices,
and a guitar fingerpicking distinctly modal figures. Lee's extraplanetary
lyrics (sung to the moon and sky) amid a haunting minor ballad described an angel making physical contact with a human to inform the
latter that she was falling in love. This song represented one of many
originals in which Lee expressed her keen interest in metaphysical,
supernatural themes, an area she spent a great deal of time studying
throughout her life.

Some films simply involved Lee contributing music or lyrics to a theme song, while others offered her principal acting roles. *The Jazz Singer* (1953) was the first important film that cast Lee in a prominent role. This picture functioned as a remake of Al Jolson's classic 1927 film by the same title. Jolson's *Jazz Singer* was, of course, the first "talkie" in film history, synchronizing for the first time both audio and visual elements via a recorded musical score, lip-synchronous dialogue, and songs with video matching the audio. This shocking juxtaposition proved both revolutionary and delightful for 1920s film audiences. Warner Brothers' release of this debut feature film precipitated the immediate demise of silent film, as competing movie studios raced to create their own talking pictures to match the technological advances presented by this pioneering picture. A humorous but relevant account of how *The Jazz Singer* influenced the evolution of filmmaking comprised a portion of the plot of the MGM classic film *Singin' in the Rain*, starring Gene Kelly and Debbie Reynolds.

In the remake of *The Jazz Singer* Peggy Lee co-starred with Danny Thomas and contributed original music as well. The score contained Lee's original song "This Is a Very Special Day," an upbeat, optimistic ditty filled with thankfulness and joy. Lee was cast as a nightclub singer (after Doris Day declined the role) and performed her Decca hit "Lover," among other songs. Although her acting performance yielded mixed, mostly lukewarm reviews, her musical performances in the film left no doubt that Lee possessed the vocal mastery and stage presence of a world-class professional.

In "This Is a Very Special Day," Lee constructed the music and lyrics to encourage her listening audience amid the daily struggles of life. Set in a major key with a light and energetic bounce, her simple, cheerful lyrics preached the uniqueness and value of each new day. She proceeded to describe how "this morning" she awoke in a spirit of gloom, but she pushed herself out of bed with the faith that her attitude would improve just by getting the day started. "This Is a Very Special Day" became one of Lee's signature original tunes, having a decidedly optimistic message, and it received ample hearing as a set piece performed by Lee in two prominent scenes in this picture.

Lee's legendary performance of Rodgers and Hart's "Lover" in *The Jazz Singer* was, by some, considered scandalous at the time the movie was released. A number one hit for Lee in 1952, the song worked the music into a frenzy of intense ecstasy at breakneck speed. Lee was no novice in the art of building tension through the course of a song, so this opportunity to create a sexy, sizzling, and boisterous rendition of a previously innocuous romantic ballad was not lost on her. On the contrary, she welcomed the challenge with surprisingly effective results. When the orchestra built up and up toward pounding climaxes at many moments in the song, Lee's smoky, breathless answers delivered in a rhythmically free, almost shouting manner strongly suggested that this was much more than a song recording—it was an aural illustration of a sexual encounter. It remains one of the earliest and most vivid illustrations of such ever recorded. Lee's acting and musical contributions to this iteration of *The Jazz Singer* marked a significant milestone in her performing career.

One year later Peggy Lee composed song lyrics for three films: *The Rawhide Years* starring Tony Curtis; a Joan Crawford film titled *Johnny Guitar* (for which Lee co-wrote the title song with Victor Young); and *About Mrs. Leslie*, starring Shirley Booth. Lee collaborated with composer Laurindo Almeida to create "The Gypsy with Fire in His Shoes" for *The Rawhide Years*. Leading actress Colleen Miller sang this song in the film, which was finally released in 1956. Lee later recorded this brisk, energetic dance for her acclaimed *Lover* album. Set against the aural foundation of a Spanish tap dance in lieu of percussion, Lee exhibited a Spanish accent and culturally informed vocal ornaments for this style. Telling the story of this gypsy dancer, Lee approximated the dialect of Spanish singers to perform her original English lyrics as authentically as possible.

Composed for a movie by the same name, the Young-Lee collaboration "Johnny Guitar" provided an exquisitely sparse backdrop for showcasing Lee's dry, melancholic vocal delivery. This title track became a sad ballad set in a minor key scored for acoustic guitar, voice, and hand percussion. Lee performed the song twice on the movie soundtrack—first to open the film and again as a reprise on the final track. Intimacy was attained through the juxtaposition of Lee's light vocal approach next to the gentle broken chords of the solo guitar. The overarching melancholy of the song's theme provided insight into the depth of Lee's attachment to her former husband, guitarist Dave Barbour, often cited as the muse for this haunting love song.

Although Lee composed lyrics to Victor Young's "I Love You So" for *About Mrs. Leslie,* the song did not appear anywhere in the film. It may have been one of many casualties on the cutting room floor, and its fate in regard to that film remains a mystery. A photographic print including the song's title appeared in a 1954 Paramount poster for the film, and Lee and Young were credited as its writers.[2]

For a 1955 Kirk Douglas film titled *The Racers,* Lee performed the romantic ballad "I Belong to You" by Jack Brooks and Alex North, which was also released as a Decca single. This wonderful piece was scored for jazz orchestra with rhythm section and soft muted horns. Lee's mastery of delivering a ballad with exquisite tenderness, warmth, and sincerity shone brightly in this lovely piece. Here she successfully wove the sentiment of faithful vows into a vocal technique that had grown into something her very own. Rich with vibrato yet slightly husky, Lee's voice balanced quiet intimacy and feminine allure with belting the promise contained in the title. At both extremes, she displayed utmost control over her expressive palette.

Lee's most renowned venture into children's film music was her 1955 collaboration with Sonny Burke on Disney's hit animated film musical *Lady and the Tramp.* Except for the inaugural *Snow White and the Seven Dwarfs,* this film grossed more in ticket sales than any other Disney animated feature up to that point, yielding approximately $7.5 million. "He's a Tramp" proved to be a true crowd pleaser, becoming one of Peggy's most treasured songs of all time. Lee's fans instantly recognized her sassy, jazzy approach to this hard swing tune presented in the context of a "worldly" female dog swooning over the thought of the Tramp, every dog's coveted companion. Lee's lyrics revealed the history and reputation of the Tramp, the coolest of canines loved by all the female dogs and envied or revered by the males. The song opened with a catchy, saloon-like walking bass introduction countered by a repeated bluesy piano riff. Lee twice spoke the lead-in text, "What a Dog!," before launching into a smoky-voiced burlesque performance by the animated canine singer, appropriately named "Peg." Replete with a howling barbershop quartet of other impounded dogs providing delightfully charming four-part background harmony as well as barks and whines for added effect, the song achieved more artistry, humor, and staying power than one would expect from a song aimed primarily at children.

"The Siamese Cat Song" from another scene in the film provided a contrasting example of Lee's imaginative prowess in depicting the fanciful language of exotic animals.[3] Sonny Burke created a decidedly Far Eastern musical atmosphere as soon as the cats arrived on the scene. Using parallel open fifth harmonies between the cats, Lee sported a mysteriously exotic accent emphasizing broken English throughout the text. Always sensitive to minute details, Lee introduced the cats in the opening line of the song, "We are Siamese if you ple-eeze . . . " and later included purrs, growls, and hisses to reveal their sinister personalities as viewed by the canine protagonist. Lyrics referring to the cats' desire to share the goldfish swimming nearby in the fishbowl completed the picture of the problem these two unwelcome visitors presented for Lady (the canine protagonist), whose intention was to protect her family. A subsequent verse betrayed the cats' sinister intention to steal milk from the new infant's bassinet. The animated movements of the two cats mirrored a *pas de deux* filled with mystery, grace, and sly agility matching the hypnotic music. Burke and Lee managed to create a measure of depth in these two feline characters even though they only appeared in a single song and scene. Sonny Burke beautifully completed the orchestration of this musical gem using a gong, drum, and finger cymbals to evoke the appropriately exotic mood.

Lee provided not only the lyrics to all the music for *Lady and the Tramp*, but she also supplied the voiceover talent for four key characters in the film including "Darling" (the human mother whose face is never shown), the Siamese cats "Si" and "Am," and the impounded canine singer, "Peg." In one scene as Darling, Lee sang a chilling lullaby, "La La Loo," remarkably softly and divinely low, showcasing her amazing vocal control and command of pitches in a range few other female vocalists would have attempted. Her breathy, gentle alto voice lent a comforting, relaxed blanket of sound to the movie soundtrack—a refreshing departure from the clear, high-pitched, hyper-energized belt so stereotypical of Disney voices.

More than three decades following the 1955 release of *Lady and the Tramp*, Lee went down in history as one of the first musical artists to aggressively pursue intellectual property rights and royalty collection for film composers in the wake of the ubiquity of home videocassettes and laser discs. Videocassettes of increasingly numerous films, stage

Peggy Lee recording *Lady and the Tramp* (1955). *Photofest.*

plays, musicals, and television series were made available to the public for home viewing by the mid-1970s. This technological advance created a major boom of film revenue by the early 1980s. As unbelievable as it may seem, film composers and lyricists had never been granted any royalties for the millions of home movie copies of their intellectual property until Lee filed her case against Disney on November 16, 1988, and was finally awarded $2.3 million in 1991. This unprecedented win over a powerhouse entertainment conglomerate proved vital in helping secure royalty distribution for film composers thereafter. The value of Lee's victory on behalf of musical artists who later collected royalties for contributing their talents to the film industry cannot be adequately measured.

In 1955 Peggy Lee appeared as a supporting actress and singer in *Pete Kelly's Blues*, a Warner Brothers film produced and directed by the film's leading man, Jack Webb. Webb played the role of Pete Kelly, a trumpeter and bandleader. Lee portrayed the tragic character Rose Hopkins. Over the course of the film, Pete employed Rose, a "once-was" nightclub singer, codependently attached to an abusive and violent gangster (the venue owner) intent on exploiting her talent. Lee's singing scenes included rehearsals for well-known songs "He Needs Me" and "Sugar," intended to be part of Rose's set list. Often inebriated as the story unfolded, alcoholic and insecure Rose eventually was pushed down the stairs by her abuser and never recovered. The story closed with a scene in which her concerned friend, Pete, visited Rose in her new home—a hospital for mentally ill patients. Rose barely acknowledged her visitor and seemed to be in a trancelike state as she cradled a doll while softly singing Lee's original song "Sing a Rainbow." Her horrified friend simply looked on in pity. Lee's hushed catatonic delivery of this simple song created a haunting, memorable image of a ruined life. The opening theme of this song simply listed several colors followed by the statement "I can sing a rainbow," as if a toddler were extemporaneously creating a lyrical melody to a simple set of words. The double meaning presented in the repeated lyrics at the bridge ("listen with your eyes") coupled with Pete's inaction when Rose needed help, together suggested an underlying moral of this tragic story: caring about others involves observantly recognizing dangerous patterns and intervening before it's too late.

In identifying with her fractured character, Lee named the doll Deloris (Lee's middle name). Her memorable depictions of Rose's growing turmoil, depression, inebriation, and ensuing brain damage following the tumble down the stairs revealed a talented actress able to tune in to human frailty and trauma at an impressive depth. Lee consequently earned a Best Supporting Actress Academy Award nomination for this exquisite performance, placing her in the annals of history among the finest actors of her day.

Lee displayed significant growth as an actress between her slightly timid performance in *The Jazz Singer* and her outstanding showing in *Pete Kelly's Blues*. In the former film, Lee seemed less at ease in her surroundings, except while singing, and sometimes delivered her lines and blocking in a self-conscious or forced manner. A. H. Weiler from *The New York Times* wrote, "Mr. Thomas and Peggy Lee, the eminent popular songstress who is his romantic vis-a-vis, are joking, wooing, and warbling in a modern idiom, but they are selling unadorned and sometimes corny sentimentality that cannot be disguised by smooth patter or snappy ditties."[4] However, in the second film Lee grasped onto elements of her character and dove into the persona of Rose with utmost commitment to a point where distinguishing Peggy from Rose became nearly impossible. This quality of unfeigned authenticity marked a well-acted role, highly worthy of remembrance.

Continuing to accept opportunities to write film music, in 1956 Lee penned the theme song for the Frank DeVol–scored film *Johnny Trouble*, starring Ethel Barrymore. The film was released by Warner Brothers the following year, with its theme song performed by vocalist Eddie Robertson.

Since so much film produced prior to 1960 was not archived in ways to ensure perpetuity, much was subject to deterioration. Some films suffered moisture damage due to being locked in vaults for decades on end. Also, documenting film history was not yet viewed as important, so care was often not taken to preserve film or to record a project's con-tributors. Thus, in many cases, researchers have relied upon assertions put forth by various parties attached to a film with the understanding that corroborating those facts may prove difficult in modern times. For instance, Lee earned songwriting credit along with Sonny Burke for the theme song in *My Man Godfrey*, a 1957 Universal film starring David Niven and June Allyson. This was a remake of the 1936 comedy by the same name. According to Turner Classic Movies and the Library of Congress, Lee and Burke penned the theme song for this picture, which was sung by Sarah Vaughan.[5] However, a question about Lee's authorship arose due to the song not being listed in the film's opening credits.[6] In another example, the movie website Fandango listed *The Pride and the Passion* (1957), starring Frank Sinatra, Cary Grant, and Sophia Loren, among Lee's film credits,[7] although the soundtrack did not mention her. While credits have been attributed to Lee on both accounts, the extent of her actual involvement with both projects has remained a mystery.

In 1958 Lee contributed music and lyrics to the children's film *Tom Thumb*. "Tom Thumb's Tune" consisted of scat syllables and simplistic words fit for a children's nursery song and exhibited Lee's ability to write music uniquely suited for children. Scored for plucked strings, xylophone, and woodwinds in its opening, then expanding to full or-chestra and brass band, the song gave the film's protagonist a happy tune to call his own.

The level of optimism of this song revealed a bit about Lee's musical outlook. Her daughter, Nicki Lee Foster, explained to the author that Lee was essentially an optimistic person and liked to write songs that encouraged people. She wanted to leave them feeling happier at the end of a performance than when they first arrived at her show. Lee claimed: "I write happy songs when I'm sad and I write sad songs when I'm happy."[8] If this statement rang true, the large number of Lee's original songs exploring themes of optimism, cheerfulness, and encour-agement shrouded the reality of loneliness she experienced throughout her personal life. Likewise, the transparency with which she composed and performed volumes of songs having emotionally charged, bitter-sweet, or melancholic lyrics revealed a compassionate soul acquainted with heartbreak and disappointment.

Lee was asked on numerous occasions to contribute to films as a songwriter—most often as a lyricist, although she was credited from time to time with composing music. Sometimes she was asked to add lyrics to preexisting themes of films already completed and released. *The Bullfighter and the Lady* was the first of such examples. The most famous instance in which this process occurred produced the eventual song "I'm Gonna Go Fishin'," in reference to the 1959 Columbia film *Anatomy of a Murder*. Duke Ellington himself asked Lee, subsequent to the release of the film, to add lyrics to his instrumental theme song. Lee recounted her work on this as follows:

> One day Duke Ellington himself brought me the tape with the theme music from the movie *Anatomy of a Murder*, and I was impressed. He just said, 'Here you are, your Highness—write this,' and he left. (Duke nicknamed me "The Queen.") When I thought about writing a lyric about a murder, it seemed like a challenge . . . I just got lucky when I found the poetic symbol. Jimmy Stewart played the detective who liked to go fishing to think about solving a case . . . So he became the symbol of the fisherman. The trout is the man who committed the crime—the one who will be caught . . . I finished the lyric and gave it to Duke Ellington. The Duke liked it all, and that was enough for me. [9]

Ellington's music burst with energy and bluesy melodic construction, providing a wonderful musical foundation for Lee's confrontational lyrics. In the film's storyline the protagonist, a town sheriff portrayed by Jimmy Stewart, adored fly-fishing and often undertook this activity to relax and think about his cases. The song described his ruminations using a metaphor of the sheriff catching a trout to symbolize his capturing a criminal. The song very effectively used metaphoric writing to achieve a specific purpose, and Lee set the tone for this film with extreme effectiveness in her crafty design of the lyrics. She capitalized on the plot point of fly-fishing—even commenting on the finer points of casting a line. The music, constantly pushing ahead, strongly suggested the forceful pressure of a rushing river or stream. Ellington's chromatic harmony (ebbing and flowing back and forth by alternating semitones) also created an unstable, watery foundation upon which the equally forceful lyrics Lee apportioned exploded. This song represented a successful collaboration by two excellent songwriters in accomplishing a precise and effective melding of music, text, and overall message. The first recording of Ellington's music with Lee's lyrics occurred in July 1960 when Lee recorded it. The song went on to be recorded, performed, and treasured by many other jazz vocalists thereafter.

Lee co-wrote "Happy with the Blues" for a 1961 television special entitled *Harold Arlen: Happy with the Blues*, which later became the title of his biography by Edward Jablonski.[10] Lee added lyrics to Arlen's song after the composer's death, making their collaboration all the more meaningful for Lee. Her lyrics expressed her contentment in being happy with a relationship that involved absence and neglect, preferring to stay with a man who brought her the blues in order to avoid being on her own. Often feeling identified with lonely souls, Lee wrote plenty of songs like this one that dabbled in troubled relationships.

For the 1966 Columbia Pictures film *Walk, Don't Run*, Lee co-wrote two songs with Quincy Jones. This film constituted Cary Grant's final performance. Peggy's health prevented her from recording the songs in accordance with film production deadlines, so vocalist Toni Clementi performed "Stay with Me, Stay with Me," and the Don Elliott Voices covered "Happy Feet" on the movie soundtrack. Lee finally recorded both originals herself at Capitol Records later that year. "Happy Feet" appeared as a brisk, energetic urban ditty featuring a cheerful whistle as part of the percussion-driven accompaniment, evoking the image of someone whistling while walking down a city street.

In 1968 Dave Grusin wrote the instrumental theme for the film *The Heart is a Lonely Hunter*.[11] Grusin and Lee collaborated in 1974 to release the album *Let's Love*, and Grusin's song, with Lee's added lyrics, appeared in a much slower version on this singular project that Lee undertook with Atlantic Records. Whether the lyrics existed prior to the release of the film has remained unknown. Lee's earnest, heart-rending words posed difficult questions about lovers truly needing each other. Was the singer's plea to simply be understood ever satisfied? Did her love go unrequited? Lee skillfully imbued many of her later compositions with such rhetorical, philosophical questions as these.

As she aged, Lee felt drawn to explore more and more modern works by youthful songwriting teams. In 1970 her voice was heard singing the theme "Pieces of Dreams" (also known as "Little Boy Lost") in the United Artists film by the same title. The Bergman-Legrand song was nominated for an Academy Award in the "Best Song" category and also appeared on Lee's 1970 Capitol recording *Make It with You*. This lush pop ballad scored for orchestra represented one of several important forays into contemporary popular music that Lee embarked on with young writers. Its melancholic empathy for a disenchanted soul found a wonderful interpreter of impressive depth in the songstress Peggy Lee. Her tender vocal quaver suggested a vulnerability not often revealed in older veteran voices. The fact that she was willing to go to such a transparent, delicate place brought believability and authenticity to the song, sealing an ideal relationship between music creator and interpreter. Ever the actress, Lee successfully embodied a song's emotional impact and intention, and this magnificent recording illustrated this talent quite well.

First appearing on *Make It with You* were Lee's lyrics to Francis Lai's music in the French film starring Charles Bronson *Le Passager de la Pluie*, known in America as *Rider on the Rain*. The theme song, "Passenger of the Rain," sparkled in the rich orchestration of its studio orchestral accompaniment. With frequent key changes and long sustained harmonic rhythms as well as drawn out melodies, it seems understandable that this piece appeared in the film without any lyrics. The original composition was evidently intended for strictly instrumental performance, evoking long passages of slowly evolving thought in the absence of natural phrase breaks. With its long, languid, harmonically strange lines, this piece failed to possess a form that was in any way songlike. Still, it represented a valuable glimpse into the mind of a lyricist willing to put forth a worthy attempt at uniting complex music with words.

Lee added lyrics to film themes in the post-production phase on a regular basis. At other times, her lyric-infused versions of film themes may have been cut from the final products prior to release, later appearing on her albums. In 1974 Lee contributed lyrics to the theme of Twentieth Century Fox's *The Nickel Ride*, a post-film collaboration with jazz composer Dave Grusin. The delicate song appeared on the Grusin-Lee Atlantic album *Let's Love*. This slow, haunting waltz explored major and minor harmonic shifts in a manner reflective of the joys and tragedies of childhood. It featured Lee's storytelling prowess and gentle vocal delivery paired with Grusin's evocative piano accompaniment in the higher registers of the instrument, strongly suggesting a child's carnival experience. In veritable Lee style, she deferred from singing to speaking midway through the song, sharing a story about her past experiences with this particular ride, accompanied by the lush piano backing of Grusin. At this juncture, Grusin provided a richer harmonic palette upon which Lee's ruminations were beautifully supported. Following the last sung verse, Lee's spoken words fashioned an ending as she portrayed a carnival barker inviting passersby to enjoy the ride for just a nickel or three rides for a dime. This gem of collaboration revealed a richness Lee often found when pairing her talent with instrumentalists and composers as excellent at their craft as she was at hers.

In the 1981 Burt Reynolds police drama *Sharky's Machine*, Lee sang a ballad called "Let's Keep Dancing" for the soundtrack. As evidenced by the aged, slightly deepening tone of her voice, Lee recorded this track expressly for the film or shortly before. This lushly orchestrated piece presented a gentle opening in a minor key featuring a restless piano line and accompanying strings. Lee joined in softly with lyrics describing two people falling in love at first sight, and their ensuing struggle to keep love vibrant. The music slightly intensified in the second verse, during which Lee expressed a common lament—that love grows cold—but implored the lover not to "let that happen to you and me."[12] The triple meter quarter notes of the drum set, the shrill repetition of high woodwinds, the tinkling bells of a xylophone, the oom-pah of a tuba, and the slowed "wind-up" start to every refrain ("Let's keep . . .") called to mind several of Lee's original songs that fixated on the theme of a carousel.

In film music then as now, hundreds of songs received consideration for inclusion before a theme song (or other songs included in the film) gained selection. This created a huge inventory of leftover songs that never made the final cut. As a frequent songwriting collaborator for films in the 1950s and '60s, Peggy Lee was no stranger to this type of scenario. In 1955, for instance, Lee collaborated with harpist Stella Castellucci to write "We" for consideration as a possible theme in the James Stewart film *The Spirit of St. Louis*, chronicling the story of famed pilot Charles Lindbergh. The song was ultimately not selected for use in the film. Later, although Lee wrote "The Land of the Leal" as a theme song contender for the 1960 H. G. Wells classic *The Time Machine*, her song was eventually cut from the film. Being the nature of a highly competitive and fickle industry, the practice of film studios turning down or cutting hundreds of song submissions occurred frequently during Lee's career. This reality presents the question: how many worthy songs by excellent composers have been cut from films or passed over and never released or heard about again?

In 1964 Lee contributed lyrics to the theme of the Metro Goldwyn-Mayer film *Joy House*, also known as *Les Felins*, starring Jane Fonda. In its nascent iteration, the song debuted in the film as purely instrumental music by Lalo Schifrin. Although the song with Lee's lyrics never appeared in the film, Lee later recorded the bluesy song in 6/8 meter under the title "Just Call Me Lovebird" for her Capitol recording *In the Name of Love*. Lee's version began softly with minimal bass and percussion accompaniment. Gradually the texture expanded, adding complexity as well as volume. The piece included an ascending key modulation that built tension as the tune progressed, as well as a lively piccolo solo contributing birdlike energy throughout the second half.

Lee's superb intuition often assisted her in composing music for use in film projects. One such example involved a scenario in 1966 when

Johnny Mandel invited Lee to write lyrics to his theme for the United Artists LP *The Russians Are Coming, The Russians Are Coming: Original Motion Picture Score*. The film had already completed production, and Mandel's theme had appeared as an instrumental piece, so this was an occasion in which Lee's lyric-writing talents assisted a theme song composer after the completion of a film. Lyrics were sometimes prized as improving the marketability of an instrumental film score and were thus used as a strategy for heightening soundtrack sales. Lee constructed one of her finest original ballads for this project; "The Shining Sea" featured singer Irene Kral performing the song on the official recording. Shortly thereafter, Lee recorded her own version on the Capitol label. Biographer Peter Richmond described the story behind Lee's involvement with the song as "one of the best illustrations ever of Peggy Lee's ability to interpret the mood of a piece of music—not just with her singing, but her words and images. If anyone ever had doubts that Lee was in touch with every stratum of song, the tale behind the creation of 'The Shining Sea' would dispel them."[13]

Lee's daughter, Nicki Lee Foster, shared with the author that Lee often felt intuitively, almost spiritually, connected to her music.[14] In this particular case, Lee produced the lyrics for "The Shining Sea" without having seen the film. Given that fact, Johnny Mandel was shocked upon his first reading of the descriptive words Lee created for his composed theme. She had written "The Shining Sea" according to what was evoked to her solely by the music. Amazed by the lyrics she had written, the composer asked her, "Do you have any idea what you did?"[15] Mandel then invited Lee to accompany him to the Director's Guild to view the scene the song had been intended to accompany. Even without her foreknowledge of any specific plot lines, Lee's lyrical depiction of a tender moment shared between lovers on a picturesque sandy beach exactly described the account of one love scene in the film. Lee had unwittingly depicted in her lyrics exactly what appeared at that moment on the movie screen. Mandel described Lee as "extremely intuitive" and the experience of writing this piece with her as simply "incredible."[16] This strong intuitive sense, according to Lee's daughter, guided much of Peggy's creative life and work.[17]

"The Shining Sea" shone forth as an outstanding example of Lee's collaborative genius. Johnny Mandel's richly beautiful theme provided an expansive, joyous backdrop for a ballad that has remained in the repertoire of many accomplished singers. Lee herself recorded a lovely debut version of the song with her lyrics, and the author also experienced the rewarding process of recording and performing this masterpiece, featuring a noteworthy improvised solo by trombonist Bill Watrous, a frequent performance collaborator with Peggy Lee. The song's melody began in a wavelike fashion with large and small intervallic distances suggesting the rising and falling of ocean waves. In a manner reminiscent of high tide rolling out into low tide, Mandel utilized phrases of calm, long, sustained melody notes alternating with wavelike phrases. This juxtaposition yielded an unusual song for the period, with recurring themes organized in tandem with contrasting sections that added interest, dimension, and compositional development via sequences, step progressions, key changes, and a climactic ending that included a satisfying denouement back into the calm rest of the sea at low tide. This song stood among its counterparts of the era as a vastly rewarding undertaking—difficult to sing well, yet worthy of study and performance for its sheer beauty, compositional merit, and its masterfully married music and lyrics.

In addition to acting in a few films, Lee occasionally engaged in television acting. In 1960 she appeared as the female lead in the series *General Electric Theatre* for an episode called "So Deadly, so Evil." She also portrayed Packer Jo in "The Furnace Flats Affair," part of the 1967 series *The Girl from U.N.C.L.E.* (derived from *The Man from U.N.C.L.E.* stories). Lee appeared on television with Anthony Quinn for skits in their 1970 Kraft Music Hall special, *A Man and a Woman.* In 1972 she filmed an episode ("Smiles from Yesterday") for the series *Owen Marshall, Counselor at Law.* Her guest appearance involved portraying a client of the law firm, and Lee's recording of a theme song for this episode appeared on the series soundtrack.

Beyond the 1970s Peggy's studio recordings took on a new life of their own, appearing in many films, television episodes, and made-for-television movies. Some examples of well-known projects that featured Lee's studio recordings include: *After Hours* (1985); *Gorillas in the Mist* (1988); *Bugsy* (1991); *This World, Then the Fireworks* (1997); the 1999 Oscar-winning Best Picture, *American Beauty*; *The Yards* (1999); *King Kong* (2005); *The Notorious Bettie Page* (2005); *About Adam* (2005); *Bernard and Doris* (2006); the HBO series *Six Feet Under* (2001–2005); and *Savages* (2007).

Lee's extensive catalog of recorded music remains an ongoing source of inspiration for film music supervisors the world over, proved by the revived interest in using her music for contemporary films over the past three decades. Because of this revival, definitively listing all the uses of her songs in visual media would involve maintaining an ever-increasing list. The resurgence in posthumous use of any artist's catalog points to the staying power and authentic legacy of that artist and generally marks the cultural significance and perceived value of that artist's work. Suffice it to say, the recorded music of Peggy Lee, via its ongoing popularity within the film industry, possesses and enjoys its own niche in twenty-first century filmmaking. Modern music supervisors and film directors continue to recognize the signature qualities that Lee's music lends. Countless emotions and idiosyncrasies known to the human experience have been explored in sound recordings and capably executed by Lee at one time or another. The seductiveness exuding throughout her rendition of "Big Spender" matched her compliant resignation of "What More Can a Woman Do?" The energetic gratitude exhibited in "I Love Being Here with You" equaled the woeful loss personified in the music of "Johnny Guitar." Her childlike innocence portrayed in "Sing a Rainbow" exuded no less persuasion or believability than her confident feminist anthem "I'm a Woman." When it came to transforming emotions and attitudes into music, Peggy Lee consistently hit it out of the park.

A film music supervisor today may feature a Lee recording to imbue a scene with poignant, meaningful symbolism or background that only the perfect song performance can deliver. In this way Lee effectively ensured her immortality in the entertainment industry, as few other recording artists captivated audiences with such a staggeringly broad range of emotions. Add to that her massive catalog of professionally recorded material, comprised of both instantly recognizable radio hits as well as obscure masterpieces for every occasion, and there may be no end to the possible uses for her timeless music.

Lee's numerous contributions to film music since the 1950s continue to reverberate indefinitely through the use of her recordings. The depth, variety, and consistently high quality of her (often original) film material reveal a great deal about Lee's unmatched talent as a singer, lyricist, actress, and voiceover artist. Literally thousands of examples of Lee's recorded output have been preserved via sound recordings, film shorts, film clips, full-length features, documentaries, television episodes, variety show clips, music videos, and other media. These serve as testaments to the uncontested value of Lee's voluminous contributions to art, entertainment, jazz, film, and popular music.

6

TELESCRIPTIONS AND CAPITOL REVISITED

Lee's experience in the radio and film industries broadened her opportunities in the music industry in ways that helped her steer the development of her career. Having been actively involved in hosting radio shows, she became familiar with the transcription technology used to create them. She then became an artist pioneer in creating early music videos. Later, as her career experienced exponential growth, her continually prolific recording activities found a welcome home at Capitol Records.

From the 1920s through the 1950s radio programmers utilized technology called Electronic Transcriptions to bolster their live broadcasts. These were phonograph recordings made much like studio records and disseminated to radio stations *en masse*. The recordings captured theatrical programs, commercial jingles, advertising spots, and musical shows specifically made for broadcast on the radio. Capitol Records utilized a radio transcription service that connected its artists with valuable radio airplay and airtime necessary to further their careers. When radio stations played the prerecorded transcriptions, the low-noise advantage provided by this technology produced sound quality that was nearly the same as live: "New methods of electronic reproduction and improved record material that produced very little background noise were developed . . . the use of old phonograph music had largely been replaced by the new electrical transcription . . . with the fidelity available, it was difficult to tell a transcription from the original artist."[1] Transcriptions employed 33 1/3-rpm records that offered longer recording options (fifteen minutes per side) than the popular 78-rpm single that allowed only three to four minutes per side. In this way extended shows could be captured onto a single disk and sent throughout the country to be played and replayed as needed for radio programming.

By 1950 radio transcriptions had opened a new door for television. In September of that year, Peggy Lee and Dave Barbour collaborated with producer Lou Snader at Hollywood Center Studios to create ten telescriptions—early music videos for syndicated television broadcasting. These sessions featured Barbour on guitar (and interacting with Lee in the videos), Jess Bourgeois on bass, Sid Hurwitz (also documented as Sid Horowitz) on piano, and Alvin Stoller on drums. Each video showed Lee performing a song in costume on a single-room movie set or stage. The telescription for "I Don't Know Enough about You" showed Lee seated at a schoolteacher's desk in front of a blackboard, sporting dark-framed eyeglasses and a teacher's uniform, with Barbour playing guitar atop a wooden stool next to her desk. The two delivered a charming musical skit as they performed in a one-room-schoolhouse setting, drawing their audience in visually as well as aurally. The video for "I Cover the Waterfront" was shot against a backdrop of wooden posts suggesting a dock upon which a fishing net was draped. Lee wore a white sailor's cap, kerchief, short-sleeved shirt, and skirt, and casually smoked a cigarette while she sang. Her vocalism included both understated, soft singing as well as fuller-voiced segments saturated with expressive passion. Here was a beautiful example of this song's introductory verse, wonderfully interpreted by this duo in their polished rubato style (having no strict tempo or steady beat). In the video "I Only Have Eyes for You," Lee and Barbour wore overcoats and engaged in a mesmerizing interplay of musical dialogue amid an outdoor urban setting viewed at night from a bridge. Their unhurried ballad created a romantic mood complemented by the rhythm section's tasteful accompaniment that featured Barbour's musical commentary to

Lee's lush and lazy phrases. The video ended with the couple exchanging a lovers' gaze at the close of their mutual serenade. The video for "It's a Good Day" included Lee singing a seldom-heard introductory verse while she cheerfully pruned window-box plants from inside a small prop house, singing out the window about the beauty of a new day. Her flouncy dress, pulled-back hair, and idyllic, domestic setting created the image of a contented housewife-next-door. Lee's seasoned familiarity with the song was exemplified in the bluesy, improvisational way she sang. Knowing that her audience knew the song already, she took many artistic liberties and reinterpreted both melodic pitches and rhythms. She closed the performance appropriately by closing the shutters and retreating indoors.

The video for "Mañana" was shot with Lee and Barbour wearing Mexican costumes, leaning against a broken-down wall. Lee bantered with Barbour in a heavy Hispanic accent amid the song's verses. The duo clearly enjoyed their adventure through the song, and the added bits of conversation from Lee created a skit built around the song's theme. This performance raised particular interest considering the controversies that surrounded this piece. The visual image of a Mexican couple too lazy to maintain their home further justified the opposition they received about the intended message. Lee essentially spoke the text on pitch, rather than singing it, which illuminated the narrative approach of the lyrics and emphasized the Mexican caricature.

Video telescriptions of "What More Can a Woman Do?" and "You Was Right, Baby" showed Lee on a performance stage with the quartet backing her on the floor as if in a live concert. These two videos captured very different attitudes and vocal approaches from Lee. The former presented the singer as an earnest, youthful, meek woman who would literally do anything for her man, while the latter exhibited a somewhat more worldly-wise persona. The former gentle ballad contrasted greatly with the heavily swung blues in "You Was Right." Here Lee displayed a bit of her versatility in manifesting two very different moods and outlooks in both her songwriting acumen as well as her performance approach.

"Why Don't You Do Right?" featured Lee onstage with the instrumental quartet in front of her on the floor. This video-recorded performance assumed a slower tempo than the more famous version she had created with the Goodman band several years prior for *Stage Door Canteen*. At the slower speed, Lee successfully placed musical accents in a way that maximized the swing of the lyrics and melded them with the music. With Lee by herself atop the stage in a spotlight, the camera rarely panned low enough to capture the band, so this video appeared to be a bit dismissive of the ensemble element inherent in the performance. However, even though the featured soloist often gleaned the most attention, the other members of the jazz combo served equal importance. The layering of distinctive music provided by the piano, guitar, bass, and drums created the harmonic tapestry and rhythmic feel that supported the soloist in a tasteful and satisfying mix of sound. In modern times live performance videos often show bands and soloists performing as a single unit, reflecting the teamwork involved in performing a piece of music.

In the video for "While We're Young," Lee wore a formal off-the-shoulder gown and proceeded to arrange a basket of flowers as she sang this ballad supported by a rubato piano accompaniment. When singer and accompanist performed in this style (out of time with no steady beat), the intense listening that occurred between them was palpable by the audience. To create such interpretive nuances by timing lyrics precisely with the music in a tempo that the singer set forth and the accompanist closely followed required extensive practice and familiarity with the phrasing and shades of emphasis for each word. Lee proved over and over again to be a master at creating spellbinding ballads using rubato time. She and pianist Sid Hurwitz created a lush rendition of this golden oldie with his thickly orchestrated chords and romantic sweeps of rich pianistic color balancing Lee's tasteful, elegant delivery of this nostalgic text.

Lee and the Dave Barbour Quartet created the video for "I May Be Wrong (but I Think You're Wonderful)" on a living room set with a window and a fancy sofa stylish for the period. Lee began the song seated while she sewed a button onto a man's shirt. She then moved toward Barbour during his guitar solo and proceeded to grasp his collar, sewing a button directly onto the shirt he was wearing, to his apparent surprise. Their flawless sense of swing and easygoing nonchalance lent a touch of everyday familiarity to this domestic scene.

The adorable pairing of this married couple in early music videos provided the public with a peering eye into their relationship. In each of these ten videos Lee and Barbour portrayed the only two actively participating characters, while the rest of the band remained offstage or out of the visual field. One could not miss the mutual affection shown on both faces during most of the videos except in "I Cover the Waterfront," during which perhaps an indifferent attitude by both had been the interpretive intention for the characters involved. All in all, these videos showed a couple deeply respectful of and esteemed by one another.

Lee's ability to maintain keen focus all the way through a song remained apparent in these videos. Few contemporary artists possess the mental acuity, attention to detail, and nuanced delivery required to fully hold an audience's attention. The zone of freedom and spontaneous creativity so highly regarded and coveted by professional musicians was, as evidenced in these videos, a place Lee knew well. The videos also provided an interesting glimpse of the professionalism and skill possessed by these musicians as they recorded no fewer than five full videos per day during an era when cameras captured complete takes of each song. The outstanding performances evidenced by these ten telescriptions attested to the high level of virtuosity possessed by each performing artist involved. They also set the bar for generations of recording artists who followed these music video pioneers. Lee's music video telescriptions have provided worthy studies for subsequent recording and performing artists wishing to learn principles of performance practice, stage presence, nuance, polish, interpretation, and ensemble interaction that have always informed outstanding live performances.

To kick off her second Capitol period, Lee engaged a recording date with the Nelson Riddle Orchestra featuring a very special conductor—

Frank Sinatra. On April 2, 1957, the ensemble met at Capitol Tower (1750 North Vine Street, Hollywood) to lay down the first tracks of their collaborative album *The Man I Love*. On that inaugural date the group obtained masters for the Gershwin-penned title track as well as "He's My Guy," the Rodgers and Hammerstein classic "Something Wonderful," and "Please, Be Kind." The richly orchestrated, emotion-laden rendition of "The Man I Love" suited the romantic exuberance that this album unabashedly displayed. Its use of sweeping string lines propelled the harmonic flow amid the gentle, understated vocal approach by Lee. Her impeccable phrasing and committed attention to the lyrics placed a professional finish onto each of these orchestral recordings.

"He's My Guy" began with a series of aural swirls featuring the harp. Except for a few rubato sections that allowed the vocals to occupy a freer space, Sinatra carefully kept the tempo at a strict, unchanging pace. His respectful, non-interpretive approach left plenty of room for both Nelson Riddle's unparalleled arrangement as well as Lee's artistic phrasing to shine through. Riddle graciously allowed for Lee's ultra-soft singing when he arranged this album for a full orchestra in a way that never overpowered Lee's delicate voice. Not to be outdone by a powerful string section, Lee girded up her breath energy and delivered a strong, intensely passionate phrase at the final climactic moment: "I'm his until I die."

Riddle's arrangement of "Something Wonderful" began in a lovely way with the introductory verse providing a bit of backstory while leading into the well-known song from the 1951 Broadway musical *The King and I*. Because the song ebbed and flowed between expressing intimate thoughts and passionate outbursts, Lee successfully navigated both her characteristic soft singing and a heavier style approaching a Broadway belt. This track displayed Lee's versatility as a singer capable of a wide vocal, stylistic, and dynamic range. While her emotional vulnerability appropriately made an appearance, her technique never faltered.

"Please Be Kind" served the album as a lover's heartfelt request for sincerity, gentleness, and kindness. Here Lee delivered an intimate message that was universal in its truth and timeless relevance. Riddle skillfully set up the lyric with an elegant violin and horn opening, then supported Lee with a gently progressing string of soft quarter notes from the rhythm section. A saxophone lightly and extemporaneously commented on the lyrics then tastefully provided some contrast during the interlude followed by the orchestra. The song moved in a more delicate, exposed direction (with only violin commentary countering Lee's vocal line) toward its climactic moment a few measures shy of the end—a standard Nelson Riddle compositional technique. The quick tapering down of dynamics, pitch, and vocal phrasing neatly placed the song's end into a beautifully shaped restatement of the title and overall theme. This album and this track truly reflected the gold standard of orchestral Great American Songbook recordings. *The Man I Love* has remained highly recommended for all fans of this genre.

The next recording date for this project, April 4, 1957, produced four tracks for the album: "There Is No Greater Love," "That's All," "Happiness Is a Thing Called Joe," and "The Folks Who Live on the Hill." Riddle's lush arrangement of "That's All" capitalized on the romantic nature of the lyrics as well as on Lee's expert ability to massage a lyric with richness equal to that of the strings through her vibrato, phrasing, and nuanced expression. "Happiness . . . " possessed a ploddingly slow tempo that taxed both the range and the breath management of the singer, resulting in a few places where Lee's vocal stability wavered and her pitch fell at the ends of several phrases. That weakness in this track may be attributed to Sinatra's too-slow choice of tempo for this particular arrangement. The long sustained notes at the ends of the melodic phrases were not balanced by enough activity in the accompaniment, so an impression of dragging ensued. This flaw reflected the inexperienced conductor's inability to correct musical challenges when faced with the responsibilities of interpreting a score and placing a soloist in the best possible light.

Living for several years as neighbors and close friends in Los Angeles, Lee considered herself and Sinatra "The Folks Who Live on the Hill."[2] This wonderful song by Jerome Kern and Oscar Hammerstein II captured Lee's sense of nostalgia and sentimental vulnerability. Her quivering tone suggested that she may have shed a tear at any moment. Nelson Riddle painted a striking landscape in the arrangement's majestic introduction. Lee continued to add to Riddle's aural artwork as she deftly delivered the lyrics in passionate brushstrokes of her own. In the passages related to building a family, Lee's heartfelt longing for a stable family sounded readily apparent. Her thirty-six-year-old self plainly presented that dream with both skepticism and hope that were palpable. Whether or not these lyrics specifically addressed sentiments she personally felt at the time of the recording, Lee succeeded in weaving threads of melancholy and deep meaning into the song beyond a point that other singers were capable of attaining. Her profound emotional connection to this particular song was hard to miss.

April 8 marked the final recording date for *The Man I Love*. This session produced masters for "(Just One Way to Say) I Love You," "If I Should Lose You," "Then I'll Be Tired of You," and the Rodgers and Hart ballad "My Heart Stood Still." These four masters yielded straightforward versions of nostalgic songs of romance without any interpretive frills. Their clean read-throughs by the orchestra and singer yielded lovely recordings of simple love songs.

In her autobiography, Lee explained the role Frank Sinatra played in the formulation and development of their collaborative album, *The Man I Love*. "Frank thought of everything to the last detail . . . the album was totally Frank's concept. He brought me a long list of great songs to choose from, and Bill Miller came over and set all the keys with me. Then Frank hired Nelson Riddle to write those lovely arrangements and Frank conducted them. A marvelously sensitive conductor, as one might expect."[3] This represented Sinatra's third project as conductor. He would embark on four more conducting enterprises through the course of his career, following Lee's 1957 album with an orchestral project for friend and fellow crooner Dean Martin, in their 1958 collaboration *Sleep Warm*.

Following the release of the classic Nelson Riddle album, Lee recorded a few singles before launching into *Jump for Joy*, another LP enterprise with the famed arranger. Recorded in December 1957, this project yielded Lee and Riddle's orchestral renditions of Jules Styne's "Just in Time"; Baum and Weiss's "Music, Music, Music"; Al Jolson's "Back in Your Own Back Yard"; the Austin/McHugh/Mills song "When My Sugar Walks Down the Street"; Harry Woods's "What a Little Moonlight Can Do"; and other classic songs. Debuting in the *Billboard* charts during the week of July 14, 1958, the album peaked at number fifteen and remained in the charts for a total of five weeks.

By this point in her career, Lee often went into the recording studio and recorded four or five masters per day, but the majority of the album-planning decisions were still delegated to others. Mixing, editing, and mastering, as well as selecting and ordering the songs, were the domains of Capitol's producers. Furthermore, Lee's recordings made on a given day were not necessarily applied toward the current album project in the queue. For instance, some of a day's masters may have been applied toward the album in production, but others were tabled for a future project. Still others were outright rejected, leaving them unheard and locked in Capitol's vaults until compiled into a "lost masters" group that was finally released for public enjoyment in the 2000s. Lee's inability to determine the final lineup of songs for her albums, partly due to the sexist environment in which she worked, resulted in a slew of quality recordings that her fans would not experience until many years later.

On May 19, 1958, Peggy attended a session during which masters for her newest album, *Things Are Swingin'*, were created, along with the single that has been associated with the Lee brand more than any other song in her catalog—"Fever." The title track for the album was a Lee original co-written by the session's conductor, Jack Marshall. This uptempo, lighthearted swing tune appropriately opened the compilation and prominently featured the trumpet section. A bright modulation finished the song in a higher key, adding even more lift. "Alright, Okay, You Win" won for Lee another definitive version of a standard. Since this recording came into public awareness it has often been the go-to rendition for Great American Songbook and jazz fans worldwide. This track earned Lee her second Grammy nomination for Best Performance, Female in 1959. The Grammy was ultimately awarded to Ella Fitzgerald for her recording of Gershwin's "But Not for Me."

"Lullaby in Rhythm" started with Lee's carefree scat followed by her gentle, almost whispering delivery of lyrics painting aural pictures of breezes, leaves, and stars. She went on to relay a swinging story about the sandman on his way to bring peaceful dreams and sleep. Her delicate vocal approach illustrated her pitch perfection and rhythmic precision while tenderly singing this lullaby. The big band played lightly, staying out of Lee's way and cradling her voice as tastefully as ever. "You're Getting to Be a Habit with Me" commenced rather slowly for this swing tune, announcing a refreshing departure from the typically faster versions that preceded this rendition. Again, Lee sang extremely quietly, creating a less-is-more paradigm with which she became so entwined and permanently associated. The admirable effort put forth by the orchestra to match her softness created a musical and artistic blend of color. Lee's swing sense, tasteful vibrato at the ends of phrases, and occasional blue notes added polish and rewarding nuance to this recording. The finely tuned qualities that made this album great showed that Lee was, in fact, at her peak during this time in her career at Capitol.

Modeled after traditional blues style, the heavy blues song "You Don't Know" represented an important part of Lee's catalog in that she recorded it on four separate occasions. The first version hailed from 1957 and was arranged by Nelson Riddle, but the master was unfortunately lost. Lee next recorded the song at a May 1958 session, intending to co-release it on the flip side of her "Fever" single. She picked it up again in 1966 to release as a single as well as for the album *Big $pender*, and finally in 1988 for her *Miss Peggy Lee Sings the Blues* album on the MusicMasters label. It later resurfaced as a bonus track on the *Things*

Are Swingin' CD reissue. Lee's attachment to the song underscored the fact that she always felt deeply rooted in and connected to the blues.[4]

"Fever" became a gem in Lee's legacy for its smoldering sizzle, essentially unaccompanied texture, novel finger snapping, which set the tempo and kept the beat, and relentlessly upward key modulations that added interest and energy to the work akin to the steady intensification of heat. The arrangement featured an acoustic bass playing a repeated riff (or motive) throughout the song, with occasional interjections by the drums. No chords, chord outlines, or chord-playing instruments were employed at all. The arrangement was essentially Lee's, according to most accounts, although conductor Jack Marshall was exclusively cited as the arranger when the song was Grammy-nominated for Best Arrangement at the first-ever Grammy Awards ceremony on May 4, 1959.[5] It also garnered a Grammy nomination for Record of the Year and earned Lee a nomination for Best Vocal Performance, Female. "Fever" reached number eight on the *Billboard* pop chart and number five on *Billboard*'s rhythm and blues chart. In 1998 Lee's rendition of "Fever" was honored in the Grammy Hall of Fame.

In addition to being overlooked as arranger, Lee was never properly credited for her contributions to the lyrics of "Fever." Originally written by Otis Blackwell and Eddie Cooley, the music and lyrics of this hit song were added to by Lee before she recorded it in 1958. After studying the song, brought to her attention by bassist Max Bennett (after Lee asked him to be on the lookout for a new torch song),[6] Lee decided to omit some original verses and add her own. In a 1984 interview with George Christy, Peggy Lee herself admitted to authoring several of the lyrics to her award-winning version of "Fever."

> I wrote some special lyrics that have now become incorporated in the sheet music. I never got any credit for it. All the stuff about Romeo and Juliet. *"Captain Smith and Pocahontas?"* That was all mine. That's a very little-known fact. *"Those are your lyrics?"* Yes. And "Everybody's got the fever, that is something you all know . . . " and "Now you've listened to my story . . . " *"All yours? 'Chicks were born*

*to give you fever, be it Fahrenheit or centigrade . . . ' Is that your
lyric, too?"* Yes. I liked to change the way songs were usually sung.[7]

The staying power of Lee's version of "Fever" can hardly be measured.
Used in films, television, commercials, radio advertising, as a cover song
for thousands of artists and albums, remixes, mash-ups, and in internet
marketing, the song has remained instantly recognizable and attribut-
able to the legacy and brand firmly established by Lee. Rightfully so,
"Fever" and Lee will forever be intertwined.

Lee recorded an album called *I Like Men* in October 1958. This was
a themed album featuring titles with men's names and songs extolling
the masculine gender. *I Like Men* was one of five Peggy Lee albums
released in 1959, including stereo versions of previously released mono
recordings *Jump for Joy* and *Things Are Swingin'*, plus Decca's previously recorded *Miss Wonderful*. The fact that *I Like Men* never charted
may be due to the gimmicky quality of this particular album. Except for
a few well-known Broadway hits ("So in Love," "I'm Just Wild about
Harry," and "Bill"), the song selection holds up rather weakly against
many of her other projects, and the arrangements seem a bit tired and
contrived next to the normally well-crafted recordings put forth by Lee
and her bands. However, *I Like Men* served as a noteworthy contrast to
Lee's finest albums, proving that not all albums could be hit records,
even for supremely talented stars.

The following spring Lee embarked upon a live-performance recording project with legendary jazz pianist George Shearing. The duo
had been slated to perform together May 29–30 at the 1959 National
Disc Jockey Convention in Miami, and attendees had been promised
recordings of the live concert. Unfortunately, technical difficulties prevented a viable recording of the full-length concert from being obtained, so in order to make good on the promise, Capitol producer
Dave Cavanaugh arranged for Lee and Shearing to record the concert
material shortly thereafter in a studio setting. With both Shearing and
Lee being Capitol solo artists, the label expected to capitalize on dual
star power when they set up a performance opportunity to create this
landmark "live" recording. The project became known as *Beauty and*

the Beat! Although at the time Capitol would not admit to this being a studio project rather than the live concert it purported to be, evidence later surfaced that left little doubt about the true order of events. The existence of several other examples of well-known purportedly live albums from that time period onward (including "live" albums by Tony Bennett, Duke Ellington, Charles Mingus, Chuck Berry, and The Rolling Stones, among many others) that also contained much studio recording before release suggested that the practice was and still is more common than one might expect.[8]

The album opened with a lightly swinging version of "Do I Love You" following a wave of applause and a brief verbal introduction of Lee, by an emcee, and her subsequent introduction of George and his

Peggy Lee and Benny Goodman (in rehearsal for a joint appearance at Melodyland, Anaheim, California). *Photofest.*

quartet. After the first number, the ensemble began a slowly swinging version of "I Lost My Sugar in Salt Lake City," which Lee would later record on her blues album with Quincy Jones. A Benny Goodman song came next—"If Dreams Come True." This song showcased Shearing's wonderful soloing talent and peerless ability to swing lightly over the keys. The lush ballad "All Too Soon" followed, briefly draping the listener in Lee's entrancing talent for musical hypnosis. A delightful instrumental number in a Latin style ensued called "Mambo in Miami." Since several of the tunes in this set were performed without repeats, "Mambo" seemed to finish before it had reached its full fruition. Next, Shearing indulged in an instrumental-only rendition of Rodgers and Hart's "Isn't It Romantic." For this the pianist created an arrangement of unison motives played by the vibraphonist and him at several places within the texture of the song. This effectively unified the piece and placed elegant final touches on it for which Shearing was well known. The minor blues "Blue Prelude" took the next place in line. Between the bluesy vocal phrases (and even on top of them), the piano and vibes provided counter-melodic activity. This beautifully complemented the lyrics and text-based improvisation Lee deftly delivered. "You Came a Long Way from St. Louis" followed suit, providing heavily swinging blues for Lee to explore with Shearing and his band. A refreshingly Latin rendition of Cole Porter's "Always True to You in My Fashion" served as the next track. With percussionist Armando Peraza providing percussive color, this selection bore a decidedly ethnic flavor. Lee's straightforward approach to this piece stayed out of the way of both the instrumentalists and the lyrics. She knew when to improvise around a text and when to keep her rendition simple and reflective of the original composition. Her choice to simply deliver the music and text as written in this example permitted a measure of taste and class appropriate to this musical situation. Her restraint allowed the performance to feature the percussion section accordingly, without the distraction of an overactive singer.

Lee's original (co-written by Hubie Wheeler), "There'll Be Another Spring," came next, featuring George Shearing, who provided a lush,

romantic chordal motif that returned repeatedly to accompany the melodic theme. During the bridge, Shearing transitioned to a bebop approach as he improvised bubbling waves of rapid-fire melodic runs. The
Cole Porter standard "Get Out of Town" came next in the form of a
Latin-swing pairing of alternating rhythmic feel. Both Lee and the
rhythm section beautifully drew distinctions between the two styles and
skillfully maneuvered between them several times during the course of
the song. A swinging instrumental version of Ellington's "Satin Doll,"
featuring bassist Carl Pruitt, closed out the set. *Beauty and the Beat!*
went on to become a cult classic in Lee's discography. In no other full
album setting did Lee have the opportunity to share the spotlight with a
jazz performing artist as accomplished and deservingly renowned as
Shearing. The pairing was excellent, and the recording that resulted
from their collaboration spent eighteen weeks on *Billboard*'s charts
beginning in September 1959, rising to number nineteen.

Lee released an impressive five long-playing albums in 1959 and an
even more shocking five in 1960. Such incredible productivity, concomitant with her continuous release of singles, plus an extended play recording, reflected a growing interest in music fans in collecting their
own copies of their favorite artists' LPs to play at their leisure on record
players at home. In fact, during postwar years American entertainment
consumers tended to stay home in the evenings to watch TV and/or
listen to records rather than to go out for dancing and live entertainment. This growing trend greatly affected both the live venue market as
well as the increased sales of albums and singles. With more families
owning their own record players and televisions, entertaining at home
became much more convenient and economical, so trips to outside
entertainment venues became less and less frequent. Large dance
bands downsized to smaller combos of a few players, large dance halls
closed, and record production skyrocketed. The relatively new industry
of home entertainment had begun.

The five albums sporting Lee's name in 1960 included *Latin ala
Lee!*, *All Aglow Again!*, *Pretty Eyes*, *Christmas Carousel*, and *Olé ala
Lee*. Her *Latin ala Lee!* album was subtitled "Broadway Hits Styled

with an Afro-Cuban Beat." Recorded on three dates in August 1959, this project yielded four Grammy nominations. The first came in the category of Best Performance by a Pop Single Artist for "Heart," a Latinized version of the hit from Broadway's *Damn Yankees*. Ray Charles won this category's award with his legendary blues rendition of "Georgia on My Mind." Lee's second nomination was for Best Vocal Performance, Album, Female, and as before, the award went to Ella Fitzgerald—this time for her live *Mack the Knife* album. Lee garnered nominations for both her album and for its leading single. She even suggested the concept for the Grammy-winning cover art designed by art director Marvin Schwartz. First appearing in April 1960, *Latin ala Lee!* reached number eleven on *Billboard* and was the longest-running LP of Lee's career—in the music charts for a whopping fifty-nine weeks.

All Aglow Again! compiled a wide swath of singles, some previously released, and some not released prior to this album. These masters ranged from sessions dating in 1947, 1952, 1957, 1958, and 1959.[9] Lee's huge hit "Fever" opened the album, followed by "Where Do I Go from Here," a smooth and moderate Latin number with tinkling bells and gentle woodwinds providing contrasting texture. "Whee Baby," a bluesy swing tune co-written by Lee and Alice Larson, came next, reiterating Lee's ongoing affection for this style. The album included the hits "Mañana" and the exuberant "Hallelujah, I Love Him So," as well as Lee's humorous version of "Louisville Lou," which added a bit of satire to the project's melting pot of themes and styles. The slowly repeating accompaniment in "I'm Lookin' Out the Window" set an appropriate backdrop for a nostalgic pop ballad hearkening back to times gone by. An uplifting, cheerful celebration of classic big band style, "It Keeps You Young" hailed the virtues and blessings of lasting love. Finishing with the rich ballad "Let's Call It a Day," Lee and her entourage bid her audience a sincere and sweet farewell. Here Lee's sincerity and commitment to expressing the sentiment of a delicate lyric shone beautifully. The light tones of a celesta suggested a bedtime lullaby and lent closure to the recording. This song stood out as more poignant and serious than the rest. Its inclusion on the LP demonstrated the reality that this project was a compilation project rather than a concept album.

Pretty Eyes was recorded at Capitol in February 1960 with the Jimmie Lunceford Orchestra providing accompaniment for Lee. Billy May, one of Lee's favorite arrangers, conducted and arranged this album as well as her next, *Christmas Carousel. Pretty Eyes* included a few well-known gems like Van Heusen and Burke's standard "It Could Happen to You" and Cy Coleman's relatively new "You Fascinate Me So." May's thickly romanticized string arrangements created a dramatic palette of color upon which Lee gently placed her lightly sung tones.

May set "It Could Happen to You" as a slow ballad without any sense of swing, just a sweeping accompaniment with a preponderance of strings. This new sound foreshadowed the emerging easy listening style of the early 1960s. Lee's vocal approach on each song of this album included more vibrato than she normally used for swing, Latin, pop, or jazz. Her more classical approach mirrored the classical sound of the symphony orchestra with its full-sounding vibrato in the violins. "Remind Me" provided an excellent example of this classical sound matched between ensemble and soloist. Even in "You Fascinate Me So," a track sporting a swing feel, Lee's vibrato was more pronounced than in a big band or jazz piece. In this way she brought consistency and unity to the overall sound of her album. Lee and May's extremely unhurried tempo in "I Remember You" lent a nostalgic moment to the album as a contrast to the more familiar swing versions of this classic Johnny Mercer/Victor Schertzinger standard. As a slow-moving ballad, the lyrics unfolded gently and effortlessly, as though Lee were experiencing a memory or daydream. In the context of the total album, this unique approach to a well-known song truly worked. Another standard, "Too Close for Comfort," assumed a relaxed, moderate walking tempo in the style of a shuffle, modulating up a half step at the outset of the second verse. This track further displayed the strict restraint that Billy May employed regarding tempo for this album. No selections, even those with more motion than the ballads, exceeded a medium tempo and even the fastest possessed unhurried refinement uncharacteristic of Lee's jazz and big band albums.

Lee's version of "Fly Me to the Moon" included the rarely heard introductory verse, which led off the song in a declamatory rhythmic style perfectly suited for this romantic lullaby. "Because I Love Him So" stood slightly apart from the other selections on the album—instead of singing in a style similar to the other songs, she wailed and improvised in her characteristically bluesy style without the excess vibrato heard on the rest of the project. Billy May beautifully scored the album's deeply rich, artistic renderings of these songs.

The elegant milieu inhabited throughout *Pretty Eyes* suggested that a mature quality had been attained in Lee's development as an artist—a willingness to try things that had not been tried before in a manner that proved she was still evolving. Indeed, Lee never shied away from adjusting her sound, approach, and musical selections to reflect the changing world she lived in. Unlike some artists whose work sounded the same in 1960 as it did in 1940, Lee unabashedly stretched as she aged. She heartily embraced musical trends and youthful composers with each new recording project, eager to remain relevant and attractive to younger audiences while pleasing her longtime fans.

Billy May and Peggy Lee continued their collaboration for the next album that Capitol released in the Lee canon: *Christmas Carousel*. Lee opened the project with fellow Capitol artist Mel Tormé's "The Christmas Song" (co-written by Robert Wells) in which she poignantly shaped the phrases and lightly caressed each sentiment with utmost tenderness. Lee contributed several original songs to this holiday album, including "Don't Forget to Feed the Reindeer," a charming children's song, and the title track, "Christmas Carousel," a song in triple time suggestive of a carnival ride. May's imaginative arrangements set each of these into an appropriate childlike setting with high woodwinds, bells, xylophone, and a lighthearted compositional touch. May's arrangement of "Santa Claus Is Comin' to Town" featured a small group of children providing background harmony and counter-melodic interjections amid Lee's delivery of the well-worn melody. Other holiday standards like "White Christmas," "Winter Wonderland," and "Deck the Halls" appeared on this album in nostalgic or festive formats. Although *Christmas Carousel* never charted in its 1960 debut (*Billboard* did not recognize holiday albums in their own category that year), *Christmas with Peggy Lee*, a 2006 compilation including nine of the original twelve tracks from *Christmas Carousel*, plus seven from other recordings, topped *Billboard*'s jazz charts at an impressive number two, four years after the singer's death. That a novelty/holiday album would reach the top ten on the jazz charts in any decade represented both an amazing accomplishment for the recording artist and yet another genre conquered by Lee.

The final album of the five Lee released in 1960 was *Olé ala Lee!* subtitled "Great Favorites Styled in Spectacular Latin Fashion." Interestingly, the cover art was a converse of the art displayed on the cover of her earlier Latin album, *Latin ala Lee!* The first album showed Lee smiling at the camera arm-in-arm with two toreadors, each facing away from the camera. For the latter album, one backward-facing toreador stood in the center of the image arm-in-arm with two mirror images of Lee flanking him and facing the camera. This clever visual trick drew fans' attention to *Olé ala Lee!* as being a sequel to the album sporting the Grammy-winning cover art on her longest-running album in the popular charts, *Latin ala Lee!*

Olé ala Lee! included such familiar songs as "Just Squeeze Me," "Love and Marriage," "Non Dimenticar," and "You Stepped Out of a Dream." Music by Cole Porter, Duke Ellington, Jimmy Van Heusen, Stephen Sondheim, and Peggy Lee graced the set list. The songs sizzled, jumped, sashayed, and sauntered at a variety of tempi, making this album interesting and unpredictable all the way through. A Lee original, the calmly sweltering "Olé," provided a cool Latin respite from the rapid-fire beats of the faster songs. "Together Wherever We Go" fell in with breakneck speed, rushing the ensemble along amid the percussion-driven frivolity inherent in this favorite from Sondheim's *Gypsy*.

Arranger Joe Harnell made ample use of the trumpets and percussion in his quest for authentic Spanish sounds to apply to Great

American Songbook standards as he co-created this project. Lee and her arrangers' habit of modifying songs initially conceived in other styles became a go-to method for reinterpreting cover songs in her live performances and recordings. Modern jazz artists have continued this tradition of reimagining the context and original settings of songs they cover. A thoroughly satisfying album, *Olé ala Lee!* wrapped up 1960 and the entire decade with a worthy sequel to Lee's Grammy-nominated *Latin ala Lee!* in a manner proving that Peggy Lee, at the age of forty, was at the peak of her recording productivity and artistic prime.

Lee's pioneering work in early music videos served as a harbinger of her continued success as one of Capitol Records' most prolific and popular artists. The 1950 Snader telescriptions, created for syndicated television broadcast as shorts when the TV industry was young, helped Lee's fans become acquainted with her visually pleasing performances. They bridged her career from radio to television and provided a chance for millions of fans who were unable to attend her concerts to watch her perform. Lee's slew of acclaimed albums and outstanding singles recorded for Capitol (with a regularity intensifying through the late 1950s) bolstered her continuing climb up the popular music charts toward superstardom and into the hearts of her public.

7

1960S BLUES AND JAZZ

The early 1960s found Peggy Lee as prolific and focused as ever and eager to collaborate with some of the most talented young musicians in the business. Her recording and performing activities throughout the next decade would cement her relevance as not only an enduring popular music artist but also a legitimate blues singer, jazz singer, and easy listening pioneer. Lee learned how to adapt to the changing musical landscape while keeping her public actively engaged.

In April and May 1961 Lee entered Capitol's recording studio to record an album called *Blues Cross Country* with a young composer named Quincy Jones, who also served as conductor of the sessions. Produced by Dave Cavanaugh (also known by his pen name, Bill Schluger) of Capitol Records, the album included classic blues tunes like "St. Louis Blues" as well as new compositions co-written by Jones and Lee. The album's theme celebrated several American cities, spotlighting the finer points of various locales from coast to coast, hence the title of the project. The song list kicked off with a high-energy arrangement of "Kansas City" played by a fully engaged horn section and an equally full-voiced Lee. This Leiber and Stoller composition quickly became a standard in the contemporary blues repertoire and is still played ubiquitously by cover bands specializing in blues and rock. The Lee-Jones version excited listeners with a loud and raucous big band arrangement that never eased off the energy but pressed full throttle to the very end. Lee's voice delivered an unusually intense vocal performance reminiscent of her approach to "Lover." Here she set into motion an album that would display her mastery of extremes in tempo, dynamic contrast, and mood. Lee's nuanced interpretation of the blues also shone brightly on this track, preparing listeners for the aural feast to follow.

"Basin Street Blues" fell next in line on this album, creating a marked contrast to the first selection in tempo and laid-back mood. This soft, gentle ballad sported a light and lively improvised piano solo and quiet dynamics alongside Lee's almost whispered stroll through the song. Soft and mellow, this selection sat sandwiched between two louder energetic swing tunes. Lee's interpretation of this old standby cut its own path in music history; most other versions relied heavily on a strong sense of swing and musical activity, whereas Lee's exemplified the power of understatement. Lee simply breathed the song lightly into the microphone and let it speak for itself.

The next song in the queue, "Los Angeles Blues," an original by Quincy Jones with lyrics by Lee, bragged about the charms of southern California from the desert to the coastline. Another carefree, optimistic song in the Lee songwriting canon, it provided appealing contrast to the traditionally melancholic lyrics of blues compositions. Its connection with the blues was more musical than lyrical, and Lee included plenty of allusions to the blues scale in her performance. She toyed with the flatted third (enharmonically equivalent to a sharp ninth) as an ornament throughout the song. Far from being in traditional blues form, this happy song in a major key relied on blue notes sprinkled throughout the melody for its nominal association with the genre.

The fourth song, "I Lost My Sugar in Salt Lake City," began with a soft walking bass line leading Lee in for a brief bass-vocal duet. Then came a loud, sudden entrance of the big band, which accompanied both singer and bassist for the remainder of the arrangement. The textural variety shown in the first four pieces on this album exhibited thoughtful programming on the part of both producer and arranger. Audiences were more likely to continue listening when each song brought a fresh approach to the blues, including variance in tempo, theme, form, and dynamic contrast. The same guideline for effective programming remains true to this day.

Staying true to the pattern of variance, "The Grain Belt Blues" possessed a boogie-woogie feel that contrasted sharply with all the previous songs. It also was the first in the series that included a key modulation to build energy between verses. Lee brought a bluesy sensibility to this lyric that paid tribute to the hard-working farmers and field workers who contributed immeasurably to the American economy and the health of its citizens and livestock. The song's form included a two-bar stop-time fragment that ended each sung verse, leaving Lee unaccompanied for those two measures each time a verse ended. This compositional device, so integral to certain types of blues, ensured that the last words (the main thrust) of each verse's lyric would be emphasized and unequivocally heard by the audience.

"New York City Blues" opened with a piano, bass, and flute introduction reminiscent of a late-night piano bar, during which Lee lamented having to say goodbye to this great city. The soft, slow, nostalgic opening paved the way for the big band's sharply contrasting entrance, which was loud, fast, and full of energy. With a Broadway belt-style ending, Lee demonstrated a wide spectrum of vocal approaches as she performed this song. She combined soft, sensual singing with straight-ahead swing. She employed call-and-response with the big band horns and drums and used a vocal belt apropos to the home of Broadway to which she was paying tribute.

"Goin' to Chicago Blues" by Count Basie and Jimmy Rushing came next in the form of a slow twelve-bar blues that wailed in both the vocal part and the horns. With a heavy swing and seemingly every blues ornament known, this track represented a classic blues masterfully played by a dynamite jazz orchestra. Lee slid and scooped amid her pitches, bending notes in true bluesy style and delivering the lyrics with the stalwart confidence of a true blues shouter.

A Peggy Lee and Milt Raskin song, "San Francisco Blues," followed suit in a brisker twelve-bar form. This swing tune possessed a bright tempo and mood as Lee listed several noteworthy places to visit in this northern California tourist stop. Not strictly a twelve-bar blues throughout, the piece contained a final extended coda and several stop-time sections that gave the ensemble a chance to experiment with alternative ways to embellish traditional blues.

The slow bluesy waltz "Fisherman's Wharf" (by the same songwriting team) struck a refreshing contrast in its departure from common time amid this album of songs having mostly four-beat groupings. Still a twelve-bar blues, this song contributed a decidedly different color to the *Blues Cross Country* tapestry with its slow swinging groups of three and upward key modulation halfway through the piece. Here Jones and Lee displayed their truly unique and innovative ideas in creating a queue of songs that held listeners' attention by varying keys, tempos, moods, meters, and styles.

The next song reinforced this trend even further. "Boston Beans" provided a strong four-beat, straight eighth-note feel. Continuing to describe the cities starring in the titles of this album, Lee highlighted the colleges, foods, and history of this northeastern American city. Even though it employed a few elements of blues including blue notes and stop-time, the song sounded more like a musical theater selection than an authentic blues.

Quincy Jones and Peggy Lee co-wrote the next song in the series, "The Train Blues." This piece described many American cities that could be reached via rail, a mode of transportation whose popularity was waning by the time two thirds of the twentieth century had passed. Like the last song, it did not qualify as blues in the strictest formal sense, but it suggested elements thereof in its bluesy, ballad-like introduction. Lee displayed her consummate attention to detailed nuance in her delicate approach at the beginning that contrasted with her laid-back, swinging narrative style in the faster section.

The album closed with the famous blues piece, W. C. Handy's "St. Louis Blues." This legendary piece first published in 1914 was one of the first blues songs to become absorbed into popular music culture— so much that it is still widely performed and recorded today. The Jones-

Lee version of this well-traveled song assumed a fast swing feel, adding a bit of reharmonization (applying new harmonic support to the original melody) to update the age-old sound. The text remained unaltered, but Lee creatively utilized text-based improvisation in which she unapologetically changed the pitches and rhythms that were originally composed. This form of improvisation was more permissible for tunes that were especially well known already than for brand-new songs. By altering pitches and timing them in her own unique way, Lee made this familiar song her own. Indeed, "St. Louis Blues" finished the Jones-Lee blues album in an outstanding way, with high-spirited energy bubbling through the innovative arrangement like a new shine on an old favorite pair of shoes.

April 12, 1961, marked the third-ever Grammy Awards ceremony, and for the third year in a row, Lee enjoyed more than one nomination. The category Best Vocal Performance, Female had been divided that year into two to honor both albums and singles. Lee was nominated for her July 26, 1960, recording of "I'm Gonna Go Fishin'," the song she co-wrote with Duke Ellington for the 1959 film *Anatomy of a Murder*. Baritone saxophonist Gerry Mulligan also scored a nomination that year for his large ensemble arrangement of the same Ellington-Lee composition. That Lee's original songs were recorded, performed, and in this case, nominated for a Grammy Award by many acclaimed peers during her lifetime spoke volumes about the quality of her songwriting and the professional respect her contemporaries paid to Lee as a song creator.

During the summer of 1960 Lee embarked on recording for humanitarian campaigns, joining forces with Nat King Cole, Nancy Wilson, and The Chipmunks for a song to promote Toys for Tots. Recorded at Capitol Tower on Vine Street in Hollywood, each artist or act had their own separate session call to complete the recording. Later that summer Lee reentered the studio for yet another humanitarian campaign. This time she recorded a song called "Meals for Millions" in an effort to promote a nonprofit humanitarian organization by the same name for which she served as chair. Gene Handsaker from the Associated Press conducted an interview with Lee about it: "Peggy Lee spun her latest recording on her turntable. Out came the familiar rich, warm voice pleading not of love or joy in living, but—soybeans!"[1] Lee's compassion and connection to her public were manifested not only in her music and lyrics but also in her proactive initiative to assist with humanitarian causes.

Recorded in February and March 1961, the *Basin Street East* sessions involved Capitol's official taping of a few of Lee's live concert performances at the famed jazz nightclub in New York. Dave Cavanaugh produced and Joe Harnell conducted the sessions. A little big band consisting of full rhythm section, three trumpets, two trombones, harp, and percussion supplied the accompaniment for this eclectic show. That year Capitol released a much-doctored, mostly studio-recorded set list called *Basin Street East Proudly Presents Miss Peggy Lee*, with the implication that this represented her live performances at the venue. However, the effort failed to reflect an actual live concert experience. Since Lee reportedly had a cold during some of the performances, and the *invited* audience heard repeated retakes of tunes instead of the natural flow of a live show, the final product included studio takes recorded at a later date with "do-overs" at the nightclub. This combination left much to be desired from a fan's perspective.

Although a great deal of time and energy went into preparing for and recording this historic performance, the recording tapes for the February 8 closing night show were thought to be lost for several decades. Cy Godfrey, the co-producer of a 2002 album that finally unveiled this unheard performance to the public, described that the tapes found mismarked in Capitol's vaults "might have been destroyed were they not listed in Capitol's computers as backup or 'safety' tapes made on February 16, 1961. It was not until they were examined and played that we realized that they were the long-lost closing night recordings made on February 8, 1961, and that February 16 was a tape transfer date."[2] This closing night concert, being one of the only truly live recordings of a Peggy Lee performance that was not excessively remade in a recording studio, has provided keen insight into how Lee presented her concert material.

The historically important recording of that live New York performance in 1961, *Peggy at Basin Street East: The Unreleased Show*, offered a rare glimpse into the extraordinary live Peggy Lee concert experience during the height of her career and worldwide fame. This 2002 release best exemplified Lee as an artist capable of casting a musical spell and holding an audience in the palm of her hand for an entire evening. The full show included various hits, originals, and several multi-song medleys.

The final night at Basin Street East began in true Peggy Lee style with an overture comprised of original songs by Lee. This fast and loud opening served to energize and excite the audience in preparation for Lee's grand entrance. As soon as she was introduced she began the Rube Bloom–Johnny Mercer standard, "Day In, Day Out." Per the conventions of the live shows of major singers of the 1960s, the song was played only once with no improvised instrumental solos, thereby funneling all the attention and musical focus onto the star. This arrangement also extended the ending a bit, adding some measures here and there to give Peggy a bit more leeway for phrasing and timing the final release. Having triumphantly sung her "hello," she thanked the audience, and the band proceeded into the next tune, "Call Me Darling," a ballad that brought the tempo down into a mellower place. Staying true to the once-through recipe, Lee sang the song with great attention to expression and provided vocal showmanship in the coda (the tail ending) replete with a bluesy pop-style run that would have given gospel singers pause. While the audience still applauded, the bassist began his walking bass line to set up the next piece, a medley of songs by Richard Rodgers including "One Kiss," "My Romance," and "The Most Beautiful Man in the World." Thus far in the performance, Lee had allowed no repeats of any songs and no instrumental improvised solos, keeping the spotlight firmly fixed upon herself. The pace of the performance also stayed moving at a rapid clip with no downtime between songs.

Lee loved medleys because they precluded the possibility that momentum would drop as musicians shifted from song to song. By linking

the songs together without stopping in between, the arrangements remained organically connected with continuous music. Medleys also
served to excite the audience. They were grouped together in themes
usually honoring one songwriter. The overture for this show was constructed as a medley of a couple of Lee's original songs, and four more
medleys were used during that evening's show. Lee's former bandmates
claimed that Lee loved to program medleys into her song lists as a
preferred way to present related material to a live audience while adding to the flow and unpredictability of the music.[3] One such related
group on this recording was a Ray Charles tribute medley connecting
four of Ray's signature songs together, each brilliantly and uniquely
performed by Lee. Connecting her repertoire in this fashion helped
Lee to avoid stopping the show's momentum for applause. It also provided the illusion that more music would be packed into one evening.
At concerts and jam sessions featuring bebop performers in those days,
most of the music would be occupied by extended improvised solos, so
the sum total of songs performed would be much smaller than the
number of songs a singer like Lee would present in one evening's medley format.

A Van Heusen medley ensued following the Rodgers medley, featuring "But Beautiful" and "The Second Time Around," each presented in
Lee's signature once-through style. To be clear, Lee often allowed instrumental solos to fill out a recorded song for a single or album (and
her arrangers wrote them in), but in a performance situation she rarely
opened up the song to showcase the soloing capabilities of her individual band members. Sarah Vaughan modeled her live performances in
exactly the same way, minimizing instrumental solos to keep all the
attention on herself for the entire duration of the performance, as did
Sinatra and many other pop stars. In this way, the star could control
both the timing allotted for each song and the attention of the audience.
Ella Fitzgerald was an exception to this trend—being a dynamite improviser herself, she relished giving her band members opportunities to
solo at her live performances, then proved she was as excellent an
improviser as any instrumentalist. Loving the element of onstage con-

trol and being unwilling to relinquish it (or the audience's attention) to anyone, Lee kept a tight rein on her band, rehearsing everything from top to bottom, including the music for bows.

Taking a great deal of time to start "But Beautiful," Lee caused the entire room to wait on the edge of its seat while she inserted a lengthy pause after each of the first two words, "Love . . . is . . . funny. . ." She milked her power over the room—knowing how to use silence and phrasing—and drew everyone's attention, especially that of the band, squarely upon herself. Her knowing rendition of "The Second Time Around" suggested that Lee had plenty of experience with serial relationships, and she delivered a melancholic yet hopeful performance. Indeed, she had been married three times by this point (after Dave Barbour to Brad Dexter briefly in 1953, and to Dewey Martin from 1956 to 1958). She was well acquainted with beginning new marriage relationships and would attempt it once more in 1965 with Jack Del Rio, only to divorce a year later.

A "Fever" ensued, and Lee addressed the raw energy of the crowd (as they recognized the opening of her signature hit) with a laugh. Taking a brisker tempo than that at which she recorded the single, Lee's masterful way of fitting in all the words even though she delayed the phrase beginnings was particularly impressive. This method of improvisation called *backphrasing* was something Lee was keen to execute effectively. It appeared that at any tempo Lee's "Fever" burned in a particularly artistic way. The burning continued as the band proceeded into a high-energy, fast waltz that, like "Fever," added heat by modulating in the upward direction. "I'm Gonna Go Fishin'" was an apropos pairing with the previous song since it also had yielded Lee a major international hit and Grammy nomination. The sheer intensity of the arrangement with the trumpet hits and call-and-response texture between singer and band created a gradually mounting frenzy that matched the drama for which it had been originally written—the film story of a sheriff hunting an elusive criminal.

Lee followed this barn-burner with an optimistic original song that became a standard. "I Love Being Here with You," co-written by Bill

Schluger (Capitol's Dave Cavanaugh), provided a warm and funny contrast to the previous song, effectively lightening the mood with a pleasantly major tonality after two consecutive songs in minor keys. Lee's deferential lyrics honoring her contemporaries in the entertainment business helped to seal the longevity of this musical gem. Mentions of the charms of Cary Grant, Count Basie, Ella Fitzgerald, Jimmy Durante, Yul Brynner, and Marlon Brando resonated immediately with modern fans, ensuring that each time Lee performed this original her public would heartily approve, as they did on this night in February 1961.

The next song in the queue yielded the first real drop in energy among the songs in this project. "By Myself" supplied a slowly simmering Latin contrast among the predominantly swinging string of songs. Unfortunately, the song's poor recording quality created a far less satisfying result than that provided by the other songs on the record because Lee's voice was not picked up well by the recording microphone. The band's volume surpassed Peggy's, and her diction was difficult to understand as a result. However, the audience apparently enjoyed the performance very much, laughing during the song in response to a joke she shared and showering her with applause afterward.

Following this Lee upped the energy with her rousing Latin version of Broadway's *Damn Yankees* hit "Heart," which she made into a hit of her own in the late 1950s. Always ready to hit this tune out of the park with her rhythmic precision, fabulous pitch accuracy, and a cheerful arrangement highlighting trumpets and Latin percussion, Lee indeed proved her ability to perform as well in a live setting as she could on recordings. Due to her success with this piece and her peerless performances of it, Lee's spirited rendition of this encouraging song remained more historically definitive than the version from the original Broadway cast recording.

"I've Never Left Your Arms" followed as an intimate moment between Lee and her audience. Flutist Bob Donovan and harpist Abe Rosen added delicate touches to the tragic undertone Lee painted. Singing freely, without reference to any steady beat, Lee created a backdrop of stark loneliness. Written by Marilyn Bergman, the text and music mesmerized the audience in Lee's interpretation, but unfortunately, she never recorded it in the studio. That fact made this long-awaited live recording even more valuable to Lee's fans. The song's eastern leanings were fully realized in the final strike of a gong ending the piece.

Next on the docket for Lee and the band was a blues-soaked medley honoring pop-soul contemporary Ray Charles. It began with a brief overture followed by a moving spoken testimony by Lee. It then moved into a rousing version of "Hallelujah, I Love Him So," which she had previously made her own in recordings and many live performances. "I Got a Man" continued the brisk high-energy feeling of authentic blues before the medley transitioned into a ballad, "Just for a Thrill," which Lee milked at a super-slow tempo and infused with note-bending rivaling any of the leading blues or gospel singers of the day. Her exquisite phrasing, energized tone, and voluptuous vibrato (when she chose to use it), topped the album with this outstanding number. The exuberant "Yes, Indeed!" completed the medley with Lee's precise syncopation and pitch accuracy, clear diction, and tasteful phrasing reverencing Ray Charles's music.

At this juncture the band began playing music associated with Lee's exit. Upon informing the audience that it seemed perhaps time she should go, the entire room urged "No!" in a wave of loving protest. Fortunately for this die-hard audience that had ventured out in a New York snowstorm, even though streets were closed and the city was in a state of emergency, Lee had an extended encore planned. Lee's full house that evening remained full to the end. She offered a gracious performance to those who had trudged through the icy weather to witness a music legend's closing night at an equally legendary jazz club.

Lee provided what her audience demanded in the final medley of the evening—several of her best-known original songs plus a few cover hits. Leading off with the first half of "I Don't Know Enough about You," Lee paused when she arrived at the bridge, and the band began playing the introduction to "Mañana." Singing only one quick chorus,

Lee and the band transitioned into the song that started it all, "Why Don't You Do Right?" After a single chorus, she segued into her fast-paced "Lover," with peculiar drum kicks on the measure downbeats. Transitioning into "It's a Good Day," Lee and the band tied up the medley with her optimistic song and its on-the-beat drum kicks completing the show. The bowing/exit music returned again, providing Lee with her comfortable show sendoff.

Always seeking to give her audience her best, Lee rarely dropped her energy throughout this live concert. She sought to maintain her excellent pitch and rhythmic sense in each section of every song. Only once at the beginning of the show did she hint at making a mistake, entering a couple of measures early, then waiting and entering again for "Day In, Day Out." This mistake greatly humanized the live recording and reminded listeners that this *was* an unretouched live performance. It also served to remind fans that in the world of live art (whether musical or theatrical) unexpected things did happen, and the finest performers simply rolled with it and got on with their performance. Audiences could not help but love a performer who acknowledged the unexpected in real time.

The summer after the famed Basin Street East run, Lee entered the recording studio several times to record an album arranged and conducted by Quincy Jones called *If You Go*. This project included such torch songs as "Deep Purple," "Here's That Rainy Day," Irving Berlin's "Say It Isn't So" and "Maybe It's Because (I Love You Too Much)," plus old standbys "Smile" and "I Get Along without You Very Well," among a few lesser-known songs. The title track revealed that this was another themed concept album, comprised this time of songs dealing with heartbreak.

In March 1962 and February 1963 Lee embarked on a series of recording sessions that would lead to the production of another pivotal album in her canon: *Mink Jazz*. Starring Jack Sheldon on lead trumpet, this fabulous outing revisited the straight-ahead jazz sensibility Lee had shown on her legendary *Black Coffee* album. With a collection of finely arranged songs and an equally long string of A-list jazz musicians at the ready, *Mink Jazz* shone brightly among the all-time greatest Capitol albums.

The album began with a dazzling display of trumpet virtuosity by Jack Sheldon in "It's a Big Wide Wonderful World." Lee was also joined by flutist Harry Klee, who provided jumping melodic delights in his solo passages. This fast swing tune barely over one-and-a-half minutes in length proved that songs did not have to be long to be impressive and effective openers. "Whisper Not," the Benny Golson composition, came next. Lee's power of understatement and bluesy feeling matched the effortlessness of Sheldon's final trumpeted statement that ended the tune. The band gave Lee a solid foundation in the ballad "My Silent Love," during which pianist Lou Levy provided musical commentary and pianistic chatter amid Lee's crooned phrases. "The Lady Is a Tramp" picked up the momentum again in a Latin feel, giving Klee another opportunity to show off his piping skills. Lee managed to sound unhurried and laid back even on this brisk, energetic, dancelike song. "Days of Wine and Roses" followed, giving Lee a palette on which to paint her expressive interpretation of melancholic poetry. Filled with nostalgia and yet at home on this jazz album, this exquisite track stood as the first heart-tugging song on the recording. Harold Arlen and Ted Koehler's "As Long as I Live" happily followed, providing a lightening of mood and a delightful swing-out for Jack Sheldon's solo trumpet, Harry Klee's flute, and the rest of the band. Lee danced lightly atop the lyrics, nailing this standard's rhythm with her authoritative but fun vocal delivery. In the words of jazz journalist James Gavin in the liner notes for the 1998 Capitol reissue of *Mink Jazz*, "Lee's swing sense drives the whole band" on this track.[4] An energetic rendering of "I Won't Dance" followed, skipping along in a lighthearted romp shared by singer and her willing entourage. Sheldon once commented on Lee's musicianship: "Her rhythm is as good as anybody's I've ever heard."[5] That spot-on rhythmic sense dazzled in this barn-burning song. Lee's poignant singing of the unknown ballad "Cloudy Morning" ensued, providing a gentle breath of fresh air amid several up-tempo songs on this project. The sheer beauty of her softly purring voice was enough amid this

sensational band's music to warrant repeated listening. Rodgers and
Hart's "I Could Write a Book" continued the set with refreshing flute
solos by Klee and laid-back, mellow trumpet solos by Sheldon. Lee
cleverly substituted "sonnet" for "preface" in Hart's lyric to suit her
fancy, and her additional lyrics at the end provided a welcome new
twist. Irving Berlin's "I Never Had a Chance" brought the tempo back
to ballad pace, presenting Lee with another opportunity to showcase
her tender treatment of a romantic lyric and her elegant phrasing. The
band effectively stayed out of her way on this track, providing a stable
backdrop upon which she freely applied her musical mastery. The mysterious "Close Your Eyes" exuded a heavy blues swing in a haunting
minor key made all the more suggestive of film noir by the sliding
virtuosity of trumpeter Jack Sheldon. A stellar version of Lee's (and
Victor Young's) original song "Where Can I Go without You?" came
next, poignantly punctuated by Harry Klee's gentle flute meanderings
around Lee's sung text. Sheldon and Klee took turns providing musical
banter to Lee's lyrics until both soloists could not contain themselves,
both providing simultaneous musical commentary during Lee's final
phrases. A truly outstanding recording of this beloved song, this track
provided a treasured look at the staying power of Lee's songwriting
talents.

The 1998 reissue album concluded with five bonus tracks not included on the original. These featured the medium-swing Fred Ah-
lert–Roy Turk composition "I'll Get By." The collective improvisational
stylings heard during Lee's lyric singing (provided by both piano and
trumpet soloists) playfully toyed with the cheeriness of this ditty. Lee
followed this with another swinger, "Please Don't Rush Me," before
revealing a track that captured her talent for sharing intimate, introspective thoughts: "I'm a Fool to Want You." Singing barely audibly,
Lee's vocal control spoke volumes through its profound tenderness and
power of understatement. This stunning track went unissued for several
decades but has since taken its place as a poignant version of this famous song. The kitschy, pseudo-Spanish Lee original "I Didn't Find
Love" came next, with silly lyrics and a heavy Mexican accent she so

loved to sport. "Little Boat," a song based on "O Barquinho" by the Brazilian guitarist Roberto Menescal, finished this reissue. The summer it was released, the original *Mink Jazz* peaked at number forty-two on the *Billboard* pop charts and hovered there for nine weeks. It carved a place in music history as one of Lee's top Capitol albums.

March and April 1962 sessions yielded Lee's *Sugar 'N' Spice* album that united her voice with treasured songs including "I'll Be Around," "Teach Me Tonight," "The Best Is Yet to Come," and "I've Got the World on a String." The album began with a light rock rendition of "Ain't That Love," appropriately suiting the contemporary sounds currently in vogue. Lee moved into a bluesy "The Best Is Yet to Come" with easy swinging big band support. "See See Rider," the sole twelve-bar blues song on the album, showcased her mastery of this timeless genre so well exemplified in the newer rock context. Her eclectic and surprising Latin rock version of "Teach Me Tonight" (arranged by Billy May) clearly aimed to bring this classic standard into the listening realm of 1960s youth. "I've Got the World on a String" served as a throwback to the swing era in a big band arrangement that swung hard with plenty of jazz inflection by both singer and band. Overall the album melded swinging blues and light rock. The mood of this project maintained an optimistic, energetic outlook and took the band out for a contemporary walk, blending genres. A couple of ballads served to remind the public that this new-sounding project starred a veteran crooner at the microphone. *Sugar 'N' Spice* entered the pop music charts in November 1962 and stayed there for twenty-one weeks, reaching as high as number forty, making this Lee's eleventh charting LP.

Other albums occupied Lee's time in the mid-1960s, including *In Love Again!*, *In the Name of Love*, *Pass Me By*, and *Then Was Then and Now Is Now!* Each album included worthy listening for Lee's fans, uniting the ongoing legacy of standards she continued to record with her penchant for exploring contemporary music. The sheer volume of her recorded output reinforced her ongoing determination to continue to grow as an artist and produce a lasting musical legacy.

On two session dates in October 1965 plus one in February of the following year, Lee recorded an album whose title track would always be associated with her: *Big $pender*. The album began with a triumphant performance of "Come Back to Me" during which Lee led her big band with confidence and steely determination. "You've Got Possibilities" followed in a sprightly Latin beat. This song pointed to a characteristic that Lee's daughter, Nicki Lee Foster, reinforced: "She was essentially an optimistic person. She liked to encourage people."[6] This song reached number thirty-six on the *Billboard* easy listening chart and remained for four weeks. The next song, "It's a Wonderful World," exuded the same positive attitude. A bit of thematic balance ensued on the next selection, "I Only Miss Him When I Think of Him." Here Lee betrayed a shade of longing that resonated with so many of her fans. Lee's heartfelt rendering of this beautiful composition communicated that even cheerful, seemingly carefree lives contended with challenges and pain. "You Don't Know" began with lyrics and a rhythmic feel similar to that of "Fever" and assumed a sassy, bluesy attitude. Lee wailed and used a speak-singing style in the manner of a subdued blues shout. Blending standards like "Alright, Okay, You Win," "Watch What Happens," and "Let's Fall in Love" with more contemporary pieces like "I Must Know" and "Gotta Travel On," Lee proved *Big $pender* to be a timeless musical exploration of male-female relationships that combined classic swing with the new easy listening sound.

Producer Dave Cavanaugh strategically placed the top-selling single from the album—also its title track—smack in the middle of the song lineup. "Big Spender," a new song by Cy Coleman and Dorothy Fields, hailed from the forthcoming Broadway musical *Sweet Charity*. Lee obtained special permission from Coleman to record the song before the original cast recording was made, releasing her version upon the premiere of the Broadway production in January 1966 to become an instant hit. Dave Grusin's arrangement of "Big Spender" towered above other contemporary big-band-style pop songs. Here stood another example in which Lee's studio debut of a Broadway show tune became even more associated with the song than its original cast recording. The album's title track entered the easy listening chart in January 1966, eventually reaching number nine. It remained on the chart for nine weeks. *Big $pender* became Peggy Lee's sixteenth album to reach *Billboard's* top two hundred, peaking at number 130 and remaining in the chart for three weeks.

July 1966 contained the Capitol session dates that eventually birthed the album *Guitars A là Lee*, sporting several more arrangements by Dave Grusin. The album contained a new Latin rendition of the Bergman/Spence song "Nice 'n' Easy" that Sinatra had used as a title track of his 1960 album. Grusin's blending of trumpets, guitar, and percussion created gentle forward motion that drove the music steadily toward the end. "Strangers in the Night" followed, again in a decidedly Latin feel, with Lee providing her entrancing vocal performance and thoughtful phrasing. "Mohair Sam," a city blues, ensued with a jazz organ providing solos and commentary on the vocal lines. Here Lee countered the organ's bluesy licks with her own stylistic panache. A slow, even eighthnote accompaniment provided the backdrop for the next original ballad, "Goodbye, My Love," co-written by Victor Young. Lee, having lost none of her tonal luster or pitch accuracy, provided the vocal control necessary to deliver a poignant performance. "Think Beautiful" reveled in the multi-guitar layering that characterized this particular album. This track provided an example of alternative orchestration techniques that were available when focusing an album concept around one particular instrument. Even though the extended solo featured a pianist for contrast, the overall textures of guitar work highlighted the resplendence of this instrument. The Luiz Bonfá song "An Empty Glass" provided Lee with another opportunity to turn heartache into fine art. Her depiction of a woman standing strong amid disappointment while bidding a lover farewell seemed remarkable in its authenticity and sincerity. "Good Times" followed, a slowly swinging big band zinger that allowed Lee to showcase both her sensitive ballad singing as well as her big bluesy belt. "Sweet Happy Life" ensued in a brisk, sunny Latin style awash in blessings and good wishes. "Touch the Earth" continued the album in a slow, meditative manner, painting an idealistic picture of life made richer through the contemplation of nature (earth, sky, and sea) and universal kindness. Here Lee preached in a barely audible, powerfully intimate vocal tone that was almost a whisper. "Beautiful, Beautiful World" came next, sounding a bit out of place in the style of a trite children's song in the milieu of an otherwise adult-oriented easy listening recording. "My Guitar" saved the day with its delicate and lovely lulling quality. Lee's unmatched *pianissimo* (very soft) singing sounded particularly haunting on this track, creating a spell in which fans could become easily entranced. The contemporary song "Call Me" followed in a sprightly mood and moderate swing, which Lee delivered in an authoritative, confident style. Overall, *Guitars A là Lee* yielded a unique album within Lee's canon that glorified an instrument she adored.

As ever throughout her career, Lee balanced album recording sessions with those devoted to singles. In September 1966 she recorded two of the latter: "So What's New?" written by John Pisano and herself, and "Walking Happy" by Jimmy Van Heusen and Sammy Cahn. This session was conducted by Dave Grusin and yielded the tenth (and last) of Lee's original songs to chart on *Billboard*. "So What's New?" first appeared in the easy listening chart in October 1966, found its apex at number twenty, and remained on the chart for seven weeks. Lee completed a session with conductor Ralph Carmichael in June 1967 during which they recorded "I Feel It." This song broke the top ten in *Billboard*'s easy listening charts, peaking at number eight and charting for ten weeks.

Carmichael also conducted for Lee's *Somethin' Groovy!* album sessions, which started with the modern song "Something Stupid" followed by the classic tune "Makin' Whoopee." Toots Thielemans whistled a solo in the former song and played a bluesy, virtuosic harmonica solo in the latter. His dynamic, unparalleled performance in "Whoopee" alone made this project a worthy listen. The overall sound of the album rendered a contemporary spin on older songs and an authentic look at 1960s easy listening music trends. The project combined light rock guitar and drum set sounds with strings as it updated classic swing repertoire like "It Might as Well Be Spring," "Love Is Here to Stay," and "Release Me," while giving newer songs like "Two for the Road" and "I'm Gonna Get It" Lee's classy gloss. For this project Lee did not sing in a jazz style, even on the standards, but instead she aimed to make her mark as a still-relevant popular singer.

Throughout the 1960s, as she continued to evolve as a performing and recording artist, Peggy Lee embraced new music and young music directors, conductors, and orchestrators. She worked with contemporary songwriters in an effort to grow her younger audience and to roll with the cultural changes. Her blues and jazz albums from the early years of the decade balanced the easy listening offerings she released later, and her consistent presence on *Billboard* charts attested to her ongoing popularity. Few artists successfully navigated this chameleonic shift as time passed, but Lee accepted the multi-decade challenge with resilience, courage, and astonishing career success.

8

TELEVISION AND THE ROAD
TO THE GRAMMYS

From the 1950s through the 1970s Lee frequently performed on television—most frequently as a guest on various star-studded variety shows. These programs, often hosted by major stars in the entertainment industry, lightheartedly showcased for the viewing public somewhat impromptu performances combining the greatest talents of the stage, screen, and radio. Lee enjoyed several of these guest invitations, and the shows benefited greatly from her outstanding performances and star power. Meanwhile, Lee's consistent production of superior quality recordings eventually led to her work with the theatrical songwriting team Leiber and Stoller, and together they traveled the road toward Lee's long-coveted Grammy.

One guest TV performance aired in October 1954 on the Sid Caesar special *Caesar's Hour*. Lee stood next to an orchestra on a sound stage and sang a snippet of "Why Don't You Do Right?" followed by an extended version of "It's a Good Day," including the little-heard introductory verse. This particular arrangement, designed for a television orchestra rather than a big band, lacked a sense of swing, yet Lee still brought her fine-tuned professionalism and musicality to the performance. Being a comedy show, *Caesar's Hour* provided an opportunity for Lee to act in a humorous scene. In this skit Caesar himself appeared, interrupting the singer's recording session of the popular song

"Hey There." In a later scene Lee performed a Great American Songbook ballad, "Come Rain or Come Shine." All of her performances on this televised program confirmed her musicianship and poise as well as her strong rapport with a live audience and affinity for cameras.

When 1955 brought Lee the opportunity to appear as a singer-actress in the feature film *Pete Kelly's Blues,* it also yielded her a television special advertising the film. This forty-four-minute broadcast, hosted by the film's star and director, Jack Webb, spotlighted the key musicians featured in this musical story—Peggy Lee and Ella Fitzgerald. Each performed songs from the soundtrack while Lee and Webb also spoke about other elements of the film project. Lee's performance of "Somebody Loves Me" was polished and well delivered in this program's live orchestral context. Her instant connection and unbroken eye contact with the audience were transfixing by comparison with those of Fitzgerald, who appeared nervous and distracted before the camera, avoiding eye contact altogether, but displaying her singing prowess nonetheless. Lee's poignant performance of "He Needs Me" provided a fine representation of the song and a beautiful peek into Lee's connection to it. This additional insight created a welcome complement to the film's iteration of the song, since in the storyline Lee's performance involved her portrayal of an alcoholic character whose mind was more on her troubles than on the music she was making. This televised video provided an opportunity for Lee to give this lovely song the clean interpretation it deserved outside the parameters, interruptive cuts, and influence of film direction.

In October 1957 Lee appeared as a guest performer along with Bob Hope and Kim Novak on the first installment of the *Frank Sinatra Show.* Singing "Listen to the Rockin' Bird" and "He's My Guy" (the latter conducted by Sinatra as a sample from their collaborative album, *The Man I Love*), Lee's voice was in fine form. Her gentle caressing of each note engaged her audience continuously from the beginning of each song to the end. During the taping Sinatra introduced Lee with compliments: "Ladies and gentlemen, one of my favorite people and all-time great singer . . . Here she is, a swingin' gal and a swingin' tune,

Miss Peggy Lee."[1] This televised performance provided Lee's radio fans with insight into her live performances. One could easily see via her television appearances how her concentration, expressiveness, vocal technique, and musicianship combined to create unforgettable concerts.

Appearing in the late 1950s on the *Steve Allen Show*, Lee performed Cole Porter's "It's All Right with Me" and the 1955 Jesse Stone hit "Smack Dab in the Middle" with a high-energy attitude and plenty of improvisational skill. These arrangements, scored for big band jazz orchestra, sizzled and jumped and kept Lee framed in her finest light. Her confidence and virtuosity soared in these guest performances.

In the late 1950s Lee performed a televised duet with Frank Sinatra. The duo performed "Nice Work If You Can Get It" in a flirtatious, humorous spot during which they sang a likely impromptu arrangement of this classic Gershwin tune. With their voices melding into a velvety thread of sound, their unison singing complemented the lyric nicely. They also took turns singing solo lines throughout the song, often speaking comments pertaining to the lyric between iterations of the verse. This refreshing clip captured the personalities of each performer quite well, and even spotlighted their affection for one another as they poked fun and nervously interacted on a personal level, mindfully aware that the camera was spying on this interlude.

Shortly after her 1959 release of "Hallelujah, I Love Him So" (a variation of the Ray Charles composition bearing a different pronoun in the title), Lee appeared on television singing this exuberant song. All the way to the end of this short video recording, Lee bubbled over with joy and musical energy that left a distinctly positive impression of the singer's infectious attitude and confidence. It remains among her most joyous performances ever caught on film. Another wonderful performance captured around the same time displayed Lee delivering a stunning performance of Hoagy Carmichael's "Misty." Her command of vocal technique, ranging from a strong high belt to a gently mixed floated tone, highlighted what a consummate and versatile artist she was. Furthermore, she consistently expressed the text and mood with nuance and subtlety.

In September 1961 Lee appeared on NBC's *DuPont Show of the Week* with Harold Arlen and Vic Damone in an episode titled "Happy with the Blues," after an original song composed by Arlen. Lee created lyrics to this song, which she recorded several years later (1988) for her *Love Held Lightly* album (1993), a tribute to lesser-known songs by this beloved Great American Songbook composer. The *DuPont* show aired for three seasons and earned eight Primetime Emmy Award nominations as well as an Edgar Allan Poe Award nomination.

Another memorable TV performance occurred when Lee joined Judy Garland on the latter's show, which aired in the 1963–1964 season. On one episode they sang a medley of comical songs beginning with Lee's 1959 album title track "I Like Men," continuing with "You Make Me Feel So Young," and including a brief reference to "Fever." The medley finished with a mention of "It's so Nice to Have a Man Around the House," before launching into "I'm Just Wild About Harry," and "Big Bad Bill (Is Sweet William Now)." A rousing chorus replete with a kickline-style half-time ending on "Bill Bailey" finished this hysterical romp led by two of the most talented singers of the century.

Lee joined Garland on another installment of Judy's self-titled variety show during which they engaged once again in a humorous duet. They sang a spruced-up version of Lee's original, "I Love Being Here with You," in which they made several allusions to other songs associated with the pair, including "It's a Good Day" and "Over the Rainbow" and replaced most of the original lyrics with those commemorating this collaborative performance. Their good-natured playfulness added a measure of viewing pleasure to the clip, as did their unmistakable musical excellence and charm. Both timeless duets performed by Garland and Lee during Garland's short-lived stint as a TV-show host united two world-class performers who shared mutual respect and admiration. Garland even opened one show by singing Lee's original song "It's a Good Day" as a tribute to Lee. The humor, musical gold, and effortless

Dupont Show of the Week **(NBC) episode "Happy with the Blues," September 24, 1961. (L–R) Harold Arlen, Peggy Lee, and Vic Damone.** *NBC/Photofest.*

mastery shared on these clips contributed to their value in the annals of popular music and television history.

One of many televised performances of Lee's signature song, "Fever," featured Max Bennett playing bass and Jack Sperling playing drums. The clip showed Lee's refreshingly improvisational approach to this familiar song. While many artists may have sung their hits exactly as they had sung them on recordings, Lee's sense of adventure would not allow garish imitation, even of herself. The video proved that Lee had mastered text-based improvisation. Though Lee rarely employed scat improvisation (using nonsense syllables), her freedom with reinventing rhythms, changing the timing of lyrics, and discovering different ways to bend blue notes knew no bounds. The mark of an expert jazz musician included performing songs differently night after night and concert after concert—never an easy task. Lee's performance on this black-and-white clip revealed the ease with which she kept the essential character and recognizability of the song without singing it exactly the same way she had sung it before. The clip clearly demonstrated Lee's advanced understanding of vocal improvisation, a point often lost on some jazz purists who fail to recognize more than one way to express improvisation vocally.

On an episode of the televised *Bing Crosby Show*, Lee joined Crosby, Sinatra, and Louis Armstrong for a delightful quartet, "I'm Glad We're Not Young Anymore." This performance went down in history via one particularly famous photograph in which the foursome stood arm-in-arm singing together; this illustrious picture became affectionately known as the "Mount Rushmore" of twentieth-century American music, and for good reason. Armstrong represented the founding voice of jazz, Crosby and Sinatra held their own as the two pinnacle male performers in popular music and film musicals through much of the century from the swing and post-swing eras, extending from the 1930s into the 1970s (Sinatra's career lasted even longer), and Peggy Lee crossed into all of the above genres, forging her own path as swing, jazz, and pop diva, songwriter, and universal artist. Witnessing the tongue-in-cheek comical performance from which the famous photo originated has remained a rewarding endeavor for fans of the four stars.

In 1967 Lee filmed a made-for-television performance during which she sang "Walkin' Happy" followed by "Little Girl Blue" looking directly into the camera. Decked out in sparkling gems, a formal pink gown, tiara, and long straight blonde hair curled neatly under, Lee displayed her belief that her visual appearance mattered as much as her polished musical performances. Lee's opening number showed that her sense of swing rivaled that of the big band that accompanied her, and her smile and carefree demeanor supported the warm sentiments the lyrics communicated. Lee's confidence and storytelling bubbled with energy. During the applause she took a slight head bow, mouthed "thank you" to the audience, and immediately focused her attention on starting the next serious piece, gathering herself and placing her arm upon a stool next to her. The stark change in character between the first and the second pieces (with no film cut in between) allowed the viewing audience to witness the level of concentration Lee poured into her songs and shows. Her ensuing ballad unfurled with professionalism, vocal lushness, and poignancy. As the song continued, Lee inhabited the meaning so completely that she seemed to etch an autobiographical moment into the broadcast. Lee appeared to be singing directly from her heart, transparently confessing through the lyrics her deepest desires for companionship. This performance captured Lee at middle age—then forty-seven—still relevant in the music business but appealing to a maturing audience of her peers. Her concentrated emotion, sustained for several minutes and captured in this televised clip, warranted repeated viewing and study by actors, singers, and fans of great performances.

Lee was finally granted her own television specials in 1966 and 1967 titled *Something Special with Peggy Lee,* each lasting an hour. Programmed as part of a syndicated series (*Something Special*), the programs showcased Lee performing long strings of songs—essentially taped concerts. These included standards like "The Best Is Yet to Come," and "Alright, Okay, You Win," as well as originals "I Love Being Here with You," and "Mañana." A song medley from her *Blues Cross Country* album also graced the televised song list. Lee's 1967 broadcast featured Ralph Carmichael and His Orchestra, Mundell Lowe on guitar, Max Bennett on bass, Lou Levy on piano, Toots Thielemans on harmonica, Jack Sperling on drums, and Francisco Aguabella on percussion. On both occasions Lee was the featured performing star, presenting twenty-one songs for the first show and seventeen for the second.

Airing January 13, 1968, the *Hollywood Palace Fifth Anniversary Show* featured Bing Crosby as host, and Peggy Lee, Jimmy Durante, and Milton Berle, among other celebrity guests. A grand production featuring a host of professional dancers, background singers, and an orchestra, this show celebrated the return of *Hollywood Palace* to its Saturday night TV programming slot. For her scene, Lee appeared in a baby-blue gown and sang "What Is a Woman?" with a rich orchestral accompaniment. Here she capably posed existential questions about youth, love, and femininity. Following a rousing ovation, she moved into a faster swing number, "Seems Like Old Times." Swinging lightly, Lee kept the energy moving forward toward a big finish for which the audience rewarded her amply with fervent applause. This performance exhibited Lee's commitment to finely tuning the visual aspects of her concerts, from hand motions to blocking and from facial expressions to turns of her head, which served to complement the music. Students of Lee's art could spend hours studying the relatively few documented televised performances that pointed toward an artist intent on perfecting every possible aspect of her craft.

Later in the show Lee joined Crosby for a long endearing medley of charming songs including "So What's New," "When He Makes Music," "Do I Hear a Waltz," "Something Stupid," the silly and fun "A Doodlin' Song," "Sing a Rainbow," "When the Blue of the Night" (about which Lee joked, "Still trying to make that song a hit?"), and "Yellow Bird," circling around again to "So What's New" to complete the medley. This clip portrayed the enduring friendship of two legendary entertainers who had by then exceeded veteran status among their peers. Their pure enjoyment of singing together after so many years of paving successful parallel careers shone forth. This performance highlighted their long professional friendship and reinforced how wonderfully both artists still collaborated together.

Lee's daughter and granddaughter shared with the author documents detailing the clothing, makeup supplies, purses, jewelry, gowns, shoes, hair products, and accessories that Lee painstakingly catalogued in an effort to keep track of all her needs while preparing for any given performance or tour.[2] She made inventory lists and travel logs of what items to pack for particular destinations. She kept careful track of which gowns she wore in each city to make sure her audiences would always see her in a different gown when she returned for a concert. She kept boxes and boxes of notebooks that organized her song lists for various concerts, ideas for albums, lists of on-stage props, wigs, and costumes, and blocking for her many shows. The extreme attention to detail she employed in preparation for each performance revealed an artist consumed by her desire to make every concert memorable and outstanding. The high polish on her televised performances thus far proved that her efforts to adequately prepare were not in vain. While critics of this obsessive type of preparation (and rehearsal) may have complained about her lack of spontaneity during performances, televised performances confirmed that Lee indeed improvised via her phrasing, rhythmic timing, and pitch choices while preserving the well-rehearsed beginnings, endings, and energy-sustaining arrangements that characterized her shows. This rare level of preparation represented one of several qualities that set Lee's musical contribution to American art apart from everyone else's in her era and thereafter.

In 1969 National Educational Television produced a program called *Miss Peggy Lee.* In this biopic, Lee gave interviews and provided video access to her performances and rehearsals. The program began with a short clip of Lee singing a harsh rendition of the heartbreaking "Don't Explain" and continued with a filmed concert planning session among Lee, musical director Mundell Lowe, arranger/scorer Dick Hazard, composer Johnny Mandel, and pianist Lou Levy. All were filmed discussing ideas for melding a classic Johnny Mandel composition ("The Shadow of Your Smile") with his new song ("I Never Told You") for a forthcoming project. In this documentary Lee revealed a bit of her strategy for staying current as musical styles perpetually changed: "I think it's keeping a constant interest in what's going on. But even now with the new trends in music, the component parts of it are really not new. They are different to the extent that they're put together in a new way." Lee went on to theorize about trends affecting the younger generation: "When bebop came in . . . then there started this whole free-form, almost selfish kind of music that left the younger generation with nothing to dance to, and not to be able to really take part in it. And I've often wondered if that wasn't what caused the younger people to find something of their own. Because we need music."[3]

Regarding her choice of modern music to perform, Lee stated: "I choose material that lets me tell a story. It's a nice way to make a living!" In describing her routine leading up to a concert, Lee narrated as the camera displayed a rehearsal in a room at Lee's home: "If there is a crucial time in all the long preparation for a show, it's here in the yellow room with the rhythm section when we start to bring our music to life. There are very important judgments to be made here: rhythmic patterns, balance in the overall interpretation, whether a song plays best as a jazz waltz, bossa nova, or a straight ballad."[4] Here Lee revealed how much band rehearsal and arranging actually took place in her personal residence prior to a recording session, live concert, or tour.

During a clip of a sound and lighting check, Lee overdubbed commentary: "You have to get acquainted with each new room—the sound, the lighting, the way I hear the orchestra behind me, all the pieces must go together before the audience arrives." Later during that same clip Lee requested a five-minute break to discuss elements of the show and the current song's progression because she disagreed with what her musical director and arranger had planned. The camera followed and caught the exchange during which Lee politely expressed her desire to change some of the music at that moment in the show because she felt it did not fit the mood she wanted. This clip revealed the tension between the star and her male team of instrumentalists who arranged the music and made most of the musical decisions. "As an instrumental, it's beautiful, but I don't think it allows me to say what I feel that the lyric says." Interrupting her before her sentence was complete, music coordinator Mundell Lowe faced the challenge of making the show work while keeping the singer contented. Her musical advisors finally conceded, "It sounds very binding." Lee asserted, "It IS." They smiled and broke the huddle, having come to a satisfying conclusion about the musical change they agreed to implement.

Lee shared thoughts about her show flow planning: "There's a kind of unseen form that develops from the music itself—a flow of moods which becomes special to this presentation. And if a song, no matter how fine it is, breaks that flow, it must be taken out." This specific rehearsal was leading up to a concert at the Mark Taper Forum in Los Angeles at which Lee performed a mix of classic standards like Lerner and Loewe's "Almost like Being in Love" and contemporary hits including Carole King's "Natural Woman." The production team had programmed some high-energy music after the first few songs during which Lee walked to both ends of the stage acknowledging the audience throughout the room, thanking them for their applause, and giving them plenty of opportunity to offer yet more. This provided a break of sorts for Lee—a brief chance to build up audience participation and enhance a willingness to applaud due to the orchestra providing intensified music specifically inserted to keep the audience clapping while she rested her voice. The orchestra thus built a musical platform upon which Lee strolled like a runway model, giving the audience some visual gratification and affection. This scoring tactic is still used today by many pop music professionals to hype up the energy of a concert by tacking on an extended ending meant to rouse the audience to a higher level of energetic applause.

While the vocal prowess of this artist may have begun to wane by the time this was filmed (perceptible in a slight stridency present in her tone and a dearth of her formerly youthful vocal color), her pristine polish and ability to deliver a completely committed performance remained strong. This documentary provided an opportunity for Lee's fans to peer into the artist's home, thoughts, and even onstage as she prepared and performed a major concert. That this (1969) was the year she finally attained a coveted Grammy award made the release of this television documentary particularly timely for Lee.

Lee's television appearances continued into the following decade, when in 1973 Lee appeared on an episode of *The Julie Andrews Hour* along with guest Robert Goulet. This clip revealed how quickly time had taken its toll on fifty-three-year-old Lee, both physically and vocally, in just four short years since her Grammy win. She sang a pop ballad called "Someone Who Cares," which revealed a striking lack of breath energy compared to all her previous work. Costume designers did Lee no favors on this show, for which she sported body-hiding waistless gowns in various tones, a pulled-back hair wig, and very thick almost surreal makeup on her face, visibly swollen from plastic surgery. Nevertheless, she strove to maintain her sense of humor and professionalism. She joined Andrews and Goulet in a rousing trio, "Lord, I'm on My Way," a Broadway-style gospel number that was more suited for the other two voices than it was for Lee. A truly touching duet ensued when Andrews joined Lee in a rendition of "Sing a Song" coupled with Lee's own "Sing a Rainbow," which Andrews layered atop Lee's delivery of the former song. The medley continued with "Up, Up, and Away," which Lee began to sing while Andrews continued on with the original "Sing a Song" motif, followed by "I Believe in Music" and several other song snippets. They worked in "Alright, Okay, You Win," and "I Want to Be Happy" before making their way back to "Sing a Song" for a lovely finish. The inclusion of this well-arranged duet in the program was fortunate for Lee as it allowed her the opportunity to be showcased with songs she sang well, joined by a gracious artist who put her in a favorable light. One could clearly see on this clip the torch passing from Lee, the music veteran, to Andrews, the youthful talent. Lee appeared again singing "Who Will Buy?" with her usual sense of style and sultry charm, this time wearing a black dress that flattered, in a setting with lighting that reflected her innate beauty. In a romantic duet with Goulet, Lee sang "Make Someone Happy," and her joy was palpable. Rejoining Andrews, Goulet, and Rich Little for the finale, Lee and friends exuberantly performed "Together" from the 1959 Broadway show *Gyp-sy*.

This fifty-minute large-scale production represented an excellent case study of the importance of considering lighting, costuming, and stage makeup for all artists over an entire televised show. During this program each scene change dramatically affected both Lee's physical appearance and aural beauty. While Lee maintained firm control over every element of her live concert appearances on tour (even bringing a lighting designer with her) she likely had very little control over how her televised performances were handled by tech crews and directors—especially when she was a guest performer on a syndicated variety show. The costumes she was given to wear for this performance presented a dowdy, almost tacky look that was highly unusual for the perfectionistic star. Given this series of anomalous costumes that did not suit Lee's normal style, it was likely that Lee was costumed by someone else for this production. Further evidence to this theory was shown in the "Sing a Song" duet for which Julie Andrews sported a bright yellow tent-like gown that matched Lee's. Both singers seemed trapped inside ridiculous-looking getups that distracted from the poignancy and quality of their charming duet. Costumes notwithstanding, Lee put forth a decent effort for this appearance, but it did not reflect her best work. Lee continued to appear on television from time to time in the 1970s and '80s, often to promote a new album or concert tour. Overall, her activity in television and film wound down by the mid-1970s as she put her energy into recording and performing new music.

Throughout her career Lee's forays into television greatly enhanced her popularity as a star of the live-music stage and radio, and it served as a marvelous platform on which to build her international fan base. As both her popularity and prolific recording output grew, she became a natural contender for Grammy Award consideration. The Recording Academy had instituted a televised award show in 1958 aimed at honoring the greatest contemporary music artists in a given year. Lee's road to the Grammys began with no fewer than seven consecutive nominations between 1958 and 1962. Her impressive string of uninterrupted nominations during the earliest stages of these coveted awards proved what colossal talent and star power she possessed and highlighted the unequivocal esteem she enjoyed from her peers in the music industry.

Lee earned her seventh nomination with the title track, by the songwriting team Jerry Leiber and Mike Stoller, from her 1962 album *I'm a Woman*. Stoller shared that this pivotal song first came into Lee's awareness through pianist Mike Melvoin, who had recently been hired to accompany Lee. Producer Dave Cavanaugh came to a session date or a rehearsal with a stack of acetate demo records and asked Melvoin to look through them to find songs that might be a good fit for performing with Lee. He selected "I'm a Woman" because he noticed it was composed by Leiber and Stoller, and he knew their songs. Later, an article announced that Lee was performing "a wonderful new song called 'I'm a Woman'" at Basin Street East, although no one had contacted Leiber or Stoller to notify them that she had added it to her repertoire: "I remember it was a freezing night and I went to Basin Street East and of course it was our song. And she was doing it just great. I'd never met her before . . . I went back and introduced myself to her in the dressing room."[5]

Recorded in March and November 1962, as well as over several sessions in January 1963, the album itself did not chart—neither did the song, even though it scored a huge hit for Lee at her live performances, became forever identified with her, and obtained Grammy attention. Like many of Lee's later albums, this project united classic standards (in this case "Come Rain or Come Shine" and a uniquely Latin rendering of "Mack the Knife") with newer rock songs ("I'm Walkin'" and "A Taste of Honey"). One refreshing quality of this album included the decidedly different presentation of older songs. Pieces generally performed as swing tunes became reinterpreted in a Latin style and traditionally fast songs slowed down drastically to ballad tempo. None of the arranging ideas that made this album unique were wasted, as they all placed Lee in a favorable light as a relevant artist whose interests included both new music and new representations of old standbys.

The single "I'm a Woman" yet again placed Lee squarely in the public eye as an artist unafraid to express herself in the most explicit and suggestive terms. This song boasted female empowerment—even domination. The strength, confidence, and firmness with which Lee delivered this powerful and striking composition proved that she alone was absolutely the right female artist to make this song her own. To this day no other artist who recorded it ever came close to eclipsing Lee's definitive version. The manner in which she deftly maneuvered between speaking rhythmic text (as she rattled off her resume of skills) and powerfully singing the song's title left no doubt as to her authority over this piece. The song's message would be used as a feminist anthem for decades. It has continued to appear in films and commercials, still effectively transmitting its phenomenal power since the day it was first released.

At the 1963 Grammy awards, Lee enjoyed her fifth straight year of nominations. (It was also the fifth year the awards had existed.) Once again Ella Fitzgerald was also nominated. Ella retained the top honors, winning the award for Best Solo Vocal Performance, Female with her album of Nelson Riddle arrangements, *Ella Swings Brightly with Nelson*. That Lee had been nominated five years in a row indicated how well her career had blossomed by this point. She continued to enjoy a substantial salary from live performing in addition to record sales and worldwide popularity.

Though Leiber and Stoller's "Kansas City" and "I'm a Woman" first introduced Lee to the team's fine songwriting work earlier in her career, it was 1969 before the trio stumbled upon a project that would finally produce the Grammy Award that had thus far eluded the singer. The songwriting duo had written a very serious philosophical song dramatizing a backward look over a life riddled with broken dreams of a safe and happy home, a lasting love relationship, and other disappointments. The shocking final verse dealt with the consideration of ending one's own life, as novel a prospect as that may have been for a popular song. The song's mood lightened each time the refrain came back around, during which the protagonist concluded that the only recourse in the face of such bleakness in life was to dance, drink, and enjoy oneself in spite of it all. "Is That All There Is?" resonated with millions of people in 1969 during the height of the Vietnam conflict, civil rights marches, the alternative lifestyle of flower children, political splintering, and American disillusionment. Arranged and conducted by Randy Newman, its carnival-like accompaniment beneath Lee's matter-of-fact spoken narration intensified the song's irony. That such a childlike, banal background could provide the foundation for a song as tragic and somber as this was truly revolutionary. The song's relevance reverberated in the lives of countless listeners experiencing distressing circumstances and angst about the state of the world. The dichotomy had grown starker between real-life problems and the party-line position that forgetting one's troubles and just getting happy held the answer. Lee's collaboration with Leiber and Stoller struck more than a chord with the American public. It shot through America's consciousness like a bolt of lightning, offering a song of empathy for those caught in the tragedies and traumas of that decade. It also offered a word of cheer, encouraging those who otherwise might have given up on life to celebrate the joys anyway, even though correction of deep-seated problems plaguing society (or individual lives) may have proved to be unattainable. Finally, this song represented an anthem to middle age—Lee shared with her generation the fine line between all they had accomplished and dreams yet unfulfilled. This welcome song encouraged a letting go of things beyond one's control, and the world received it gratefully.

In writing the song, Mike Stoller explained, the sung refrain was the last part to be composed. Lyricist Jerry Leiber had penned the stories that were to be spoken, and Stoller had composed the music that accompanied the spoken recitation. British chanteuse Georgia Brown heard the songwriting team perform the song, and when invited to consider performing it herself she exclaimed, "I'd love to—I'm going to do this, but it needs something for me to SING!" Leiber replied, "Let me think about that—I'll work on some lyrics." Stoller went home and wrote some new music, and when the team reconnected, neither wished to hear the other's work first, fearing that each of their perfect ideas might be forced into a compromise. After arguing about who would reveal first, they discovered that the words and music fit together perfectly with no tweaking necessary: "We didn't have to change a syllable. It never happened like that before or since. And that's how it got that refrain and the title, 'Is That All There Is?'"[6]

Almost immediately upon receiving the song in 1969 from Leiber and Stoller for recording consideration, Lee replied: "If you send this song to anybody else, you're gonna be in a lot of trouble . . . that song is mine!"[7] Georgia Brown had already followed through with her promise to premiere it on BBC TV in 1966, but Lee was the first to secure the rights to record it. She felt that it was autobiographical in more than one way; the song mentioned a house burning down, which Lee experienced as a young child. She also had recently grieved the death of the man she considered to be the love of her life, Dave Barbour, in 1965. The song became emblematic of her own life and was ever associated with Lee from that point onward.

After over thirty takes in the recording studio, "Is That All There Is?" finally attained the apex of its perfection, but unfortunately, the recording engineer failed to record the penultimate, best vocal take. Lee gave it one more try and the producers were left with the task of editing previous takes in an effort to cobble together the rendering that was finally adopted. Interestingly, the eventual release of the song embodied an uphill battle with Capitol Records. Capitol's producers believed the song to be too unconventional for practical use as a single. In an effort to prove them wrong, Lee performed it on television for *The Joey Bishop Show* where it was warmly received by the viewing public. She then insisted that the song be released and promoted under penalty of her resignation from the label, and they conceded. The song quickly made it into the top twenty pop hits chart and won the Grammy Award despite all the controversy surrounding it.

Regarding the arrangement of the song, John Chiodini (Lee's musical director from the 1980s) shared: "She knew exactly what she wanted. She wanted that Kurt Weill, 1930s Nazi Germany sound. When

Mike Stoller, Peggy Lee, and Jerry Leiber. *Courtesy of the Leiber & Stoller Archive.*

you think of that time in history, it was totally 'Is that all there is?' Boy did he (Randy Newman) deliver. I think that was his first professional arrangement."[8] Mike Stoller added: "The music for the first two of the four spoken verses was reimagined brilliantly by Randy Newman. Those and his exquisite orchestration enhanced both the song and the Peggy Lee recording immensely."[9]

Many of Lee's talents came together in the recording of this Grammy-winning song. Her penchant for poetry and habitual recitation of it at many of her live performances set the stage for the spoken portions. She narrated with a somewhat disengaged persona, simply letting the story speak for itself without melodrama added. Still, she infused this storytelling venture with sincerity, tenderness, and understatement, which powerfully allowed the song to be interpreted in a number of different ways. Lee's singing came into play during the refrain, and her performance reflected a life of experience and wisdom utterly foreign to the sensibilities of teen idols and pop music doo-wop groups sharing the airwaves. Lee's song towered over the competition as one the older generation refused to let drown among more trite radio and jukebox selections. That "Is That All There Is?" received the sweeping support it did from the Recording Academy confirmed the taste and quality requirements of that organization in that decade, both traits that have since, unfortunately, been called into question in the field of modern popular music. Lee's timing of the spoken text also greatly enhanced the message, as she intuitively knew how to pull, push, and shape a phrase in a way that enthralled her audience and left them wanting more. With "Is That All There Is?" that was the whole point, and she skillfully delivered on that expectation.

Five years later, with her Grammy in hand, Lee embarked on another Leiber and Stoller collaboration, this time co-creating an album titled *Mirrors* aimed to give the decorated singer an entire recording project in which to relish the rich songwriting legacy of this unique team. Their Grammy-winning masterpiece, "Is That All There Is?," opened *Mirrors*. A theatrical piece based on the Thomas Mann novel *Disillusionment*, the award-winning song perfectly set the stage for a project consisting purely of theatrical pieces. In describing the duo's style, Peter Stoller (the composer's son and remix producer of the 2005 *Peggy Lee Sings Leiber & Stoller* album) remarked, "It was their melding of R&B with the craftsmanship of Tin Pan Alley—and particularly the musical theater—that truly distinguished their songwriting and production."[10] The team benefited even more from the highly skilled arranging work provided by arranger-conductor Johnny Mandel. When asked by journalist David McGee about her impression of Mandel's arranging for *Mirrors*, Lee replied: "I think he is one of the greatest ever and he's a marvelous conductor. We have always worked together very well. That was a joy."[11]

On the other hand, Lee's tensions with Leiber and Stoller produced sparks in the studio. Mike Stoller commented: "Apparently she worked off of anger. She might be extremely angry but then when she sang, there was that wonderful voice. . . . So it was difficult working with her at times and wonderful working with her at other times. But ultimately it was the sound of her voice that just was so, so beautiful, so special."[12]

A primary goal for the 2005 restoration of *Mirrors'* tracks involved lifting Lee's voice from its too-deep setting in the final mix. Peter Stoller remarked: "The Peggy Lee album was a victim of, among other things, a lot of bad timing. It kept getting released when record companies were changing ownership, and it never got much of a shake in the digital domain. Also, it wasn't the greatest sounding record."[13] Tape hiss complicated the editing process, as Lee's singing volume remained very low at this point in her career. Because her subtle, understated vocal qualities were comparatively soft amid the other recorded sounds, restoring them fully proved to be challenging. Further complicating the restoration of *Mirrors* stood the unfortunate fact that the original masters were already deteriorating by the time the decision had been made to clean up the recordings. Regarding the project, Jerry Leiber insisted: "These are the best songs we ever wrote, and the best songs we ever will write."[14] The eleven tracks on the album were later reordered when presented in the 2005 release, and four additional tracks were included. The reworked set accomplished long-awaited clean renderings of the team's songs, albeit several decades later than necessary to provide Lee with an opportunity to hear the restored work.

The disappointing *Mirrors* venture, unappreciated by the rock-soaked culture and harshly reviewed by some critics as being "tuneless and wordy"[15] and "pretentious,"[16] was unable to revive Lee's declining popularity through the 1970s. Misunderstanding and under-appreciating the concept album, the disco-hungry listening public failed to recognize it as the treasure Johnny Mandel described: "I think it's classic and it's timeless."[17] Even amid this disappointment, however, the dreams of Leiber and Stoller to eventually release an album project that beautifully showcased their tireless work with Peggy Lee, placed their finest compositions in the best light, and vindicated the outstanding performances Lee rendered in the recording studio were ignited. Those dreams, though put on hold for thirty years, would ultimately transform *Mirrors* into the skillfully reworked *Peggy Lee Sings Leiber and Stoller*.

Lee attained many triumphs between her early guest work on televised variety shows (near the infancy of that genre) and her eventual acquisition of the top award in music. Her decades of experience in television helped to solidify her international appeal, and her continuing work in that medium provided illustrative documentation of her development as an artist. Her growing familiarity with the songs of Jerry Leiber and Mike Stoller eventually led her toward a collaboration that would yield a Grammy Award. Her instincts about the inherent qualities of a hit record proved to be correct once again in her fight to release "Is That All There Is?" and the road to the Grammys finally rewarded her with long-sought-after gold. This long-awaited Grammy win finally acknowledged Lee's many years of outstanding performing and scores of Capitol hits, truly marking the pinnacle of her career.

9

LATE ALBUMS AND BROADWAY

Before and after Lee's Grammy win with the Leiber and Stoller hit, she continued to churn out singles for Capitol Records. One record contract led to another through the 1970s and '80s as a string of labels extended recording opportunities to the star after her Capitol contract expired. Lee's continued commitment to live performing led to an opportunity to write, produce, and star in her own show on Broadway. Her performing career continued to thrive, leading eventually to a satisfying series of Grammy-nominated albums late in her career. Lee's artistic longevity—health notwithstanding—seemed to have no end.

Lee's longtime producer, Dave Cavanaugh, had left Capitol in 1967 and was replaced at several of her sessions by independent producers Charles Koppelman and Don Rubin. This new production team created a new recording process to which Lee was expected to adapt. One major change to the protocol involved Lee no longer discussing and rehearsing arrangements before recording sessions but coming into the studio and overdubbing her vocal part onto a prerecorded instrumental track. For an article appearing July 1, 1968, in *Melody Maker*, Lee shared:

> I was used to hearing demonstration records, talking over material, rehearsing the rhythm section, selecting my arranger, deciding on a style of interpretation. Under the new system, they just sent me lead

sheets and I waited for them to call me up. I had nothing to do with
the instrumental aspects of the records. When I found out Shorty
Rogers was going to arrange and conduct the first session, I felt a lot
more secure. . . . It wasn't a mechanical process at all. They'd put a
lot of creative effort into it, preparing backgrounds so that I could
just step in and bring my own interpretation of the lyric to whatever
they had set up for me. [1]

In April that year, Lee made a live album titled *Two Shows Nightly*.
Accompanied by a band of the finest jazz instrumentalists anywhere,
Lee undertook a set list of mostly contemporary songs and made plans
to record her album live at her New York haunt, the Copacabana. The
fourteen-member ensemble (Lou Levy and His Orchestra) featured
Levy at the piano, drummer Grady Tate, guitarist Mundell Lowe, saxo-
phonist/flutist Hubert Laws, trombonist Bill Watrous, and harmonica-
playing whistler Toots Thielemans, among several others, including a
trumpet section, trombone section, and French horn.

During the mixing and mastering stages of album production Koppelman and Rubin decided to insert applause tracks after each song and
tweak the vocal masters to further refine the recordings. The inserted
applause sounded artificial to Lee's ear, and she, rightfully, objected.
Remaining on the 2009 release of this project, the applause suggested a
much larger audience than could have been present in a nightclub. The
density of clapping suggested several hundred audience members instead of a more appropriate number for the venue, and the arbitrary
starting and stopping of the applause made its artificiality obvious. Lee,
preferring to keep the natural, unadulterated quality of the recording as
intact as possible, adamantly opposed those changes. After expressing
her distaste for the resulting sound to the producers, Lee ultimately
withdrew the album and prevented it from being released. As a result,
although it was essentially finished, *Two Shows Nightly* never saw day-
light, but remained locked in Capitol's vaults until after Lee's death. It
did, however, receive an initial pressing, and a very small number of
LPs (only ten to fifteen at the time of this writing) have been located in
the United States. Even with Lee's objections to the muddy sound

quality, collectors have highly prized this extremely rare recording. The outstanding arrangers for the project included an all-star lineup: Billy Byers, Mundell Lowe, Shorty Rogers, Ralph Burns, and Dave Grusin. It seemed unfortunate that Capitol's producers and engineers could not meet Peggy Lee's criteria for excellence in delivering an adequate final product, given the proven strength of the arrangements and world-class performers on this unreleased project.

In 2009 the original twelve tracks were finally brought into the light under the original album title, *Two Shows Nightly—Deluxe Edition*, and released along with a dozen bonus songs, most of which had been obscure singles. The collection has been viewed as a treasure trove of outstanding recordings of Lee in her prime and has remained a favorite of collectors since its release.

The remade album kicked off with an emcee announcing Peggy's stage entrance during the energetic introduction to "Do I Hear a Waltz?" Lee's exuberant opening song burst out of the gate like a race-horse and generously displayed her effortless pitch precision, rhythmic exactitude, and musical expression. The album then moved into a very slow ballad, "By the Time I Get to Phoenix," which Lee delivered with maximum effectiveness and tender detachment apropos to the song's message. With its heartbreaking text, Lee and harmonica soloist Toots Thielemans painted a lush landscape of the melancholic journey away from a lover. More often sung by a man, the song melted in Lee's hands, coming through as a statement of unfortunate yet inevitable change rather than cruel abandonment. "Reason to Believe" followed in a straightforward manner balanced by heavy horn backgrounds and hits. "Didn't Want to Have to Do It" continued the project with its slow swingy ballad in a 12/8 feel, creating a beautiful contrast in beat structure with all the previous songs. The band provided melodic echoing throughout the texture of the piece, repeating the titular melody in a call-and-response manner immediately after Lee presented it. As per usual in Lee's live shows, these songs were not weighted down by lengthy instrumental breaks or soloing but rather stood as relatively brief vocal features that kept the spotlight and attention firmly on Lee for the duration of the show.

Lee then introduced the next song, expressing that she nearly felt that Cy Coleman and Dorothy Fields wrote "Personal Property" (from the film version of the Broadway musical *Sweet Charity*) especially for her rather than for Shirley MacLaine (who starred in the 1968 film). This song about New York resonated for Lee, as evidenced by the conviction and sincerity with which she performed it.

"Hand on the Plow" followed with its brisk energetic drive in the style of a non-swinging, minor blues. Lee's purely focused, no-nonsense manner of singing strict, simple rhythms suited this simple blues perfectly. Her syncopation always landed right "in the pocket," maintaining a groove as well or better than her instrumental compatriots. The extended, repetitive, horn-driven ending suggested this was a juncture in the performance when Lee took bows or otherwise worked the crowd to prolong and maximize applause. The set continued with "Until It's Time for You to Go," a sentimental ballad with sparse broken-chord accompaniment provided by the piano and guitar. This piece dropped the energy significantly after the faster songs in front of it, yet the contrast created a refreshing moment of relative stillness, albeit a song of pathos so typical of pop music in that time period.

The C. Carson Parks song "Something Stupid" came next, with Toots Thielemans providing whistled backtalk during Lee's rests between phrases. This speedy song brought the energy back to a rousing level through Thielemans's lighthearted contributions that enhanced Lee's vocal lines. The song's relatively short duration balanced the previous ballad's length, again showing Lee's prowess for creating performance flow that kept an audience's attention riveted upon her.

The ballad "What Is a Woman?" ensued with lovely guitar and piano lines occasionally interjecting accompaniment as Lee warmed into the song from a relatively solitary beginning. The texture gradually became denser and denser as more instruments were added to provide a climactic moment toward the end of the first vocal chorus. The arrangement opened up into a lush instrumental interlude that led Lee back in at the midpoint (bridge) of the song's form. Here Lee competently displayed her mastery of dynamic control, performing both soft and loud singing (and everything in between) while the energy of the piece ebbed and flowed as naturally as the ocean's tide.

"Alright, Okay, You Win" began with Lee introducing every member of the band. The song's humorous arrangement spotlighted the instrumentalists verbally echoing the title words in a call-and-response texture at the beginning and end of the piece. Lee displayed marvelous pitch precision, breath energy, and rhythmic sense as she sang confidently and authoritatively, proving she truly owned the song. This version of an oft-performed standard has remained well worth collecting and may be Lee's finest rendition available.

Lee's original song "Here's to You," co-written by Dick Hazard, stood alone as a blessing that Lee bestowed upon her audience. With lyrics bidding good health, happiness, wealth, and friendship in a multitude of languages, Lee's intent in writing and sharing this very slow waltz revealed a bit of her idealistic, optimistic nature. In her spoken introduction to this song she expressed not only her heart's desire to spread positive energy and encouragement to the whole world but also her faith in humanity that all people shared the same wish: to bless others and to receive a blessing in return. The band played a short fully orchestrated encore—an extension of the song in a different key—to give Lee another opportunity for a bow and to greet her audience, much in the style of a television orchestra filling downtime with a brief overture or medley of familiar themes related to that show.

Lee ended her recorded Copacabana set with "Come Back to Me," a high-energy barn burner that kept the band on its toes playing at breakneck speed. The applause track inserted by the production team had been mixed in with the song's opening music, creating a slightly distracting situation as she resumed the show, since it did not mesh at all with the venue's actual audience capacity. Lee delivered two full verses of lyrics with a band arrangement requiring utmost virtuosity by all the performers. Lee's pointed articulation and precision shone on this final song and revealed her extraordinarily high level of musicianship. There were no signs of an aging voice or a drop in breath efficiency, which began to creep into Lee's performances and recordings just a few years later. This recording used vocal overdubs (vocal retakes recorded in a studio) to re-create the live performance at the Copa. It captured the singer at the peak of her vocal and musical powers. Live or not, it has continued to impress fans ever since its public release only a decade ago.

In January 1969, Lee recorded a version of "Spinning Wheel" that debuted in the easy listening charts in May, just months prior to the Blood, Sweat, and Tears rock rendition, which peaked at number two in the pop charts. Lee's take on the song maxed out at number twenty-four and stayed in the charts for six weeks. Pianist/arranger Mike Melvoin conducted and played organ on this big band chart. The song became part of Lee's 1969 album *Natural Woman*, a big band exploration of contemporary pop and rock music. Bobby Bryant and Mike Melvoin shared arranging and conducting credits for this Capitol album.

The first song on the album, "My Heart Sings," betrayed a problem that began to haunt Lee at this period in her life and never let her go. Lee began to have difficulty sustaining energy and pitch all the way through a phrase. These issues stemmed from breathing difficulties that developed from decades of smoking cigarettes, which later worsened after a bout with pneumonia. The singer eventually needed to transport tanks of oxygen to her performances and studio sessions. Breathing deeply from a respirator backstage, Lee discovered that she required supplemental oxygen to get through her live performances and recording dates. Her tone quality began to wane and her breath energy decreased to a fraction of what it used to be. Lee's singing started to become less consistently energized and pitch-accurate as the 1970s progressed, but she continued to perform and record nonetheless. Even with a compromised breathing system, Lee successfully navigated her phrasing and other aspects of musicality and artistry, making her later work all the more remarkable given her physical limitations. Peter Stoller remarked about Lee's 1975 *Mirrors* sessions: "She was not at her technical peak and I don't think that's any mystery, but one of the things that's remarkable . . . is that she was somebody who dealt with significant physical problems that limited what she could do as a singer. . . . Because she had health problems that required her to bring tanks around to breathe, [she put] a song across through nuance and phrasing and time rather than through sparkle and volume and dexterity."[2]

One very old jazz standard, "Don't Explain," was included on *Natural Woman*. Since the song bore a strong association with Billie Holiday, Lee's version cleverly possessed elements that identified it as contemporary music. A symphonic arrangement with orchestra, modern big band, French horns, and electronic organ helped set Lee's rendition apart from the classic Holiday version. At the outset, Lee paid homage to Holiday with her understated, hushed singing in which she toyed with the pitches and vibrato in the way Holiday had done in her glory days. However, Lee made her own unique vocal statements in the song, too, choosing alternate notes to sing on the title text, and reaching much lower on "explain" than Holiday ever did. At the end, Lee made the song her own with heartbroken wailing in a high register, almost in the style of a crying belt. This huge versatility helped illuminate why Lee's singing style could not be categorized. Her ability to make her voice create an astounding number of sounds, dynamic changes, vibrato speeds, timbres, ranges, and styles has remained unparalleled in the canon of jazz and popular music.

"Change My Mind" further demonstrated Lee's struggle with pitch and sustaining energy, while "Lean on Me" gave Lee a hard-swinging blues to sink her teeth into. This bit of extra firmness and confidence were enough to firmly establish Lee's voice in a familiar, proven genre that, even with her physical challenges, allowed her to be showcased at her finest. Lee literally leaned more into each pitch when she sang the blues, so the extra energy and emphasis with which she delivered her vocal lines provided ample support for her pitches and rhythms. Overall, *Natural Woman* provided fans with some new music presented in classy Lee fashion. While her blues and token jazz standard remained solidly outstanding from a musical standpoint, her vocal strength faltered a bit on the contemporary material. A few of the tracks, including "Dock of the Bay," "Everyday People," and "Please Send Me Someone to Love," featured a small ensemble of background (gospel-Motown) singers who added a great deal of stylistic quality to the recording. Initially recorded in January and February 1969, the album received remastering treatment in 2003, enabling modern fans to enjoy the recording with advancements provided by modern technology. Proud to have avoided tampering with her vocal sound in the Capitol studio, Lee expressed in a *Los Angeles Times* interview: "There's no overdubbing on the album, no sweetening."[3]

In the early 1970s Lee endured a battle with pneumonia that permanently altered her voice and lung health. Although her smoking habit finally ceased due to this illness, the damage to her breathing organs had rendered her incapable of singing at her previous masterful level. Once able to sing intricately complex rhythms and pitch series at a wide variety of ranges, tempi, and volume levels, she hereafter was forced to lean more heavily on her power to interpret lyrics and time her phrases. Her ability to sustain long lines of music suffered, as did her lung capacity and overall health, although these continued to fluctuate for many years. In the late 1970s her health challenges escalated when she experienced facial paralysis and a Ménière's disease diagnosis, but Lee pressed on, determined to continue her work and creative activity despite severe physical limitations.

Labels with which she worked in her post-Capitol years between 1974 and 1995 included Atlantic, A&M, Polydor, DRG, Harbinger Records, MusicMasters, and Chesky Records. *Let's Love*, an album collaboration with Dave Grusin and Paul McCartney, occupied Lee's efforts in 1974 at Atlantic Records. The album's genre and mood fit perfectly with Lee's gentle, somber timbre and sentimental interpretation. For this project Lee interpreted Grusin's "The Heart Is a Lonely Hunter" and McCartney's title track as easy listening selections. The up-tempo, gospel-inflected "Sweet Lov'liness," supported by a gospel choir in the background, provided an uplifting moment of inspiration amid sadder love songs. A particularly funky rendition of Irving Berlin's "Always" displayed the artist's commitment to Great American Songbook repertoire while bringing modern relevance and an impressively contemporary (even hip) sound to the repertoire for the benefit of younger listeners. Lee's exquisite rendition of Henry and Felice Mancini's "Sometimes," originally recorded in 1971 by The Carpenters, reminded listeners that heartfelt ballads were this singer's forte, and would remain her interpretive strong suit for the rest of her career.

Following her 1978 or 1979 attempt to negotiate another album with EMI Capitol Records, a member of the Artists and Repertoire division there recommended that she contact Hugh Fordin, the owner of the independent label DRG, and shop her idea to him. She was signed to the label for three LP records, but for reasons unknown, only produced one. This recording deal resulted in the 1979 album *Close Enough for Love*. The project included several quality compositions from that era, including the opening disco tune by Tom Snow called "You," a funky original ballad co-written with Dick Hazard titled "Easy Does It," and Melissa Manchester's hit "Come in from the Rain." Lee's rock ballad interpretation respected Manchester's lyric while relying on blue notes and relaxed timing. Johnny Mandel's title track yielded an intimate, tantalizingly tender moment of supreme softness. Even in her fifty-ninth year Lee demonstrated her amazing ability to weave a spell of seduction in this marvelous song. Marvin Hamlisch's "Through the Eyes of Love" received a relatively straightforward rock ballad reading while Lee's original, co-written with pianist Marian McPartland, "In the Days of Our Love" gave the singer an opportunity to showcase her nostalgic song. The most surprising selection on this album was a fast disco rendition of the Cole Porter classic "Just One of Those Things." The eclectic arrangement's rapidly moving chord progression kept the electric bassist and keyboardist playing at maximum speed. The album swung its pendulum between ultra-fast disco arrangements and ultra-slow contemporary ballads, always staying true to its modern slant.

While maintaining a busy performance calendar in 1980, Lee turned to live theater to gain experience in yet another performance genre. She was cast in *Side by Side by Sondheim*, a musical revue of songs by the esteemed Broadway composer that was produced in Detroit's Birmingham Theater for a month, beginning June 20, 1980. Pianist Paul Horner performed with Lee in this project and became her collaborative composer for the autobiographical Broadway musical *Peg* that they would produce together in 1983. The short Sondheim revue was supposedly intended for Broadway following the Detroit stint, but that never came to fruition, perhaps because Lee and Horner began working immediately on ideas for their own musical.[4] Lee's performance in the Sondheim run gained favorable reviews overall. In the May 6, 1980, issue of *The Ledger*, Lawrence DeVine wrote: "As the hostess of this get-together, Peggy Lee distracts attention from the rest of the crew by her very considerable presence, biding her time while the others carry on until it's time for Miss Peggy Lee to get up and sing."[5]

Armed with the positive response both had achieved in the Sondheim effort, Lee and Horner began crafting a musical centered around the story of Lee's life. Although the original intent was to write the entire show together, certain persons with influence persuaded Lee to also include many of her hits in the score. Much to Paul Horner's chagrin, the services of successful Broadway arranger/composer Cy Coleman were eventually solicited, and Coleman's musical ideas sometimes conflicted with Horner's. In the end, the score consisted of a mixture of Lee's cover hits, Coleman's arrangements, and Horner and Lee's new originals written to propel the story along. Rather than a dramatic storyline, however, the end result comprised a musical revue.

Thematically, *Peg* consisted of a long string of songs that Horner and Lee created specifically for the musical, including "Daddy Was a Railroad Man," a brisk tune orchestrated with the distinctive sounds of a train whistle and locomotive engine. "One Beating a Day" was a controversial song about child abuse set to an energetic Latin beat. Through this song Lee described how her stepmother treated her as a child. Critics felt this song trivialized the pain of abused children and poked fun at childhood trauma. Lee maintained that she was trying to stay lighthearted while keeping the story honest. "That's How I Learned to

Sing the Blues" brought the mood up and gave Lee a familiar place to land—in the swing of a blues song.

The ensemble support for the show consisted of a rhythm section (which remained onstage throughout the entire production) staffed by Lee's touring band: Jay Leonhart on bass, Grady Tate on drums, Mike Renzi on piano, and Bucky Pizzarelli on guitar. A twenty-six-member orchestra conducted by Larry Fallon also provided musical support at the back of the stage, and a small group of background singers was situated next to the instrumentalists. Lee herself, serving as narrator, remained onstage from beginning to end. Although a cast of twenty-two actors plus a dance troupe was originally envisioned in re-creating Lee's life story, the final production consisted solely of Lee fronting a one-woman show. Her poetic dialogue was accompanied by the orchestra. Band members recited lines corresponding to the characters of Benny Goodman, Dave Barbour, and others, which unfortunately diminished the storytelling potential of the musical. With Lee forced to bear the entire burden of the story herself, the project became an overwhelming task and massive disappointment for the star.

When the time came for Horner and Lee to mount their original show on Broadway, Lee found the advertising and publicity to be terribly insufficient. Her autobiography revealed that she had complained to her producers when they could not identify an opening date, and she attested that nothing advertising her show was ever displayed on the marquee at the Lunt-Fontanne Theater. One full-page advertisement was run in the *New York Times*, but the wrong phone number was shown. Amid these challenges, *Peg* opened December 14, 1983, and closed just a few days later on December 17, in part due to poor ticket sales.

The production elicited criticism mainly centered on the libretto. The show opened with Lee reciting poetry to describe her entrance into the world. Critics interpreted this, along with the tone of the rest of the show, as self-glorification. A review published in *Variety* offered: "A simpler, more modest approach would have been more winning. . . . [The] writing, which omits introspective insights, ironically distances

Peggy Lee in *Peg: A Musical Autobiography* (1983 Broadway show). *Photofest.*

her from the audience . . . It's not that the singer is an unattractive or cold personality. . . . But *Peg* is a Broadway show at Broadway prices, and its unsatisfying narrative presentation will probably limit its longevity."[6] Furthermore, the show's pianist, Mike Renzi, related that the

tragic subject matter was unwisely trivialized in an attempt to add humor: "Everyone warned her, by the way, about the show. It was a very
good show, but it got ridiculous, all that stuff about the beatings, and
the depression. You can allude to it, but she was trying to make it funny.
It was not."[7]

In spite of less-than-desirable critiques of the libretto and tone of
Peg, the performers earned praise from even the staunchest critics for
the show's musical excellence. Lee and her cohorts were lauded unequivocally by various reviewers, most notably in *Variety*:

> When Peggy Lee is singing, *Peg* is an entertaining show. . . . Lee's
> voice remains one of the glories of popular music. It's a distinctive
> instrument capable of delightful tonal variations, and her subtle
> phrasing and expressive lyric interpretations are unimpaired. Backed
> by an outstanding onstage orchestra, the star delivers tasty versions
> of some 26 songs, including the obligatory hits, along with a handful
> of pleasant new songs co-written with composer Paul Horner. Musi-
> cally the show is virtually flawless.[8]

A music critic from the *New York Times* wrote of the musical:

> Dressed in a flowing gown of white and silver, her head crowned by a
> halo of glitter, Peggy Lee takes to the stage of the Lunt-Fontanne
> like a high priestess ascending an altar. And *Peg*, the "musical auto-
> biography" that Miss Lee has brought to Broadway, is nothing if not
> a religious rite. In this evening of song and chat, one of our premier
> pop singers presents herself as a spiritual icon. There is some enter-
> tainment in *Peg*, not to mention some striking musicianship, but the
> show is most likely to excite those who are evangelistically devoted to
> Peggy Lee and God—ideally in that order. . . . Though Miss Lee's
> voice is a small instrument, it is usually sure in pitch. Her rhythmic
> attack can't be beat.[9]

Following the experience of mounting her own autobiographical Broadway show, with hit Capitol singles becoming achievements of her increasingly distant past, Lee continued to pursue the release of album

projects. Two particularly noteworthy albums made late in her career included projects for which Lee received more Grammy nominations. *Miss Peggy Lee Sings the Blues* came in 1988 after guitarist and music director John Chiodini suggested to Lee that she record an entire blues album. The recording session in February of that year was called during a two-week stint at The Ballroom in New York, which extended to five weeks due to the group's success and high demand. Excited about the enthusiastic audience response and the sound they had achieved, the ensemble piled into a recording studio and laid down the tracks in just two days. The album began with the classic "See See Rider," a blues waltz that set the tone for the entire album of head arrangements (songs everyone knew in their head without requiring a written chart). "Squeeze Me" continued the recorded set in its heavily swinging yet lighthearted character. Lee's consistently musical and expressive performances solidified her previously uncontested musicianship to the extent that the album received a great deal of attention. "You Don't Know" came next, providing a style of blues that contrasted with the previous selections. Having recorded this before, Lee proved that she still had all the swing, rhythmic sense, expressive compass, and pitch accuracy that characterized her artistry throughout her career. John Chiodini and Jay Leonhart contributed outstanding performances on this track, showcasing in particular Chiodini's adventurous guitar soloing, replete with blues, rock, and jazz influences. The Billie Holiday staple "Fine and Mellow" ensued in a manner that paid tribute to the late singer. The clear allusions to Holiday's style suggested that Lee, despite a lifetime of comparisons with Holiday, fearlessly aimed to honor this important contemporary influence. Pianist Mike Renzi and vibraphonist Mark Sherman both played solos on this track, providing a distinct contrast with the classic Holiday version that featured tenor saxophone soloist Lester Young. "Baby Won't You Please Come Home" provided a bluesy ballad for Lee to explore alongside the tender and poignant four-bar solos taken by Renzi, Sherman, Chiodini, and Leonhart, respectively. Lee's effective penchant for moving her audience with a heartfelt ballad enhanced this track, proving that age was no match for her perennial artistry. Her timing and phrasing, matched with a secure sense of pitch and innate blues style, provided everything the singer needed to effectively paint a performance of lasting value. The brief but beautiful solo passages offered by each member of her quartet clinched the fact that this was a recording master to be treasured.

The Leiber and Stoller hit "Kansas City" followed, yielding a familiar tune for the ensemble. This arrangement was necessarily simpler and more raw than the 1966 Quincy Jones version had been, as the latter was scored for a much larger band, and this particular recording session was planned rather quickly. The lack of any planned arrangements made this session even more special for Lee's fans, as it featured pure, completely improvised jazz. Critics of Lee who considered her exclusively a popular artist—not a jazz artist—ought to have taken notice of this particular outing that proved she was as skilled an improviser as anyone. Her band delivered stunning performances on this recording and proved that they belonged among the finest jazz performers in the world when the album was nominated for a Grammy award.

"Love Me" proceeded at a powerful yet slow swing pace. Chiodini's rhythmically playful solo revealed his predilection for exploring a variety of metrical tricks including double-time. Mark Sherman's vibraphone solo provided another taste of the aural diversity of this band. "Beale Street" continued the common blue thread woven by each of the previous songs, lightening the mood and giving the impression that Lee may have been poised to begin an entirely new career as a blues singer. Her remarkable ease with the style gave a resplendent glow over this and other songs on the album, firmly fixing her name among the greatest blues singers of all time. "Ain't Nobody's Business If I Do" gave Lee an opportunity to place her original mark on this storied tune. The superslow pace of this song, an aspect that often defeated lesser singers, proved that no tempo was too slow for Lee to maintain her unique mastery over her audience's attention. The enormously talented and well-partnered band created a deep groove that highlighted Lee's ineffable timing and phrasing talents. The recording ended with a memorable and tender rendition of Billie Holiday's signature song, "God Bless the Child." On this track, the Holiday influence reappeared, yet Lee's own style and musicianship won out as the predominant qualities governing this glorious version of a timeless song. That this masterpiece of an album attained a Grammy nomination came as no surprise; it captured the essence of Lee's genius in crafting moment after moment of improvisational gold with her extraordinary band. Blues fans ought not to discount this outing on the basis of the singer's relatively advanced age—musical greatness and fresh interpretive ideas drip from every song.

In late August and early September 1988, Lee undertook an ambitious project of recording a collection of songs by iconic American composer Harold Arlen—many of which were unfamiliar to the general population. The lack of familiar Arlen classics on this recording posed unique marketing challenges for her producer and made it difficult to find financial backing. Fourteen songs were recorded with an octet led by producer-arranger Keith Ingham. Lee, faced with the pressure of recording an unknown collection of works by a timeless composer such as Arlen, delayed the album's release until 1993 when the Harbinger label was found to be a good fit. Rarely heard selections on this album included a gentle rendering of the title track "Love Held Lightly," a swinging arrangement of "Love's a Necessary Thing" with trombone and trumpet solos, the humorous and nonsensical "Buds Won't Bud," a Truman Capote lyric set to a slow bossa nova "Can You Explain?" and a moderately swinging "Wait'll It Happens to You." "Come on, Midnight" sported a slowly descending melody line exploring half steps and dissonant intervals, which gave Lee no trouble whatsoever navigating her pitch precision. "Bad for Each Other" possessed a tongue-in-cheek sentiment made more interesting with the vibraphonic commentary between Lee's sung phrases and unique instrumental orchestration.

Lee's final noteworthy album, *The Peggy Lee Songbook: There'll Be Another Spring*, took shape around a group of her original songs. Recorded in early November 1989, this second album on the MusicMasters label also earned a Grammy nomination and was produced by her guitarist and collaborative composer, John Chiodini. Considering a wide swath of time from early in Lee's career to the present, the group brought together her signature song, "Fever" (albeit with newly written verses), several originals from decades past, four brand-new songs co-written by Chiodini, and one interesting collaboration, "Circle in the Sky," co-written by composer Emilio Palame. The album successfully represented a microcosm of Lee's original work that spanned more than four decades but emphasized her newer compositions co-written by contemporary collaborators. "Over the Wheel," a Chiodini-Lee piece, dealt with letting go of the past. Their "Boomerang" sported a playful promise of returning to a loved one "just like the hound dog do."

Pianist Emilio Palame performed with Lee from 1984 to 1995, eventually serving as her musical director. He related that he began playing a tune during a rehearsal with Lee, and, liking the melody, Lee sat down with him and began writing lyrics. "Pretty amazing—actually it all came out at once," he remarked.[10] Unable to finish the tune at the rehearsal, Lee called Palame around midnight that evening and without saying hello, began to sing what would become the bridge: "Forever, forever, I'll love you forever." Palame remembered going to the piano and filling in the chords over the phone. The only part of the process on which they disagreed was the final line. Lee wanted "circle in the air" while Palame preferred ending with the title line, "circle in the sky."[11] Lee won out and the song's transcendent finish left the listener with a metaphor that defied concise definition.

Some of Lee's well-worn originals made an appearance on this recording, dressed up in new arrangements. These included the Mandel collaboration "The Shining Sea," of which John Chiodini shared: "When she got to 'his hands, his strong, brown hands,' I could see them. That's never happened. I could actually see them. Not imagine them . . . actually see them by this person planting that in my head."[12] The recording also featured new versions of the Sonny Burke collaboration "He's a Tramp" and two Victor Young settings of Lee's lyrics: "Where Can I Go without You" and "Johnny Guitar." While these late versions lacked the peak of Lee's vocal beauty captured decades earlier, they maintained her emotional connection to the text and music and evoked her innate skill for effective phrasing.

Lee's determination to continue recording in spite of her worsening physical health yielded this final product that was respected and admired by her peers. However, signs of her vocal decline were readily apparent throughout the project. Needing oxygen to sustain her during these studio sessions, her previously strong energized breath simply could not produce the supported tone of more youthful days, so her vocal timbre suffered. However, her timing and phrasing, having long been her strong suits, continued to serve her well.

The strength of this album lay not so much in Lee's performing abilities but in her songwriting skill. Finishing her illustrious career with a recording celebrating her writing talent rather than her singing allowed Lee to place one more outstanding album into her large discography of recorded work, regardless of her current state of vocal health. This collection was intended as the first of a series planned both by Lee and the MusicMasters label to highlight her as a songwriter. When informing the press, the record label announced the project as "a release of our first of a multi-volume project entitled *The Peggy Lee Songbook.*"[13] Lee had considered making the second volume devoted entirely to music she had written with Dave Barbour, but for unknown reasons no further albums were recorded or released. The long impressive era of her six-decade recording career had come to an end, and Lee secured her fourteenth Grammy nomination to show for it.

Lee's success as a prolific Capitol Records artist extended into the sixth decade of her life and the fourth decade of her career. With help from other record labels, Lee continued to record outstanding albums and pack performance venues, even as she approached her seventieth year. Though her venture into the world of Broadway yielded a somewhat less noteworthy result than the rest of her work, Lee moved forward with confidence. The phenomenal success of her later albums served as testimony to the artist's staying power, immense talent, and much-deserved respect among her peers.

10

THAT'S NOT ALL THERE IS

Following her victory at the Grammy Awards in 1969, Lee released a few more records with Capitol that explored the changing landscape of American popular music in the direction of rock and contemporary pop. Her work in 1970s' pop music reflected an important transitional stage in her artistic development. During this period she proved her willingness to evolve with the changing tastes of music consumers by honoring contemporary composers. Her recording diligence led her to more Grammy attention in the 1980s and elicited invitations to continue performing at some of the world's most acclaimed venues, even in the 1990s, her eighth decade. After her death in 2002 Lee's popularity surged again. This opened the door for Capitol Records, in cooperation with Lee's estate, to put forth a string of recordings comprised of material that Lee had recorded but had never released, as well as previously released songs that were treated to twenty-first-century improvements in engineering and sound production. Lee's six-decade career included forays into a wide variety of genres, over one thousand recording masters, and success in radio, film music, acting, and songwriting, in addition to the outstanding live performance legacy for which she was revered. Trends observed when investigating Lee's original music have shed new light on the value of her catalog. Lee's peers and collaborators have offered overwhelmingly positive assessments of the artist's talent, legacy, and consistently impressive body of work.

Although Lee was not known for her work in the rock realm, she released an album in 1970 called *Make It with You* that highlighted new music by young songwriters John Lennon, Paul McCartney, Neil Sedaka, Paul Anka, Gordon Jenkins, Lew Spence, and David Gates, among others. Jazz great Benny Golson arranged and conducted most of the sessions, though pianist Mike Melvoin did the honors for "You'll Remember Me," which became a hit for Lee on the easy listening chart. The songs on this album created a nostalgic backward-looking mood of longing so appropriate for Lee at this point in her career and middle-aged life. Even this unlikely genre (contemporary '70s pop) inspired complimentary feedback for Lee: "Many who participated in (this) process now concur that these songs may very well be receiving their until-now untold best circa '70 treatment. From Peggy Lee. Magnificent. Natural. . . . An entertainer who relishes her music, beguiles her audiences . . . Sings . . . straightaway in a 24-carat absolutely bewitching style. Peggy Lee touches on all the best . . . songs from all seasons and sources . . . gives each of them an astonishing, thoughtfully-wrought interpretation."[1] For this project Lee tackled "The Long and Winding Road" and "Make It with You," both famous songs amid a slew of less-well-known modern songs. Her soft-spoken approach to the album was cradled supportively by Golson's soft rock arrangements, making this recording fit in well with Lee's evolving easy listening catalog.

The 2008 EMI rerelease of this album included four additional songs: "Pieces of Dreams," "Didn't We," "You're Driving Me Crazy," and "No More"; each of which fit well with the melancholic theme firmly established by the original album. Lee's ability to pull heart-strings was never better illustrated than in the first two added tracks. "You're Driving Me Crazy" provided a much-needed moment of light-hearted, bluesy swing before finishing the recording with another blue ballad. This project's poignancy and truth proved that Lee was still evolving as an interpretive artist and worth continuing to watch.

Other contemporary pop albums Lee released after her Grammy win included *Bridge Over Troubled Water* from April 1970 and *Where Did They Go* from 1971. The former recording, conducted by Mike

Melvoin, contained material comprising a concept pointing toward difficult love relationships. The title track showed Lee singing with more vibrato than usual, possibly to match the volume of the large accompanying ensemble. The blues-soaked "The Thrill Is Gone" impressed with its strong instrumental orchestration exploring a touch of 1970s' funk, giving Lee a chance to wail amid her text-based improvisation. This album seemed more heavily influenced by blues and rock than her previous album, convincingly presenting an entirely different sound than anything Lee had recorded. "What Are You Doing the Rest of Your Life?" suited Lee well as a relatively new Academy Award–nominated song. Written for the 1969 film *The Happy Ending*, "What Are You Doing" was penned by the acclaimed songwriting team Alan Bergman, Marilyn Bergman, and Michel Legrand.

Where Did They Go also included tracks composed by young contemporaries Kris Kristofferson, Burt Bacharach, Joe Raposo, George Harrison, Stephen Sondheim, and Andrew Lloyd Webber. The title track amply opened the project asking the question that set the stage for the rest of the album. A mellow exploration of heartfelt sentiments followed, ranging from remembering lost love, to asking to be loved, to encouraging the world to sing. The varied repertoire ranged from musical theater pieces to radio pop songs. Joe Raposo's "Sing" cheerily provided an up-tempo reminder to keep a positive attitude through music while the Bergmans' "I Was Born in Love with You" gave Lee another haunting ballad through which to weave her symphonically enhanced spell. Ending with Beatle George Harrison's "My Sweet Lord," Lee finished the project with an air of spirituality appropriate to the soul-searching and longing theme woven throughout the album.

Lee's final album for Capitol Records was appropriately titled *Norma Deloris Egstrom from Jamestown, North Dakota*, effectively bringing her marathon Capitol career full circle. Her title suggested a backward look over her years at the label and ended her tenure there precisely where she began thirty years earlier. However, instead of featuring career hits and highlights, the album bravely broke new repertoire ground while bidding her Capitol listening audience farewell. The album continued Lee's projection into the contemporary pop trend she had embraced and adapted to throughout her career. The project opened with "Love Song," Lee's final single for Capitol, which peaked at number thirty-four on *Billboard*'s easy listening chart. Lee utilized her characteristically large ensemble to provide a wealth of musical colors and plenty of power behind her. The rest of the material followed suit, both stylistically and thematically, and centered around contemporary pop explorations of male/female relationships, always with a hint of longing. The project ended with two Great American Songbook standards. "The More I See You" presented a meaningful and novel small-ensemble take on an old familiar song, featuring guitar and percussion factoring prominently in the accompaniment. For her final song, Lee delivered a poignant "I'll Be Seeing You," famously a swan song for many artists, projects, and concerts due to the emotional goodbye it expressed. Lee's quivering voice in the last few phrases evoked strong emotions of sadness at parting. One critic remarked about the album: "By the standards Peggy Lee herself has set (no others can take her measure), the new album isn't particularly outstanding. But, as always, there are three or four stunning bands here —'I'll Be Seeing You,' 'I'll Get By' and 'Someone Who Cares'—that reach the highest level of her accomplishments, and that is high indeed."[2]

These late Capitol records, while perhaps not selling millions of copies, still afforded Lee a strong showing in the changing musical landscape during the splintering of musical styles that characterized the 1970s. That decade broke popular music into streams of rock, pop, metal, disco, funk, jazz fusion, easy listening, soft rock, and other genres. Though by no means attempting to try every style, Lee paved her own way in the newer pop sound. Like jazz trumpeter Miles Davis, Lee patently avoided the tendency of most aging recording artists to stay focused on early stylistic successes and hits as years passed. Instead, Lee adapted to changing tastes while gravitating toward her strengths of textual interpretation, high-quality arranging, and gentle singing. Her commitment to expressing a well-written lyric never dimmed, nor was her talent for it surpassed.

In the 1980s Lee's lifelong work was confirmed and rewarded by Jim Henson when he created a Muppet with a name bearing a striking resemblance: "Miss Piggy Lee." The "Miss Piggy" character, decked out in formal stage performance clothes, a glamorous demeanor, false eyelashes, and a penchant for singing, underwent a name shortening to avoid a too-close-for-comfort association with the living star. Lee expressed that she was flattered to be imitated and slightly caricatured in such a way. She was pleased that the younger generation was introduced to her performing legacy and delighted to have been chosen as the model for the preeminent female puppet character in the family of Muppets.[3]

The Quintessential Peggy Lee, a video-recorded concert from the summer of 1984, was released in 1985 and has remained one of the only key resources that captured both video and audio for an entire live performance given by Lee and her touring band. This film documented Lee's performance with the New Jersey Symphony Orchestra at Resorts International in Atlantic City, and it featured Mike Renzi on piano, John Chiodini on guitar, Jay Leonhart on bass, Vinnie Johnson on drums, and Mark Sherman on vibraphone and percussion. Though edited and shortened from the actual live performance, the video captured twenty-seven songs the diva performed at that concert. Concertgoer George Kurek shared his thoughts about attending this performance:

> This was a free concert of a seemingly endless string of Peggy's songs. As an appreciative member of that audience I marveled at her stamina—her health was not robust at the time, but she drew strength from the cheering audience song after song. Near the end of the concert fans had left their seats and crowded the area below the stage (despite her caution about violating fire regulations) and strained to be near to the star. The live program generated an excitement that the video could only hint at. . . . Peggy's show lasted much longer than the edited tape; cut was some warm banter that Peg made with the audience. . . . At the concert's end both star and her fans were left exhausted—she from her singing, we from applauding.[4]

This video recording holds a vital place in Lee's recording output along-side her more than one thousand in-studio audio recordings. The concert visibly displayed Lee's command over musical details including instrumentalists paying close attention to her gestures, head motions, and guiding vocal nuances, and her unmistakable rapport with her audience. Even at sixty-four, Lee's mastery over pitch, rhythm, style, stage presence, song list construction, poise, and lyrical interpretation were visually and aurally documented in this recording.

Throughout her career Lee gleaned compliments from leaders in the music industry as well as her peers. In the liner notes of her 1988 *Miss Peggy Lee Sings the Blues* album, Gene Lees gushed:

> There have been few careers in American music to compare to Peggy Lee's. Miss Lee evolved into our greatest singing actress, producing in her performances of songs—many of which she wrote—indelible character sketches of women in all walks of life. Her work has never flagged, the quality of it has never faltered, and she is still at it. . . . I think of her work as Stanislavskian, because instead of projecting a song "at" you, she illuminates it from within. . . . It's as if her songs are not so much heard as overheard.[5]

Peter Clayton, a jazz critic from Great Britain, asserted that Peggy Lee was "quite simply the finest singer in the history of popular music."[6] Such lofty compliments and accolades gathered around Lee as her fans and longtime followers watched her approach the end of her career. Peggy Lee's legacy not only endured subsequent to her passing in 2002, it continued to grow. Several new album projects compiled from her unreleased work and prior recordings were treated to twenty-first-century technological improvements. These additional collections have continued to be churned out to this day, shedding new light upon the expanse of work Lee accomplished during her lifetime. This rich and prolific period of posthumous work has testified to her music's relevance and value.

One such noteworthy compilation remade the 1975 A&M album *Mirrors* as a thirtieth anniversary project in 2005. Modern fans have reaped the benefit of hearing the painstakingly restored best possible versions of those recording sessions since the reissue became available. *Peggy Lee Sings Leiber and Stoller* included songs from *Mirrors* as well as four others by the songwriting duo that had not been part of the original album's sessions. The remake began with "Kansas City," a rousing performance of the duo's best-known songs, arranged by Quincy Jones for his 1962 *Blues Cross Country* project with Lee. Lee's confident bluesy singing with the muted trumpet created a strong start to this celebration of Leiber and Stoller gems. The album continued with several theatrical songs relying on Lee's storytelling prowess. "Some Cats Know," "Don Juan," and "I Ain't Here" required drama and context, which Lee generously provided, although never to the degree of creating melodrama. The latter two were, like "Kansas City," additional songs Leiber and Stoller added for the reissue. Remix producer Peter Stoller explained: "'Don Juan' and 'I Ain't Here' are two tracks that were rejected from the original album. When they started working on *Mirrors*, they looked at going in a couple of different directions. One was more of a pop album and one was a more experimental album. Once they picked a direction . . . these tracks no longer fit. They didn't stylistically make sense with the album they decided to make. As a consequence, they sat in the can from 1975 until we put this out."[7]

"I'm a Woman" followed as the fifth track, representing a decidedly strong moment of female assertiveness in an album that explored a variety of viewpoints and perspectives. This well-known Leiber and Stoller hit was the final song in the quartet that was added to the previous *Mirrors* lineup, and for good reason. With it Lee had already scored a Top 100 placement at number fifty-four on the 1962 pop charts; and she used it as the title song on her 1963 Capitol album. The song was a reminder of the successful partnership Lee had already forged with this acclaimed songwriting team.

Though the 2005 reissue included all of the original songs on *Mirrors* (and then some), Peter Stoller noted: "The entire album was resequenced from the original *Mirrors* album. Jerry [Leiber], in particular, was very involved in the idea of reconceiving the entire album rather than just putting things before and after the original record in its original sequence."[8] Since the concept and direction of the album had changed since the 1975 experience, the production team decided to order the songs in a manner that reflected their new focus and additional repertoire.

Peter explained that he viewed the project as having two acts. Act One included the first five tracks: "Kansas City" through "I'm a Woman," referring mostly to a separate period and style, whereas Act Two constituted the rest of the project, which contained exclusively tracks that had been included in *Mirrors*, although in a different order. "Ready to Begin Again (Manya's Song)" began this second act reflecting a more mature persona than that shown in the previous songs. It depicted an aging woman whose teeth and hair were no longer her own. The "boom-chick" of the accompanying texture brought to mind "Is That All There Is?" and effectively replied to the inquiry of the Grammy-winning song with a resigned air of measured decisiveness. "Professor Hauptmann's Performing Dogs" opened with the sounds of a circus. A bark-like vocal call, tuba, cymbals, and comical instruments like whistles and toy xylophones painted clear images of big top–style entertainment. The theatrical bent of the second act songs unified them strongly. "A Little White Ship" ensued, set to themes of Stoller's previously composed *Suite Allegro* for violin, clarinet, cello, and bassoon. It dealt with Tennessee Williams's play *Camino Real* and served as a sample of music Stoller wrote for a possible musical adaptation of the Williams play. Lee skillfully wove the chromatically challenging musical tale with deftness and pitch-perfect precision.

The next track, "Tango," appeared as a tribute to the recently murdered silent film actor Ramón Navarro. Lee's approach to this unusual song included spoken text at the initial vocal entrance, followed by a gentle ballad offering tenderness and tragedy. The team effectively portrayed a skipping record in two sections by repeating a short segment over and over again in a meter contrasting with the rest of the song—an overtly theatrical effect timed with the reference to a tango found on an old broken record: "over it plays . . . over it plays."[9] This song showcased the ease with which Lee's artistry complemented the literal depictions of theatricality teeming throughout the songs of Leiber and Stoller.

In sharp contrast to the previous song, "I've Got Them Feelin' Too Good Today Blues" followed lightheartedly with a whimsical, carnival-like accompaniment providing the foundation for Lee's cheery vocal line. Composed for the film *The Phynx*, Johnny Mandel's burlesque-style arrangement of this song represented a throwback to ragtime and vaudeville. "The Case of M. J." recalled the strange Truman Capote short story *Miriam*, as a psychoanalytical exploration of the tale set to another theme from Stoller's *Suite Allegro*. This selection blurred the lines between literature, theater, and music, effectively merging the three in a fresh uncharted manner. Lee alternated between singing and speaking, as if transitioning back and forth between performing a song versus reciting lines of a play. Her comfort with this genre-busting work proved she was no amateur in such complex ventures.

Based on a haiku poem, "I Remember" retained a sparseness and simple beauty that offered Lee a blank canvas on which she hummed lightly amid the delivery of a few brief lines of text. Her simplicity and straightforward performance served well the minimalism embodied in the short song. Composed for *The Madwoman of Chaillot*, "Say It" was intended to be sung by an older woman to a younger man. According to the album notes, this song was Lee's favorite piece from the *Mirrors* sessions. Opening with a piano solo, the rich orchestral arrangement boasting robust strings, muted trumpet, and harp provided a lush back-drop for Lee's tender declarations and invitations. The vocal energy Lee utilized for this piece remained strong and well supported, demon-strating that her technical skill was still present in spades. Truly a beau-tifully sung performance, "Say It" deserved far more widespread atten-tion than it ever attained. The album continued with "Longings for a Simpler Time," a song highlighting memories of yesteryear. Replete with the classic Leiber and Stoller chromatic pickup notes, rubato (out of time) passages, fermatas (holds on one note), and challenging melod-ic intervals, this song painted a picture of nostalgia made even more poignant via Johnny Mandel's wonderful arranging skill.

The Grammy-winning masterpiece "Is That All There Is?" finished the album. Not included on the original *Mirrors* outing, the song was first added to the project (as the opening song) in a 1989 A&M reissue of *Mirrors.* "Is That All There Is?" represented an appropriate swan song for the 2005 project in more ways than one. It proudly stood as the pinnacle of Lee's collaboration with the Leiber and Stoller songwriting team and ended the recording with the strongest song the trio had ever created together. Moreover, it also posed the consummate existential question, which made it impossible to conceive placing it anywhere in the song list except at the end.

Peggy Lee Live in London captured an outstanding March 1977 performance by Lee and her touring band at the Palladium in London. This three-CD plus DVD set was released in 2015. Representing the singer at age fifty-seven after years of health challenges that left her lungs weak, this four-disc recording showed her resolve and power of expression to be stronger than ever. In Neil Sedaka's "The Hungry Years," Lee's full-sounding vibrato enhanced the pop ballad with an air of authentic longing and an emotional connection to the lyric. "Here, Now" featured background gospel singers, horns, and strings in a beautifully harmonized ensemble blend that made this track stand out as particularly uplifting. The total sum of these recorded performances revealed Lee's continued commitment to balancing her concert repertoire with selections that varied tempo, mood, key, style, and emotional intensity.

Following the concert, the artist remained apparently unconvinced about the recording's readiness for release. *Jazz Times* writer Christopher Loudon reported that "Lee, notoriously picky about live albums, wasn't fully satisfied with the results and asked that another Palladium concert also be recorded a week later. But Polydor rushed the album's release, only using material from the first date."[10] She may have been relieved to have known that future audiences would have the benefit of both concert recordings via the 2015 reissue, which also released the second date's recordings for the first time.

In 2004 Capitol Records released a video documentary of Lee's career called *Fever: The Music of Peggy Lee.*[11] It shared twenty film and television performance clips of the star, some of her Snader telescriptions, and numerous interviews with family, friends, and music colleagues. In addition, the project showed her *What's My Line?* game show appearance, and even a shampoo commercial in which Lee had been cast. Duets with Mel Tormé, Andy Williams, Judy Garland, and Bing Crosby revealed the collaborative side of Lee, while other clips showed her broad spectrum of musical and artistic development from her early years until her final performances. The documentary created an overview of Lee's career from the viewpoint of her closest family members, friends, and musical collaborators, as the film included several interview clips quoting those who knew Lee best.

Even amid challenges of lung illness and physical weakness that confined her to a wheelchair onstage in her final years, the star continued to present memorable quality performances. Lee's final public performances solidified her legacy as a perennially professional, nuanced, outstanding performing artist. Pianist Marian McPartland described watching Lee perform at the 1993 Concord Jazz Festival in a wheelchair and sunglasses:

> Her voice was sinuous and soft and beguiling. You could hear every word. It wasn't loud. In contrast to the way some people think they have to shriek . . . I remember she had on this beautiful headdress, or headband . . . She just looked gorgeous . . . she really made a very attractive picture and she did a very good show. Needless to say, there were millions of people milling around, wanting to give her a hug. I was pleased that she was so glad to see me. That might have been the last time I saw her.[12]

Neither Lee's seventy-three years nor her failing health kept her from maintaining a public presence in the music world through her eighth decade of life. She determined to continue performing, and she still managed to receive invitations from world-class venues to the very end.

On May 9, 1994, the International Ballroom of the Beverly Hilton
Hotel resounded with cascades of applause and loving affirmation of a
timeless music legend. Peggy Lee was honored that evening with a gala
tribute event in Beverly Hills by the Society of Singers, an organization
whose mission was to help fellow musicians struggling with financial
crisis. They honored Lee with a Lifetime Achievement Award at the
Beverly Hilton, and other singing artists Natalie Cole, Rosemary Clooney, and k.d. lang paid fitting musical tributes to Lee, performing "I'm a
Woman," "Heart," and "Black Coffee," respectively. When a microphone was handed to the wheelchair-confined Lee, the room became
utterly silent. "You know," she began, "it's been said by many great
philosophers that love is the greatest force in the universe, and I think
I've felt and heard more love here in this room tonight." She went on to

Peggy Lee and Mike Stoller performing at a 40th-anniversary event. *Courtesy of the Leiber & Stoller Archive.*

compliment the level of talent shown by those gathering to honor her and finished with "I don't think I'd better say much more, or I'll cry. So I'll try singing."[13] Starting with Gershwin's "'S Wonderful" and ending with a fitting gesture of appreciation for the organization's public honor, Lee closed with a touching, heartfelt rendition of her original song "Here's to You," originally written for Cary Grant to sing to his daughter. Through this peerless song, Lee melodiously bid farewell and wished those in attendance "good luck" and "Godspeed" in several languages before closing with her favorite blessing, "angels on your pillows," a bedtime prayer she used to bid good night to her daughter, Nicki. The masterful timing, meticulous phrasing, and tear-jerking expression that were Lee's alone shimmered through this penultimate performance. Pop music arranger, songwriter, and pianist Artie Butler expressed: "She cast a spell over the whole room. The spell was her secret weapon, you know. . . . In a tiny voice, she did more with that song than I ever heard anyone do with a song in my life."[14]

Lee's final public concert occurred at the Hollywood Bowl on August 2, 1995, with longtime cohorts from Capitol Records Mel Tormé and George Shearing. Both male stars, for whatever reason, would not speak to their female co-star. Back in 1992 Lee had been paired with Tormé for a Hollywood Bowl performance that exhibited Tormé's lack of collegiality. The wife of Shearing's manager shared: "Mel Tormé was a very, *very* difficult person . . . so multitalented, but anger and spitefulness penetrated everything he did. He was a man who wanted and needed all the attention, and he did some very mean-spirited things to see that he got it."[15] Younger Tormé even arranged for Lee to open for *him* whenever they shared a performance. In 1992 the audience would have none of that, offering Lee far more adulation and applause than Tormé received.[16]

Lee's pianist for the 1995 Bowl show, Emilio Palame, remembered Lee's attitude backstage before the concert: "She cared so much about what people thought of her. . . . And she took it really seriously. She wanted people to know how much it meant to her. She wanted to connect with them. To have them feel what she felt."[17] Although this was to be her final major performance, Lee's harpist and friend Stella Castellucci confirmed that her co-stars, Shearing and Tormé, "completely ignored her. She was very hurt."[18] Regardless of the stings strewn her way by fellow Capitol legends, Lee's final Hollywood Bowl concert (her final large public performance) was warmly received by the public, as shown by the almost two-hour procession of fans she greeted backstage following the show.

Lee's final studio recording was taped later that month at Group IV Studios, Hollywood, for *Benny Carter Songbook*, a celebration of Carter's original songs, accompanied on alto saxophone by Carter himself, John Heard on bass, Gene DiNovi on piano, and Sherman Ferguson on drums. Performing together "I See You," Lee still possessed her pitch and rhythmic accuracy, as well as meaningful phrasing and poignancy. Carter's thoughtful commentary played alongside Lee's sung lines—filling whenever she sustained long notes or rested—revealed a sincere and beautiful conversation between old friends. A deliciously authentic rendering of this lovely song, "I See You" fittingly stood as Lee's final recording.

Following this session, Lee's health grew more and more weak, and planned performances had to be canceled. In October 1998 Lee suffered a debilitating stroke and never recovered fully. Her daughter accepted her Songwriters Hall of Fame Award in June 1999 in New York, alongside other recipients Tim Rice, Bruce Springsteen, Bobby Darin (posthumously), and Bart Howard. That she was honored during her lifetime as a major songwriter, along with other famous hit makers, cemented Lee's creative legacy as one standing among the legacies of the most important song creators of the twentieth century.

In January 2002, Lee and over one hundred other music artists won a lawsuit against Universal (which owned the rights to Decca) for underpayment of royalties. This victory once again marked Lee as a proponent of artists' rights in a world increasingly hostile toward music creators. The lawsuit helped set the stage for the ongoing battle modern songwriters have continued to wage against music piracy and streaming platforms intent upon cheating songwriters out of their due earnings.

This cause has faithfully been taken up by countless composers and lyricists who lobby with Congress to pass laws protecting songwriters' rights to a fair wage for their work. Lee maintained that music must not be free because it costs songwriters and performing artists many thousands of dollars and hours to create. Artists who continue this fight may thank Peggy Lee and her contemporaries for pioneering the path toward fair pay.

Passing away from a heart attack on January 21, 2002, Lee finally drew her last breath. Her storied career and musical legacy turned the page to a chapter yet unwritten. From her pop recordings of the early 1970s that celebrated young songwriters and the changing musical landscape of the last third of the twentieth century, to posthumous releases, Peggy Lee's recording legacy continued to grow. Scores of contemporary artists have maintained an affection for Lee's work by arranging her timeless songs to suit the evolving jazz and traditional pop genres of the twenty-first century.

Upon consideration of Lee's work as a prolific song creator, patterns emerge that reward deeper exploration. Characteristics of her singing style necessarily informed her compositional style. Lee composed songs for her own voice to sing, so her poetic style perfectly matched her musical sense of understatement and conversational delivery.[19] This ideal union of poetry and voice resulted in countless recordings that jazz aficionados esteem among the finest ever produced. Few other great jazz singers (if any) benefited from a vast amount of repertoire written specifically for their own voice by the very same poetic mind that governed that voice. The breadth of Lee's work showed staggering diversity and versatility. Genres ranged from the blues to pop standards, and from Broadway musical songs to film scores, while her range of themes also exhibited unconventionality and enormous expanse. Lee's talent for wedding words to music manifested itself in songs that bestowed directness, clarity, sophistication, irony, humor, sensitivity, romance, poignancy, and impressive depth upon the grateful listener.

When considering the element of variety within songs written by Lee, one must not neglect the plethora of methods through which she transferred her themes and ideas. Poetic style and prosody were indispensable tools she utilized to tailor her lyrics to the corresponding music. Direct, descriptive communication of an idea versus the use of metaphor or symbolism represented an important distinction in Lee's work. In eliciting a speech-like, casual style she deftly timed the rhythm of the musical line in perfect synchronicity with the rhythm of the lyrics being sung. In "I Don't Know Enough about You" Lee managed to fully embody the sense of rhythmic swing with the swinging pattern of the words she selected to match the music. Here she exhibited her talent for placing proper emphasis on key words and syllables at musically appropriate moments without disrupting the flow and swing of the music. In "He's a Tramp" Lee delivered a direct, conversational, yet sensual lyric in a song composed for a dog to sing to other dogs while describing a dog she loved. The tremendous success of this song owed a great debt to the vivid imagination of this gifted lyricist.

"I Love Being Here with You" proved Lee's ability to express directly through description or narration. Lee's lyrics described a litany of items she loved, almost in the manner of a list, topping all of them with the statement embodied in the title. This "list" method also appeared in "Where Can I Go without You?" (composed by Victor Young), showing Lee's penchant for a descriptive, concise poetic style. In "There'll Be Another Spring" (composed by Hubie Wheeler) Lee's lyrics flowed extemporaneously, exuding a natural, gentle feeling of calm declamation. Johnny Mandel's "The Shining Sea," from the 1966 film *The Russians Are Coming! The Russians Are Coming!*, included some repetition of phrases in a highly nostalgic manner, as though the singer daydreamed her way through the song.

Aside from a direct, declamatory style of writing, Lee also frequently explored a metaphorical approach. In so doing she proved that she could not only compose concise, beautifully descriptive lyrics but also imply meanings behind a veil of symbolism. In "I'm Gonna Go Fishin'," co-written by Duke Ellington for the film *Anatomy of a Murder*, Lee discreetly used metaphors to represent characters in the film. In this case, the "trout" represented a man who would be hunted by the sheriff, himself an avid fisherman.

In "Circle in the Sky" by Emilio Palame, Lee's symbolist approach to describing an eternal love relationship produced the ethereal, transcendent message contained in her lyrics. The circle never received full explanation, and the vague, nebulous words of the song reached new heights through their sheer ineffability. These lyrics evoked romanticism through the symbolic nuances of implied meaning. "Forever our love is stronger than a star" and "the circle will be everywhere, the circle in the air."[20] begged further explanation, but none was provided. This nebulous style of poetry called to mind the work of French symbolist poets from the late nineteenth and early twentieth centuries (Stéphane Mallarmé, Arthur Rimbaud, and Paul Verlaine) who specialized in exploring suggestive, implied meaning in their poetic works.[21] Lee's willingness to venture into such diverse poetic styles exhibited her versatility and creativity as a song lyricist.

Mike Stoller, Peggy Lee, and Jerry Leiber (1990s). *Courtesy of the Leiber & Stoller Archive.*

Lee's compositions possessed a number of distinctive characteristics in the realm of phrase structure. In many of her songs Lee opted for short phrases and subphrases, often inserting rests between related sections of text. This practice fared consistently with Lee's understated singing style and preference for silence to balance vocal phrases. In one of Lee's most celebrated ballads, "There'll Be Another Spring" by Hubie Wheeler, words were sung only in pairs followed by brief silences, leaving the audience hanging on every word. This method proved to be quite effective in depicting a wistful, melancholic scene while causing the audience to listen much more intently. One- and two-measure phrases appeared commonly in Lee's slow and medium-tempo pieces, giving the vocalist only a few seconds to impress the audience with a bit of text. This structure placed a greater emphasis on the lyrics and less on the vocal quality itself. Another salient aspect of Lee's phrase construction dealt with anacrusis and crusis. She tended to begin her songs' phrases on an anacrusis (pickup or offbeat) rather than on a crusis (strong downbeat). This quality appeared consistently throughout one of Lee's most famous songs, "I Love Being Here With You." Beginning phrases of text before or after the beginning of the corresponding musical phrase set Lee's songs apart from those of many other songwriters and contributed to the unpredictable, conversational nature of so many of her finest songs. Significantly, the time Lee most often chose to place the phrase onset in synchrony with the musical phrase (often on the downbeat) occurred at the bridge of many songs. This provided added strength and reinforcement to the bridge as the climactic moment of the work. Examples of songs that utilized anacrusic phrase beginnings in the main theme while using crusic phrase beginnings at the bridge included "I Love Being Here with You" and "I Don't Know Enough about You." Lee not only experimented with anacrusic textual phrases preceding musical phrases but also frequently began phrases of text *after* the start of the musical phrase (as in "The Shining Sea" and "Where Can I Go without You?"). Her intentionally shifting overlap of text versus musical phrasing allowed her to create songs that were rich in extemporaneity and originality.

One particular aspect of Peggy Lee's lyrical composition that greatly impressed composer John Chiodini included her vast range of themes.[22] Lee herself confessed: "I have a love of singing, of music in general, and I sort of like to feel as though I could play the role of whatever the song might require . . . and I like a song to tell a story . . . I like to have the music fit that mood."[23] Lee possessed a vivid imagination for thematic ideas and was able to construct innovative pathways for the execution of those ideas. Many of her songs shared the theme of optimism and encouragement, including "Take a Little Time to Smile," "It's a Good Day," "This Is a Very Special Day," and "There'll Be Another Spring." Lee's daughter, Nicki Lee-Foster, asserted that Lee's themes arose from her interest in writing about things currently happening on a given day:

> She liked to write about what was going on in her life at that time. "It's a Good Day" was written literally when she was just having a wonderful day. It *was* a good day! It's so simple in one way to have a song like that come out of . . . simple activity. It's really cool. She was writing about what she was experiencing right then. It was a good day for paying the bills, a good day for losing your ills—everything to gain and nothing to lose. That was the attitude of that day. It was just going beautifully.[24]

When Lee wrote lyrics for a love song, she found a unique thematic angle that had not yet been explored in other songs rather than simply settling for a thoughtless gush of romantic sentiments. For instance, to describe a budding young relationship she wrote "I Don't Know Enough about You," in which the singer ruminated about a man she wished she knew better. In "Circle in the Sky," Lee poignantly depicted a more serious, mature, boundless love with overtones of eternal destiny sweeping through the song's lyrics. In the nightclub spoof "He's a Tramp," Lee managed to believably portray the love of a street-wise canine waxing on about the dog she adored. For "Where Can I Go without You?" Lee sensitively constructed the unsuccessful journey of a heart seeking escape from a lost love. "What More Can a Woman Do?"

presented the story of a woman willing to go to extremes to show her lover how much she cared. A highly original depiction of love enveloped "Happy with the Blues," in which the singer expressed a strange contentment with an imperfect relationship. Clearly, Lee's imagination and heartfelt truth illuminated her body of original lyrics as a catalog steeped in authentic human experience.

The various genres for which Lee provided lyrics exemplified the breadth of her songwriting output to an impressive degree. The scope of her compositions covered the blues, jazz standards, popular songs, Latin songs, children's songs, film scores, country songs with blues and gospel leanings, novelty songs, and an entire Broadway musical. The diversity of genres represented in her total work revealed a truly versatile lyricist.

General trends observable upon careful study of Lee's lyric writing, including elements of poetic style, phrase structure, rhyme schemes, range of themes, and various representative genres, illustrate the depth and breadth of her abilities and help explain her demand as a leading songwriter during her lifetime. These elements of lyric writing experienced several permutations and manipulations in the hands of this master lyricist, depending on the composer setting the music and the context of the work.

Partnering with Lee's guitarist and collaborative composer, John Chiodini, the author released a 2008 album on the Rhombus Records label called *Dear Peg* that honored Lee's songwriting talents and featured a wide swath of new arrangements of her original songs, spanning several decades of Lee's output. The album also debuted a new song that was added to the Peggy Lee Songbook: "Burn It Slow," from a poem Lee had privately published in her book of poems *Softly, with Feeling*, was set to bossa nova music composed by the author. The album gained Grammy consideration for Best Traditional Pop Album in 2009. The author recently engaged in another rewarding recording session for an album on the Blujazz label called *Tish Oney with The John Chiodini Trio: The Best Part*, featuring Chiodini on guitar, Chuck Berghofer on bass, and Ray Brinker on drums. This project, celebrating contemporary songwriters, included three never-released songs that Lee wrote with Chiodini in the 1980s. The album at last unveiled Lee's smooth, Latin-grooved song "Most of All—I Love You"; a swinging blues titled "I've Got a Brand New Baby"; and the country ballad "I've Been Too Lonely for Too Long." "Most of All" attained Grammy consideration in 2019 for Song of the Year, Best Improvised Jazz Solo (by John Chiodini), and Best Arrangement, Instrumental/Vocal, also credited to Chiodini. Being heavily soaked in the blues, "I've Been Too Lonely" earned Grammy consideration for Best American Roots Song. Lee's prolific songwriting efforts somehow ensured that even after her death "new" works continued to stream from this gifted writer of American popular song. Her timeless and transcendent talent still received a fresh welcome from her listening public nearly eighteen years after her death.

With her depth and breadth of performing talent, her first-rate arrangements, her A-list musicians, and her discriminating ear for perfecting recording quality, Lee's recorded output overwhelmingly proved to be worth hearing over and over again. Songwriters were fortunate to have their songs covered by Lee, as her pitch-perfect, rhythmically precise, and tastefully phrased renditions reflected utmost technical attention and emotional expression, yielding some of the finest recordings of American song obtained in the twentieth century. On the occasion of Lee's centennial birthday in 2020, and beyond, listeners and fans may expect more releases, remixed and remastered recordings, and possibly even more recordings that have remained cloaked in vaults or private collections until the right time has come to share them. Reflecting upon these more recent collections, critics and reviewers consistently declare that Lee's talent and genius do not disappoint.

Throughout her life Lee's voice evolved from a youthful, canary-like treble clarity into a bluesy, conversational, breathy tone, and yet, her pitch precision and vocal beauty remained intact. This gradual transformation from a youthful sound to a worldly, womanly voice began during her early work with Benny Goodman. From then on she explored the extent of quietness she could achieve in a performance, built her emotional range, mastered the art of phrasing, and fueled her constant pursuit of perfection both onstage and in the recording studio. Even in her later years, her health challenges did not hold back her continued development of rhythmic exactitude, phrase delivery, and emotional commitment, which remained paramount in defining her relevance and longevity in the music business. Her pivotal roles as a lyricist, bandleader, and arranger forged new pathways for women in the industry, and her commitment to advocating for music creators' rights helped spawn the movement that has recently facilitated the passing of the Fair Play Fair Pay Act of 2017 and other legislative advancements for artists in the United States Congress.

Lee's diverse talents as a performer, recording artist, actress, voice-over artist, bandleader, and songwriter must not be discounted in the present day, when it is unheard of for a musical artist to successfully pull all these strings of the entertainment business simultaneously into a well-balanced ribbon of success. Add to all this the fact that Lee remains unparalleled as a leading interpreter of the Great American Songbook—1940s, '50s, and '60s popular songs, jazz, blues, and theatrical music—and the significance of her accomplishments shines unmistakably bright. Frank Sinatra himself noted Lee's outstanding qualities when he reveled in her peerless abilities and asserted: "Her talent should be studied by all vocalists, and her regal presence is pure elegance and charm."[25]

EPILOGUE

Several years ago I met Nicki Lee-Foster at the International Association for Jazz Education national conference. She stood in a room filled with nearly six hundred jazz singers and announced, "My name is Nicki, and Peggy Lee was my mother." The audience immediately responded, showing their love and respect for the legendary singer by answering this surprising statement with a torrent of applause lasting nearly a full minute. After sharing with us the fact that her mother had not only sported an enviable career as a successful jazz and pop singer but that she also had written over 250 original songs, Ms. Lee-Foster invited us to consider adding her mother's songs to our repertoire.

At the time I was a doctoral student at the University of Southern California's Thornton School of Music, majoring in jazz studies and minoring in voice pedagogy, musicology, and choral music. I was actively keeping my eyes and ears open twenty-four hours a day in case a worthy dissertation/lecture recital topic presented itself. (The requirements were such that the dissertation document needed to culminate in a lecture recital, so I had to choose an area of focus that I could both sing and present as a written document.) Attending the conference was one strategy I utilized to mine for potential topics that had not yet been researched. I instantly realized that this (Lee's original music) was perhaps the topic for which I had been on high alert. My jazz voice teacher, Tierney Sutton, cautioned me to carefully consider the material first to determine whether the songs were worthy of such a deep and thorough investigation. Indeed, I pursued Nicki's help in procuring the body of work and soon realized that I had not only plenty of quality music around which to build a compelling dissertation and recital, but I had discovered a treasure trove of art that would feed my heart and soul (and my own songwriting predilection) for many, many years.

In planning the recital Tierney suggested that I "book a gig and invite the faculty." The manager of the Pasadena Jazz Institute asked for three performances instead of one and urged me to make it a ticketed event because he was sure we could sell the show I envisioned. I created a lecture recital from the dissertation, hired Lee's former musical director (guitarist John Chiodini) as well as fabulous drummer Kendall Kay and outstanding bassist Joel Hamilton, arranged a seventy-five-minute show, and produced three full multimedia concerts called *The Lyrical Genius of Peggy Lee* at the Pasadena Jazz Institute to fulfill my last performance requirements for the doctoral degree. I invited Nicki Lee-Foster and her daughter, Holly Foster Wells, who both thoroughly loved our presentation. There and then they affectionately named me the world's foremost expert on the original music of Peggy Lee. With their endorsement and help, *The Peggy Lee Project* was born.

The inaugural band and I went on the road with this unique touring concert that, unlike every other Peggy Lee tribute show, illuminated Lee's songwriting talents by including *only* her original material. We performed *The Peggy Lee Project* throughout the United States and have continued to accept engagements at performing arts centers, jazz festivals, and concert series worldwide. The project thrives because Lee's music speaks for itself. Many thousands of fans have expressed their thanks and appreciation over the years to John and me for introducing them to this artist's wonderful songwriting talents, to which most of her listening public was previously oblivious.

Although today my performance repertoire extends far beyond the music of Peggy Lee, I am personally grateful to her for her beautiful recordings, her painstakingly attentive work on refining her live performances, and the love with which she infused so much of her music. I am grateful to sing her songs and to continue her legacy as an excellence-seeking performer, recording artist, songwriter, arranger, and author. I am grateful that our mutual love for Peggy brought friendship and collaboration with John, Holly, Nicki, and so many other outstanding people into my life. I am grateful for the difficult conversations Peggy had with chauvinistic colleagues, and for her standing her ground because she knew what was best for her career and for the songs and albums in question. I am grateful she fought for artists' rights to royalties and fair compensation. I am grateful for her outstanding talent and genius and for the privilege of sharing them with thousands of lovers of great music. Although we never met, I feel deeply honored to have participated in her ninetieth birthday celebration via my *Peggy Lee Project* and her one hundredth birthday with the publication of this book. Happy birthday, *Dear Peg*, and here's to you . . .

NOTES

I. A VOICE FOR THE BIG CITY

1. Peter Richmond, *Fever: The Life and Music of Miss Peggy Lee* (New York: Picador, 2006), 52.

2. Richmond, *Fever*, 19.

3. Mary English, "Softly . . . with Feeling," *Record Whirl*, October 1955. http://www.peggylee.com/library/551000.html.

4. David McGee, "Peggy Lee: A Consummate Artist," *Record World*, December 27, 1975, http://www.peggylee.com/library/751227/html.

5. Iván Santiago-Mercado, "The Benny Goodman Years (1941–1943)," The Peggy Lee Bio-Discography and Videography, accessed November 23, 2018, http://www.peggyleediscography.com/p/Goodman.php.

6. Benny Goodman, *Peggy Lee & Benny Goodman: The Complete Recordings 1941–1947,* Columbia Legacy C2K65686, CD liner notes, 1999.

7. Jack Zaientz, "Lost in Translation–Di Grine Kuzine (The Greenhorn Cousin)," *Teruah Jewish Music*, accessed 13 September 2019, http://teruahjewishmusic.blogspot.com/2009/01/lost-in-translation-di-grine-kuzine.html.

8. Oren Jacoby, *Benny Goodman: Adventures in the Kingdom of Swing* (Culver City, CA: Sony Pictures, 1993).

9. A well-known maxim among recording artists has endured through the ages: when covering a song, improve it, reframe it, or skip it! This unsuccessful recording may have been a case in point.

10. Nat Shapiro and Nat Hentoff, *Hear Me Talkin' to Ya: The Story of Jazz as Told by the Men Who Made It* (New York: Dover Publications, 1966), 320.

11. George Christy, "Peggy Lee: Still at Fever's Pitch," interview by George Christy, *Interview* (October 1984).

2. A CAPITOL IDEA

1. Peter Richmond, *Fever: The Life and Music of Miss Peggy Lee* (New York: Picador, 2006), 160.

2. Dave Dexter Jr., *Playback* (New York: Billboard Publications, 1976), 52.

3. James Gavin, *Is That All There Is?: The Strange Life of Peggy Lee* (New York: Atria Books, 2014), 135.

4. Gavin, *Is That All There Is?* 89.

5. John Chiodini, interview by author, Spartanburg, SC, digital recording, April 23, 2013.

6. Gavin, *Is That All There Is?* 91.

7. Iván Santiago-Mercado, "The Capitol Years, Part I: 1943–1945," The Peggy Lee Discography, accessed November 24, 2018, http://www.peggyleediscography.com/p/preCap.php.

8. John Chiodini, interview by author, Los Angeles, digital recording April 4, 2007.

9. Santiago-Mercado, "The Capitol Years, Part I."

10. David Torresen, *Peggy Lee: The Lost '40s & '50s Capitol Masters*, EMI Music Special Markets, CD liner notes, 2008.

11. Jack Garner, "Peggy Lee: The Lost '40s & '50s Capitol Masters," *Rochester Democrat & Chronicle*, accessed September 13, 2019, https://www.peggylee.com/new-cd-dvd-releases/the-lost-40s-and-50s-capitol-masters/

12. Ron Wynn, *Nashville City Paper*, accessed September 13, 2019, https://www.peggylee.com/new-cd-dvd-releases/the-lost-40s-and-50s-capitol-masters/

13. Will Friedwald, *New York Sun*, accessed September 13, 2019, https://www.peggylee.com/new-cd-dvd-releases/the-lost-40s-and-50s-capitol-masters/

3. CAPITOL HITS AND *THE PEGGY LEE SHOW*

1. Iván Santiago-Mercado, "Chesterfield Supper Club (On the Radio, Part III)," Peggy Lee Discography, accessed November 28, 2018, www.peggyleediscography.com/p/LeeRadioSupperClub.php.

2. Margaret Whiting, *It Might as Well Be Spring: A Musical Autobiography* (New York: William Morrow, 1987).

3. Santiago-Mercado, "Chesterfield."

4. James Gavin, *Is That All There Is?: The Strange Life of Peggy Lee* (New York: Atria Books, 2014), 108.

5. Will Friedwald, *Peggy Lee: The Singles Collection*, Capitol Records/ EMI 724353975623, CD liner notes, 2002.

6. Santiago-Mercado, "Chesterfield."

7. Iván Santiago-Mercado, "A Date with Peggy Lee/The Rexall Show (On the Radio, Part IV)," Peggy Lee Discography, accessed November 28, 2018, http://www.peggyleediscography.com/p/LeeRadioRexall.php.

8. Peggy Lee, *The Peggy Lee Show*, CBS Radio Network, New York, July 15, 1951, accessed November 30, 2018, https://youtu.be/Yb8wLQpIMrI.

9. Santiago-Mercado, "The Rexall Show."

10. Philip Furia, *Skylark: The Life and Times of Johnny Mercer* (New York: St. Martin's Press, 2003), 141–42.

11. Ibid.

12. "Hoagy Carmichael Biographical Timeline," Hoagy Carmichael: The Official Website, accessed September 22, 2019, https://www.hoagy.com/biography.

4. EARLY ALBUMS AND THE DECCA YEARS

1. Iván Santiago-Mercado, "The Capitol Years Part II: 1948–1952," Peggy Lee Discography, accessed November 17 2018, http://www.peggyleediscography.com/p/capitoleela.php.

2. Julia Blackburn, *With Billie: A New Look at the Unforgettable Billie Holiday* (New York: Vintage Books, 2006), 194.

3. Philip Furia, *Skylark: The Life and Times of Johnny Mercer* (New York: St. Martin's Press, 2003), 163.

4. Iván Santiago-Mercado, "The Decca Years: 1952–1956," Peggy Lee Discography, accessed December 28, 2018, http://www.peggyleediscography.com/p/decca.php.

5. Iván Santiago-Mercado, "Observations on the Arrangement of 'Lover,'" Peggy Lee Discography, accessed December 28, 2018, http://www.peggyleediscography.com/p/LeeResearchLover.php.

6. Peggy Lee, *Miss Peggy Lee: An Autobiography* (New York: Donald I. Fine, 1989), 185.

7. Lee, *Autobiography*, 188.

8. Holly Foster-Wells, interview with author, digital recording, February 12, 2019.

9. Stella Castellucci and Edgar Amaya, *Diving Deep for Sea Shells* (Los Angeles: LitFire Publishing, 2015), 55.

10. Castellucci and Amaya, *Diving Deep for Sea Shells*, 59.

11. Will Friedwald, *Peggy Lee: Black Coffee*, Decca DL8358/Verve, CD liner notes, 2004.

12. Santiago-Mercado, "The Decca Years."

5. A FLAIR FOR FILM

1. Nicki Lee Foster, interview by author, Los Angeles, digital recording, April 11, 2007.

2. Iván Santiago-Mercado, "A Photographic Showcase of Lee's Movie Soundtrack Contributions," Peggy Lee Discography, accessed November 30, 2018, http://www.peggyleediscography.com/p/PhotosMovieSoundtrack.php.

3. *Lady and the Tramp* (Los Angeles: Walt Disney Productions, 1955), DVD, 75 min.

4. A. H. Weiler, *New York Times*, accessed September 25, 2019, https://www.peggylee.com/new-cd-dvd-releases/the-jazz-singer/.

5. "My Man Godfrey," Library of Congress, accessed March 2, 2019, https://www.loc.gov/item/jots.200023299/.

6. Santiago-Mercado, "Movie Soundtrack Contributions."

7. "Peggy Lee Filmography," Fandango, accessed March 2, 2019, https://www.fandango.com/people/peggy-lee-385072/film-credits.

8. Foster, interview.

9. Peggy Lee, *Miss Peggy Lee: An Autobiography*, (Los Angeles: Dutton, 1989), 177.

10. Peter Richmond, *Fever: The Life and Music of Miss Peggy Lee* (New York: Henry Holt, 2006), 386.

11. Richmond, *Fever*, 327.

12. *The Soundtrack Music from Burt Reynolds' Sharky's Machine*, Warner Brothers B000R0ML28, Vinyl LP, 1981.

13. Richmond, *Fever*, 298.

14. Foster, interview.

15. Johnny Mandel, interview by author, Van Nuys, CA, digital recording, March 5, 2007.

16. Mandel, interview.

17. Foster, interview.

6. TELESCRIPTIONS AND CAPITOL REVISITED

1. Henry B. D. Davis, *Electrical and Electronic Technologies: A Chronology of Events and Inventors from 1900–1940* (New York: Scarecrow Press, 1983), 73–74.

2. Nicki Lee Foster, interview with author, digital recording, April 11, 2007.

3. Peggy Lee, *Miss Peggy Lee: An Autobiography* (New York: Donald I. Fine, 1989), 220.

4. Peter Richmond, *Fever: The Life and Music of Miss Peggy Lee* (New York: Picador, 2006), 132.

5. Iván Santiago-Mercado, "The Capitol Years, Part IV (1957–1959)," Peggy Lee Discography, accessed March 21, 2019, http://www.peggyleediscography.com/p/capitolee2a.php.

6. Iván Santiago-Mercado, "Observations about the Song 'Fever,'" Peggy Lee Discography, accessed March 21, 2019, http://www.peggyleediscography.com/p/LeeResearchFever.php.

7. George Christy, "Peggy Lee: Still at Fever's Pitch," *Interview*, October 1984.

8. Iván Santiago-Mercado, "Research and Inquiry over the *Beauty and the Beat Dates*," Peggy Lee Discography, accessed March 29, 2019, http://www.peggyleediscography.com/p/LeeSpecBeauty.php.

9. Santiago-Mercado, "Capitol Years, Part IV."

7. 1960S BLUES AND JAZZ

1. Gene Handsaker, "Peggy Lee's Famous Voice Promotes 'Meals for Millions,'" PeggyLee.com, accessed April 9, 2019, https://www.peggylee.com/2013/01/18/peggy-lees-famous-voice-promotes-meals-for-millions/.

2. Cy Godfrey, *Peggy at Basin Street East: The Unreleased Show*, Capitol Records, CD liner notes, 2002.

3. John Chiodini, interview by author, Los Angeles, digital recording, April 4, 2007.

4. James Gavin, *Peggy Lee: Mink Jazz*, Capitol Records, CD liner notes, 1998.

5. Gavin, *Peggy Lee*.

6. Nicki Lee Foster, interview by author, Los Angeles, digital recording, April 11, 2007.

8. TELEVISION AND THE ROAD
TO THE GRAMMYS

1. Frank Sinatra, *The Frank Sinatra Show*, ABC-TV, October 18, 1957.

2. Nicki Lee-Foster, interview by author, Los Angeles, digital recording, April 11, 2007.

3. Peggy Lee, *The World of Peggy Lee*, directed by Nick Cominos (National Educational Television, 1969), video recording, 90 min.

4. Ibid.

5. Mike Stoller, interview by author, digital recording, August 5, 2019.

6. Ibid.

7. Peter Stoller, *Peggy Lee Sings Leiber & Stoller*, A&M Records, CD liner notes, 2005.

8. John Chiodini, interview by author, Los Angeles, digital recording, February 14, 2019.

9. Mike Stoller, interview.

10. Peggy Lee, *Leiber & Stoller*, liner notes.

11. David McGee, "Peggy Lee: A Consummate Artist," *Record World*, December 27, 1975.

12. Mike Stoller, interview.

13. Peter Stoller, interview by author, digital recording, June 19, 2019.

14. Jerry Leiber, *Leiber & Stoller,* liner notes.

15. Stephen Holden, *Rolling Stone*, December 18, 1975.

16. Peter Reilly, *Stereo Review*, March 1976.

17. Gavin, *Is That All There Is?: The Strange Life of Peggy Lee* (New York: Atria Books, 2014), 373.

9. LATE ALBUMS AND BROADWAY

1. Iván Santiago-Mercado, "The Capitol Years, Part VII (1968–1972)," *The Peggy Lee Discography*, accessed July 11, 2019, http://peggyleediscography.com/p/capitolee2c.php.

2. Peter Stoller, interview with author, June 19, 2019.

3. John Hallowell, "Peggy Lee Is Very Different from You and Me," *Los Angeles Times*, April 12, 1970.

4. Iván Santiago-Mercado, "Performances for the Theater (Live, Part II)," accessed July 23, 2019, *Peggy Lee Discography*, http://peggyleediscography.com.

5. Lawrence DeVine, "TipOff," *The Ledger*, May, 6, 1980.

6. Iván Santiago-Mercado, "Observations about the Artist's Broadway Show," *The Peggy Lee Bio-Discography and Videography*, updated November 21, 2018, http://peggyleediscography.com/p/LeeSpec1983Peg.php.

7. Santiago-Mercado, "Observations about the Artist's Broadway Show."

8. "Peg," *Variety*, December 21, 1983, https://www.peggylee.com/all-about-peggy/concerts/the-eighties/.

9. Frank Rich, *New York Times*, December 15, 1983, https://www.peggylee.com/all-about-peggy/concerts/the-eighties/.

10. Emilio Palame, interview with author, Los Angeles, April 15, 2007.

11. Palame, interview.

12. John Chiodini, interview with author, Los Angeles, February 14, 2019.

13. Iván Santiago-Mercado, "The MusicMasters and Harbinger Contracts (1988–1990)," accessed August 11, 2019, *Peggy Lee's Bio-Discography*, http://peggyleediscography.com.

10. THAT'S NOT ALL THERE IS

1. Phil Wright, *Peggy Lee: Make It with You*, Capitol Records, ST-622, liner notes, 1970.

2. Peter Reilly, "Norma Deloris Egstrom from Jamestown, North Dakota," *Stereo Review*, October 1973.

3. Nicki Lee Foster, interview by author, Los Angeles, digital recording, April 11, 2007.

4. George Kurek, "Live, in Concert," *The Peggy Lee Bio-Discography*, accessed October 11, 2019, http://peggyleediscography.com/p/LeeLive.php.

5. Gene Lees, *Miss Peggy Lee Sings the Blues*, MusicMasters 5005-2-C, CD liner notes, 1988.

6. Peter Clayton, quoted in *The Peggy Lee Songbook* (Milwaukee: Hal Leonard), 4.

7. Peter Stoller, interview by author, digital recording, June 19, 2019.

8. Peter Stoller, interview.

9. *Peggy Lee Sings Leiber & Stoller*, A&M Records B4169-02, CD, 2005.

10. Christopher Loudon, "Peggy Lee: Live in London," *Jazz Times*, April 4, 2016, https://jazztimes.com/reviews/albums/peggy-lee-live-in-london/.

11. *Fever: The Music of Peggy Lee*, produced by JoAnn Young and Jim Pierson (Capitol Records, 2004), DVD, 90 min.

12. Marian McPartland, quoted in Peter Richmond, *Fever: The Life and Music of Miss Peggy Lee* (New York: Picador, 2006), 507.

13. Peggy Lee, quoted in Richmond, *Fever*, 509.

14. Artie Butler, quoted in Richmond, *Fever*, 510.

15. Ellie Fuerst, quoted in James Gavin, *Is That All There Is?: The Strange Life of Peggy Lee* (New York: Atria Books, 2014), 497.

16. Gavin, *Is That All There Is?* 497.

17. Emilio Palame, quoted in Gavin, *Is That All There Is?* 504.

18. Stella Castellucci, quoted in Gavin, *Is That All There Is?* 504.

19. Tierney Sutton, interview by author, Van Nuys, CA, digital recording, March 26, 2007.

20. Peggy Lee, *The Peggy Lee Songbook: There'll Be Another Spring*, MusicMasters 5034-2-C, CD, 1990.

21. Graham Johnson and Richard Stokes, *A French Song Companion* (Oxford: Oxford University Press, 2000), 94.

22. Chiodini, interview by author, Los Angeles, digital recording, March 27, 2007.

23. *Fever: The Music of Peggy Lee*, DVD.

24. Lee-Foster, interview.

25. Frank Sinatra, quoted in *The Peggy Lee Songbook* (Milwaukee: Hal Leonard), 4.

SELECTED BIBLIOGRAPHY

BOOKS

Blackburn, Julia. *With Billie: A New Look at the Unforgettable Billie Holiday*. New York: Vintage Books, 2006.

Castellucci, Stella, and Edgar Amaya. *Diving Deep for Sea Shells*. Los Angeles: LitFire Publishing, 2015.

Epstein, Daniel Mark. *Nat King Cole*. New York: Farrar, Straus & Giroux, 1999.

Furia, Philip. *Skylark: The Life and Times of Johnny Mercer*. New York: St. Martin's Press, 2003.

Lee, Peggy. *Miss Peggy Lee: An Autobiography*. New York: Donald I. Fine, 1989.

Richmond, Peter. *Fever: The Life and Music of Miss Peggy Lee*. New York: Picador, 2006.

Roland, Paul, ed. *Jazz Singers: The Great Song Stylists in Their Own Words*. London: Octopus Publishing Group, 1999.

Santiago-Mercado, Iván. *The Peggy Lee Bio-Discography and Videography*. www.peggyleediscography.com.

Whiting, Margaret. *It Might as Well Be Spring: A Musical Autobiography*. New York: William Morrow, 1987.

Yanow, Scott. *The Jazz Singers: The Ultimate Guide*. Milwaukee: Backbeat Books, 2008.

VIDEOS

Fever: The Music of Peggy Lee. Capitol Records, 2004.

The Quintessential Peggy Lee. Kultur International Films, 1984.

The World of Peggy Lee. National Educational Television, 1969.

WEBSITES

Peggy Lee Associates, LLC. http://www.peggylee.com.
Santiago-Mercado, Iván. *The Peggy Lee Bio-Discography and Videography*. http://www.
peggyleediscography.com.

INDEX

ABOUT THE AUTHOR

Tish Oney has enjoyed an active lifelong career as an international jazz performer and recording artist. Having released her fifth critically acclaimed jazz album, *The Best Part*, in 2019, Tish has maintained a busy career performing, composing, arranging, conducting, and producing albums. As a widely recognized music pedagogue she also teaches singing and writes books and articles about music. Having earned a DMA in jazz studies from USC Thornton School of Music and MM in voice performance from Ithaca College School of Music, Dr. Oney has taught music at eight universities and colleges and has served as artist-in-residence at several more. She performs on tour worldwide as a soloist with symphonies, big bands, jazz combos, and choirs and as a solo pianist/ singer. Pursuing a dual career in performance and pedagogy she has earned widespread recognition as a master teacher of voice, musicology, and jazz. She frequently presents master classes on multi-genre singing for the National Association of Teachers of Singing, as well as choral workshops and musicology/jazz theory lectures. She arranges and performs tailor-made concerts at professional venues and institutions throughout the world. She is a contributing author for the *Journal of Singing* and writes a popular jazz column called "Anatomy of a Standard" for *All About Jazz*. She is currently authoring a book titled *Jazz Voice: A Singing Pedagogy* for Rowman & Littlefield. Connect with Dr. Oney online at www.tishoney.com.

CPSIA information can be obtained
at www.ICGtesting.com
Printed in the USA
LVHW091908051020
667981LV00011B/210